3rd Workshop on Computational Linguistics for the Political and Social Sciences (CPSS 2023)

Ingolstadt, Germany
22 September 2023

ISBN: 979-8-3313-1646-4

Printed from e-media with permission by:

Curran Associates, Inc.
57 Morehouse Lane
Red Hook, NY 12571

Some format issues inherent in the e-media version may also appear in this print version.

Printed with permission by Curran Associates, Inc. (2025)

For permission requests, please contact the Association for Computational Linguistics at the address below.

Association for Computational Linguistics
209 N. Eighth Street
Stroudsburg, Pennsylvania 18360

Phone: 1-570-476-8006
Fax: 1-570-476-0860

acl@aclweb.org

Additional copies of this publication are available from:

Curran Associates, Inc.
57 Morehouse Lane
Red Hook, NY 12571 USA
Phone: 845-758-0400
Fax: 845-758-2633
Email: curran@proceedings.com
Web: www.proceedings.com

CPSS 2023

The 3rd Workshop on Computational Linguistics for the Political and Social Sciences

Proceedings of the Workshop

September 22, 2023

Order copies of this and other ACL proceedings from:

Association for Computational Linguistics (ACL)
209 N. Eighth Street
Stroudsburg, PA 18360
USA
Tel: +1-570-476-8006
Fax: +1-570-476-0860
acl@aclweb.org

Foreword

This workshop is the *3rd edition of Computational Linguistics for the Political and Social Sciences (CPSS)*. The main goal of the workshop is to bring together researchers and ideas from computational linguistics/NLP and the text-as-data community from political and social science, in order to foster collaboration and catalyze further interdisciplinary research efforts between these communities.

Submission format: We had two types of *workshop submissions*:

- archival papers describing original and unpublished work
- non-archival papers (abstracts) that present already published research or ongoing work.

This dichotomy met the different needs of researchers from different communities, allowing them to come together and exchange ideas in a "get to know each other" environment which was likely to foster collaborations.

Potential topics:

- Modeling political communication with NLP (e.g. topic classification, position measurement)
- Mining policy debates from heterogeneous textual sources
- Modeling complex social constructs (e.g. populism, polarization, identity) with NLP methods
- Political and social bias in language models
- Methodological insights in interdisciplinary collaboration: workflows, challenges, best practices
- NLP support to understand and support democratic decision making
- Resources and tools for Political/Social Science research
- ... and many more

Message from the Program Chairs

A special thank you goes to our amazing program committee for their invaluable input and dedication to the review process:

Ronja Sczepanski, ETH Zurich

Tobias Widman, Aarhus University

Indira Sen, GESIS

Robert Huber, USalzburg

Valerie Hase, LMU

Christian Rauh, WZB

Lisa Zehnter, HU Berlin/ Manifesto

Moritz Osnabrügge, Durham University

Agnieszka Falenska, UStuttgart

Dominik Stammbach, ETH Zurich

Ines Reinig, UMannheim

Maximilian Splithöver, UHannover

Tornike Tsereteli, UMannheim

Manfred Stede, UPotsdam

Eva Maria Vecchi, UStuttgart

Invited Speakers:

- **Lucie Flek**, University of Marburg and Bonn-Aachen International Center for Information Technology
Title: On "fixing" the framing: Is bias detection a pair-wise comparison task?
Abstract: NLP techniques for framing analysis can shed new light on fundamental questions in social science research, helping to understand biases towards entities and concepts e.g. in educational textbooks, news media or social networks. In this talk, I will present our studies on discovering indoctrination frames in historical event descriptions, showcasing their validity for contemporary media studies. I will further discuss the case for perspectivist annotation schemes and its relevance for the social grounding of LLMs.

- **Sebastian Padó**, University of Stuttgart
Title: Computational construction of discourse networks for political debates.
Abstract: Political debates form a crucial component of democratic decision processes and their structure and dynamics are highly interesting for political scientists. In this talk, I will present a series of interdisciplinary studies bringing together political scientists and NLP researchers with the goal of integrating manual and automatic approaches to constructing discourse networks. Topics include semi-automatic annotation, fairness, and hierarchical classification.

Organizing Committee

Christopher Klamm is an interdisciplinary PhD student at the University of Mannheim. His research efforts and interests are in the areas of Natural Language Processing and Computational Political Science, with a focus on automatic rhetoric and framing analysis.

Gabriella Lapesa is an interdisciplinary Computational Linguist working at the Institute for Natural Language Processing at the, currently leading the BMBF-funded independent research group E-DELIB, which works towards the development of NLP methods which would support deliberative discourse via (semi)automatic moderation.

Valentin Gold is a postdoctoral researcher at the Institute of Methods and Methodological Foundations in the Social Sciences at the University of Göttingen. He is currently coordinating the Deliberation Laboratory – an interdisciplinary project funded by the Volkswagen Foundation bringing together social science, computational linguistics and argument and ethos mining.

Theresa Gessler is an Assistant Professor for Comparative Politics at European University Viadrina in Frankfurt (Oder). Her research interests include the use of NLP methods to study political conflict around democracy, immigration and gender.

Simone Paolo Ponzetto holds the chair of Information Systems III (Enterprise Data Analysis) at the University of Mannheim, where he leads the Natural Language Processing and Information Retrieval group. His research interests include research on text understanding and its interdisciplinary application in the Social Sciences and Humanities.

Table of Contents

Conference Program

Friday, September 22, 2023

9:00–9:15 ***Opening***

9:15–10:30 *Invited Talk by Sebastian Pado: Computational construction of discourse networks for political debates*

10:30–10:45 Coffee Break

10:45–12:00 Poster Session

Automatic Emotion Experiencer Recognition
Maximilian Wegge and Roman Klinger

Personalized Intended and Perceived Sarcasm Detection on Twitter
Joan Plepi, Magdalena Buski and Lucie Flek

SpeakGer: A meta-data enriched speech corpus of German state and federal parliaments
Kai-Robin Lange and Carsten Jentsch

Multilabel Legal Element Classification on German Parliamentary Debates in a Low-Ressource Setting
Martin Hock and Christopher Klamm

Bubble up – A Fine-tuning Approach for Style Transfer to Community-specific Subreddit Language
Alessandra Zarcone and Fabian Kopf

According to BERTopic, what do Danish Parties Debate on when they Address Energy and Environment?
Costanza Navarretta and Dorte H. Hansen

Friday, September 22, 2023 (continued)

12:00–13:30 Lunch Break

13:30–15:00 Panel Session

The UNSC-Graph: An Extensible Knowledge Graph for the UNSC Corpus
Stian Rødven-Eide, Karolina Zaczynska, Antonio Pires, Ronny Patz and Manfred Stede

Deep Dive into the Language of International Relations: NLP-based Analysis of UNESCO's Summary Records
Joanna Wojciechowska, Mateusz Odrowaz-Sypniewski, Maria W. Smigielska, Igor Kaminski, Emilia Wiśnios, Bartosz Pieliński and Hanna Schreiber

Evaluating the Quality of the GermaParl Corpus of Plenary Protocols (v2.0.0)
Christoph Leonhardt and Andreas Blätte

15:00–15:15 Coffee Break

15:15–16:30 Poster Session

16:30–17:45 *Invited Talk by Lucie Flek: On "fixing" the framing: Is bias detection a pair-wise comparison task?*

17:45–18:00 Closing

Friday, September 22, 2023 (continued)

18:30 **Dinner**

Automatic Emotion Experiencer Recognition

Maximilian Wegge and **Roman Klinger**
Institut für Maschinelle Sprachverarbeitung, University of Stuttgart
`{firstname.lastname}@ims.uni-stuttgart.de`

Abstract

The most prominent subtask in emotion analysis is emotion classification; to assign a category to a textual unit, for instance a social media post. Many research questions from the social sciences do, however, not only require the detection of the emotion of an author of a post but to understand who is ascribed an emotion in text. This task is tackled by emotion role labeling which aims at extracting who is described in text to experience an emotion, why, and towards whom. This could, however, be considered overly sophisticated if the main question to answer is who feels which emotion. A targeted approach for such setup is to classify emotion experiencer mentions (aka "emoters") regarding the emotion they presumably perceive. This task is similar to named entity recognition of person names with the difference that not every mentioned entity name is an emoter. While, very recently, data with emoter annotations has been made available, no experiments have yet been performed to detect such mentions. With this paper, we provide baseline experiments to understand how challenging the task is. We further evaluate the impact on experiencer-specific emotion categorization and appraisal detection in a pipeline, when gold mentions are not available. We show that experiencer detection in text is a challenging task, with a precision of .82 and a recall of .56 (F_1 =.66). These results motivate future work of jointly modeling emoter spans and emotion/appraisal predictions.

1 Introduction

Computational emotion classification is among the most prominent tasks in the field of textual emotion analysis. It is typically formulated as either a classification or regression task, depending on the underlying emotion theory and intended application and domain: Texts can be classified into one or multiple discrete emotion categories, following the concept of basic emotions by Ekman (1992) or Plutchik (2001), as continuous values within the vector space of valence, arousal and dominance (Russell and Mehrabian, 1977) or based on the emoter's cognitive appraisal of the emotion-eliciting event (e.g., the level of *control* or *responsibility*; Smith and Ellsworth, 1985).

Recent work has emphasized the relevance of perspective, i.e., whose emotion is considered given an emotion-eliciting event. Typically, emotions are investigated from either the writer's or the reader's perspective, with only few approaches that consider both (e.g., Buechel and Hahn, 2017). Although not exclusively focused on it, perspective is also addressed in the context of semantic role labeling ("Who is feeling the emotion?"), besides the emotion target ("Who is the emotion directed towards?") and cause ("What is causing the emotion?") (Mohammad et al., 2014; Bostan et al., 2020a). Troiano et al. (2022) build upon this idea and extend the investigation to all potential emoters affected by an event. For each entity, they consider their emotions and the appraisal of the corresponding event, which allows to disambiguate the individual emotions.

Consider the example "Ken Paxton: Texas House votes to impeach Trump ally"[1]. Here, "Ken Paxton" could be attributed *guilt* because of the impeachment process following a potential appraisal of *self responsibility*. "Trump" being described as an ally might develop *anger* because he might evaluate the situation differently and assign an appraisal of *other responsibility*. "Texas House" could be considered a named entity, but does not represent an emoter. The writer's emotion is presumably irrelevant in such news headline. Experiencer-agnostic approaches can only assign emotions and appraisal to the entire text, thus oversimplifying the relations between individual experiencers.

Wegge et al. (2022) compare experiencer- and text-level emotion/appraisal predictors on self-

[1] `https://www.bbc.com/news/world-us-canada-65736478`

Proceedings of the 3rd Workshop on Computational Linguistics for the Political and Social Sciences, pages 1–7
September 22, 2023.

reported event descriptions. They find that an experiencer-specific predictor is able to capture the individual information, while a conventional classifier averages over all individual (potentially contradictory) information in the entire text. While they provide a computational approach for experiencer-specific emotion and appraisal classification, they rely on gold annotations of experiencer-spans. They do not investigate whether these spans can be predicted reliably and what consequences this would have on the classification task.

In this paper, we evaluate (i.) the performance of an automatic experiencer-detection model and (ii.) the impact of the imperfect automatic prediction on emotion and appraisal classification. We show that there is a substantial drop in the pipeline model in contrast to using gold annotations, which motivates future joint modeling work.

2 Related Work

Computational emotion classification is commonly grounded in theories of basic emotions, i.e., Ekman (1992) or Plutchik (2001), while regression models often handle emotions as tuples of continuous values within a vector space, for instance of valence, arousal, and dominance (Russell and Mehrabian, 1977). Emotion intensity prediction combines both classification and regression tasks by assigning not only an emotion category but a corresponding intensity score as well (Mohammad and Bravo-Marquez, 2017). In appraisal theories, emotions depend on the emoter's cognitive evaluation of the event (Smith and Ellsworth, 1985; Scherer et al., 2001) and are either defined by it directly or are understood to emerge out of it, depending on the respective theory (Scarantino, 2016).

This cognitive appraisal can be modeled with variables that represent the emoter's event evaluation, for instance whether the emoter could anticipate the consequences of the event (*outcome probability*) or whether the emoter is responsible for what is happening (*self responsibility*) rather than another entity (*other responsibility*). The appraisal theories make an obvious aspect explicit: the emotion is developed by an entity that is part of an emotional episode. This work therefore puts emphasis not only on a cause or expression of an emotion, but also by whom it is perceived.

Emotion classification received substantial attention in a variety of domains like social media posts (Mohammad and Bravo-Marquez, 2017; Stranisci et al., 2022; i.a.), news headlines (Bostan et al., 2020a) or literary texts (Alm et al., 2005). Most work focused on the emotions from a single perspective. Semantic role labeling does consider more than one perspective, but is primarily focused on the relations between experiencers, targets, and causes (Bostan et al., 2020a; Mohammad et al., 2014; Kim and Klinger, 2018a). The work on emotion experiencer detection is a more direct access to the emotion experiencer (Wegge et al., 2022; Troiano et al., 2022). In comparison to emotion role labeling, that is a simplification that enables a more straight-forward modeling. These modeling differences are similar to representing aspect-based sentiment analysis as an aspect classification task rather than finding full graph representations of evaluative phrases and mentioned aspects (compare the two shared task setups described by Barnes et al., 2022; Pontiki et al., 2014).

Appraisal theories already motivated some NLP research (Troiano et al., 2023; Hofmann et al., 2020; Stranisci et al., 2022), but only recently, Troiano et al. (2022) investigate all potential perspectives involved in an event with their x-enVENT corpus, based on self-reported event descriptions (Troiano et al., 2019). The corpus is annotated with potential emoters, their respective emotions and 22 appraisals (score from 0–5 for each dimension). Wegge et al. (2022) proposed first models to assign emotions and appraisals to experiencer mentions, but did rely on the experiencer annotations. Therefore, it is still an open research question what the challenges of emotion experiencer detection are; the gap that we aim at filling with this paper.

3 Methods

Our methods consists of a pipeline of (a) experiencer detection followed by (b) experiencer-aware emotion/appraisal detection. For the second step, we follow Wegge et al. (2022) who purely relied on gold annotations for the first step.

The experiencers consist of sequences of tokens within a text (we assume experiencer-spans to be non-overlapping). The writer's perspective is represented with such annotation on a special token prefix `writer`. One text can contain multiple experiencer spans. Each experiencer gets assigned a set of emotion labels (6 Ekman emotions + other, no emotion, and shame) and a set of up to 22 appraisal dimensions (see Table 3 for a list of classes).

Our pipeline consists of two steps: (i.) the detection of experiencers and (ii.) the prediction of emotions/appraisal dimensions for each experiencer.

Models. For detecting the experiencer-spans, we fine-tune a transition-based named entity recognition model (NER) from the spaCy library (Honnibal et al., 2020) on the x-enVENT corpus (Troiano et al., 2022). The data set consists of 720 instances which we split into 538 for training (of which we use 61 for validation) and 107 for testing. We omit 14 instances that contain overlapping spans.[2]

Our goal is to ensure comparability with previous work on experiencer-specific emotion and appraisal classification. Therefore, we apply the same models as Wegge et al. (2022), by fine-tuning Distil-RoBERTa (Liu et al., 2019, using Hugging Face's transformers library, Wolf et al., 2020) with a multi-output classification head to jointly predict all emotion labels (see their paper for implementation details). Experiencer-spans are encoded via positional indicators in the text (cf. Zhou et al., 2016). We differ from the previous approach in formulating the prediction of appraisal dimensions as classification instead of regression to have a straight-forward access to an evaluation of the overall pipeline in which additional experiencers might appear that are not available in the gold annotation. To this end, we use a threshold of 4 to discretize the continuous appraisal scores. The appraisal classification head is analogous to the one for emotions.[3]

Evaluation. We evaluate the performance of our pipeline by calculating the F_1 in two settings. In the *strict* evaluation, only exact matches of token spans make true positives. In the *relaxed* setting, we additionally accept partial matches with at least one token overlap as true positives.

We apply the experiencer-specific classifiers to the experiencer-spans detected in the first pipeline component instead of the gold spans. We consider this in the calculation of F_1 by treating every predicted emotion or appraisal label as a false positive if the associated experiencer-span has no correspondence in the gold data (we accept overlapping spans). Analogously, if a gold experiencer-span was not recognized by the experiencer-span detector, we consider each gold emotion and appraisal label that was associated with that span a false negative. We compare our results against the performance values on gold-annotated experiencer spans.

[2]We use the default spaCy configuration, learning rate 0.001, weight decay, dropout 0.1, Adam optimizer.

[3]Our code is available at `https://www.ims.uni-stuttgart.de/data/appraisalemotion`.

	P		R		F_1	
	s	r	s	r	s	r
incl. WRITER	90	93	77	80	83	86
excl. WRITER	74	82	50	56	60	66

Table 1: Span-prediction results (s: strict; r: relaxed).

	GOLD SPANS			PIPELINE			
Emotion	P	R	F_1	P	R	F_1	ΔF_1
anger	73	53	61	77	45	57	−4
disgust	76	81	79	64	56	60	−19
fear	82	60	69	68	57	62	−7
joy	48	82	60	49	69	57	−3
no emotion	54	79	64	47	47	47	−17
other	33	5	9	50	5	9	±0
sadness	61	77	68	57	65	61	−7
shame	57	73	64	54	59	56	−8
Macro avg.	49	66	56	40	62	49	−7
Micro avg.	55	72	62	43	67	52	−10

Table 2: The experiencer-specific emotion classifier is evaluated on expert-annotated (GOLD SPANS) and automatically detected (PIPELINE) experiencer-spans.

4 Results

We report results for both pipeline components.

4.1 Experiencer-Span Detection

Table 1 reports the precision, recall and F_1 of the span-detector for all non-writer experiencers (excl. WRITER) as well as to all experiencer-spans (incl. WRITER). Recognizing the `writer` token as an experiencer is trivial (F_1 =1.0).

As to be expected, the performance of the span-predictor is lower in the evaluation setup that considers only the non-writer experiencers. There is a considerable difference in the exact and relaxed evaluation setup, which shows that the model sometimes only finds a subset of the experiencer tokens. The task is challenging: while the precision is acceptable, only half of the experiencers are found. This is to some degree a result of the annotation of the data – the corpus authors tasked the annotators to only label the first occurrence of each mention of an experiencer in a text – a property that is challenging to be grasped automatically.

4.2 Emotion and Appraisal Classification

Table 2 reports the results of the emotion classifier applied to the automatically predicted experiencer-spans (PIPELINE setting) as well as the baseline results (GOLD SPANS) that were obtained on expert-annotated experiencer-spans. Across almost all

Appraisal	GOLD SPANS P	R	F_1	PIPELINE P	R	F_1	ΔF_1
suddenness	67	65	66	64	59	62	−3
familiarity	0	0	0	0	0	0	±0
pleasantness	8	87	83	78	78	78	−9
understand	80	100	89	77	82	80	−9
goal relev.	38	33	0.35	29	22	25	−10
self resp.	64	95	76	61	70	65	−11
other resp.	73	73	73	64	60	62	−11
sit. resp.	52	79	62	45	68	54	−8
effort	67	29	40	20	14	17	−23
exert	0	0	0	0	0	0	±0
attend	50	17	25	50	17	25	±0
consider	72	66	69	65	57	61	−8
outcome prob.	55	75	63	51	62	56	−7
expect. discrep.	72	63	67	67	56	61	−6
goal conduc.	59	62	60	60	57	59	−1
urgency	0	0	0	0	0	0	±0
self control	58	89	70	58	64	61	−9
other control	75	55	63	63	45	52	−11
sit. control	52	78	62	46	67	55	−7
adj. check	75	75	75	72	53	61	−14
int. check	33	12	18	25	12	17	−1
ext. check	0	0	0	0	0	0	±0
Macro avg.	46	64	54	42	48	45	−9
Micro avg.	58	86	69	54	69	61	−8

Table 3: Appraisal classification results of the appraisal classifier evaluated on expert-annotated (GOLD SPANS) and automatically detected (PIPELINE) experiencer-spans.

emotion categories, the PIPELINE classifier performs worse than the GOLD SPANS baseline, which is expected as the evaluation method penalizes erroneously detected experiencer-spans. However, the drop in performance differs between emotions. For *anger*, *joy*, *sadness*, *fear*, *shame* the difference is less than 10pp F_1– for these emotions, experiencers can be found more reliably than for *disgust* (19pp) or *no emotion* (17pp).

The notable decrease in performance for *no emotion* is in line with the observation that predicting non-writer spans is more challenging than predicting writer-spans. From all spans annotated with *no emotion*, 84% are non-writer spans. However, the classification performance also drops for emotion classes that are frequently annotated in writer-spans; The pipeline classifier shows its biggest decrease in performance (19pp) for *disgust*, although 76% of all spans annotated with *disgust* are writer-spans. This is due to the span-predictor's low recall: a low number of recognized spans leads to a higher number of false negatives for all emotion classes associated with these spans. The biggest increase in FN introduced by the span-predictor is observed for *disgust* (71%), the lowest for *other* (21%).

Analogous to the emotion classifier, we observe a decrease in performance for the appraisal predictor, reported in Table 3. Again, there is a substantial difference in the drop of performance, with *effort* and *adjustment check* showing the highest loss (23pp and 14pp, respectively) and *goal conduciveness*, *internal check*, *attend* being the lowest (1pp or no difference). Both *effort* and *adjustment check* appear only seldom in writer-spans (33% each), while *goal conduciveness*, *internal check* and *attend* appear more often in writer spans (between 39% and 44%) and are less prone to unrecognized spans (44%/40% of FN are introduced through missing spans for *goal conduciveness/attention*, 29% for *internal check*; cf. Table 7). However, the individual differences are less pronounced than for the emotion classification results, due to the sparseness of some appraisal dimensions.

We show more detailed emotion/appraisal-specific statistics of writer spans and false negatives in the appendix.

5 Discussion and Conclusion

In this paper, we presented the first evaluation of experiencer detection in text and the impact of these predictions on the emotion/appraisal classification. We found that experiencer detection is challenging but the results are promising.

The emotion/appraisal detection interacts with the span prediction task. This indicates that a joint model that can explore interactions between experiencer and emotion/appraisal dimensions might work better than the pipeline setting. Such model is however not trivial to be build, because the emotion/appraisal classification depends on a variable number of spans. Possible approaches include a purely token-level classification task or multiple sequence labeling setups. Such engineering attempts can also find inspiration in emotion–cause pair extraction models (e.g., Yuan et al., 2020).

Our work also motivates other follow-up studies, namely to extend the experiments to corpora that are fully annotated with emotion role graphs (Campagnano et al., 2022), from which some contain experiencer annotations (Bostan et al., 2020b; Kim and Klinger, 2018b; Mohammad et al., 2014). We expect our approach to show improvements over full graph predictions for the subtask of experiencer-specific emotion prediction due to fewer model parameters.

Acknowledgements

This research is funded by the German Research Council (DFG), project "Computational Event Analysis based on Appraisal Theories for Emotion Analysis" CEAT (project number KL 2869/1-2).

References

Cecilia Ovesdotter Alm, Dan Roth, and Richard Sproat. 2005. Emotions from text: Machine learning for text-based emotion prediction. In *Proceedings of Human Language Technology Conference and Conference on Empirical Methods in Natural Language Processing*, pages 579–586, Vancouver, British Columbia, Canada. Association for Computational Linguistics.

Jeremy Barnes, Laura Oberlaender, Enrica Troiano, Andrey Kutuzov, Jan Buchmann, Rodrigo Agerri, Lilja Øvrelid, and Erik Velldal. 2022. SemEval 2022 task 10: Structured sentiment analysis. In *Proceedings of the 16th International Workshop on Semantic Evaluation (SemEval-2022)*, pages 1280–1295, Seattle, United States. Association for Computational Linguistics.

Laura Ana Maria Bostan, Evgeny Kim, and Roman Klinger. 2020a. GoodNewsEveryone: A corpus of news headlines annotated with emotions, semantic roles, and reader perception. In *Proceedings of the 12th Language Resources and Evaluation Conference*, pages 1554–1566, Marseille, France. European Language Resources Association.

Laura Ana Maria Bostan, Evgeny Kim, and Roman Klinger. 2020b. GoodNewsEveryone: A corpus of news headlines annotated with emotions, semantic roles, and reader perception. In *Proceedings of the Twelfth Language Resources and Evaluation Conference*, pages 1554–1566, Marseille, France. European Language Resources Association.

Sven Buechel and Udo Hahn. 2017. Readers vs. writers vs. texts: Coping with different perspectives of text understanding in emotion annotation. In *Proceedings of the 11th Linguistic Annotation Workshop*, pages 1–12, Valencia, Spain. Association for Computational Linguistics.

Cesare Campagnano, Simone Conia, and Roberto Navigli. 2022. SRL4E – Semantic Role Labeling for Emotions: A unified evaluation framework. In *Proceedings of the 60th Annual Meeting of the Association for Computational Linguistics (Volume 1: Long Papers)*, pages 4586–4601, Dublin, Ireland. Association for Computational Linguistics.

Paul Ekman. 1992. An argument for basic emotions. *Cognition & emotion*, 6(3-4):169–200.

Jan Hofmann, Enrica Troiano, Kai Sassenberg, and Roman Klinger. 2020. Appraisal theories for emotion classification in text. In *Proceedings of the 28th International Conference on Computational Linguistics*, pages 125–138, Barcelona, Spain (Online). International Committee on Computational Linguistics.

Matthew Honnibal, Ines Montani, Sofie Van Landeghem, and Adriane Boyd. 2020. spaCy: Industrial-strength Natural Language Processing in Python.

Evgeny Kim and Roman Klinger. 2018a. Who feels what and why? annotation of a literature corpus with semantic roles of emotions. In *Proceedings of the 27th International Conference on Computational Linguistics*, pages 1345–1359, Santa Fe, New Mexico, USA. Association for Computational Linguistics.

Evgeny Kim and Roman Klinger. 2018b. Who feels what and why? annotation of a literature corpus with semantic roles of emotions. In *Proceedings of the 27th International Conference on Computational Linguistics*, pages 1345–1359, Santa Fe, New Mexico, USA. Association for Computational Linguistics.

Yinhan Liu, Myle Ott, Naman Goyal, Jingfei Du, Mandar Joshi, Danqi Chen, Omer Levy, Mike Lewis, Luke Zettlemoyer, and Veselin Stoyanov. 2019. RoBERTa: A robustly optimized BERT pretraining approach. arXiv:1907.11692.

Saif Mohammad and Felipe Bravo-Marquez. 2017. Emotion intensities in tweets. In *Proceedings of the 6th Joint Conference on Lexical and Computational Semantics (*SEM 2017)*, pages 65–77, Vancouver, Canada. Association for Computational Linguistics.

Saif Mohammad, Xiaodan Zhu, and Joel Martin. 2014. Semantic role labeling of emotions in tweets. In *Proceedings of the 5th Workshop on Computational Approaches to Subjectivity, Sentiment and Social Media Analysis*, pages 32–41, Baltimore, Maryland. Association for Computational Linguistics.

Robert Plutchik. 2001. The nature of emotions. *American Scientist*, 89(4):344–350.

Maria Pontiki, Dimitris Galanis, John Pavlopoulos, Harris Papageorgiou, Ion Androutsopoulos, and Suresh Manandhar. 2014. SemEval-2014 task 4: Aspect based sentiment analysis. In *Proceedings of the 8th International Workshop on Semantic Evaluation (SemEval 2014)*, pages 27–35, Dublin, Ireland. Association for Computational Linguistics.

James A Russell and Albert Mehrabian. 1977. Evidence for a three-factor theory of emotions. *Journal of research in Personality*, 11(3):273–294.

Andrea Scarantino. 2016. The philosophy of emotions and its impact on affective science. In *Handbook of emotions*, chapter 4, pages 3–48. Guilford Press New York, NY.

Klaus R Scherer, A Schorr, and T Johnstone. 2001. *Appraisal considered as a process of multi-level sequential checking*, volume 92. Oxford University Press.

Craig A Smith and Phoebe C Ellsworth. 1985. Patterns of cognitive appraisal in emotion. *Journal of personality and social psychology*, 48(4):186–209.

Marco Antonio Stranisci, Simona Frenda, Eleonora Ceccaldi, Valerio Basile, Rossana Damiano, and Viviana Patti. 2022. APPReddit: a corpus of Reddit posts annotated for appraisal. In *Proceedings of the Thirteenth Language Resources and Evaluation Conference*, pages 3809–3818, Marseille, France. European Language Resources Association.

Enrica Troiano, Laura Oberländer, Maximilian Wegge, and Roman Klinger. 2022. x-enVENT: A corpus of event descriptions with experiencer-specific emotion and appraisal annotations. In *Proceedings of The 13th Language Resources and Evaluation Conference*, Marseille, France. European Language Resources Association.

Enrica Troiano, Laura Oberländer, and Roman Klinger. 2023. Dimensional Modeling of Emotions in Text with Appraisal Theories: Corpus Creation, Annotation Reliability, and Prediction. *Computational Linguistics*, 49(1):1–72.

Enrica Troiano, Sebastian Padó, and Roman Klinger. 2019. Crowdsourcing and validating event-focused emotion corpora for German and English. In *Proceedings of the 57th Annual Meeting of the Association for Computational Linguistics*, pages 4005–4011, Florence, Italy. Association for Computational Linguistics.

Maximilian Wegge, Enrica Troiano, Laura Ana Maria Oberlaender, and Roman Klinger. 2022. Experiencer-specific emotion and appraisal prediction. In *Proceedings of the Fifth Workshop on Natural Language Processing and Computational Social Science (NLP+CSS)*, pages 25–32, Abu Dhabi, UAE. Association for Computational Linguistics.

Thomas Wolf, Lysandre Debut, Victor Sanh, Julien Chaumond, Clement Delangue, Anthony Moi, Pierric Cistac, Tim Rault, Remi Louf, Morgan Funtowicz, Joe Davison, Sam Shleifer, Patrick von Platen, Clara Ma, Yacine Jernite, Julien Plu, Canwen Xu, Teven Le Scao, Sylvain Gugger, Mariama Drame, Quentin Lhoest, and Alexander Rush. 2020. Transformers: State-of-the-art natural language processing. In *Proceedings of the 2020 Conference on Empirical Methods in Natural Language Processing: System Demonstrations*, pages 38–45, Online. Association for Computational Linguistics.

Chaofa Yuan, Chuang Fan, Jianzhu Bao, and Ruifeng Xu. 2020. Emotion-cause pair extraction as sequence labeling based on a novel tagging scheme. In *Proceedings of the 2020 Conference on Empirical Methods in Natural Language Processing (EMNLP)*, pages 3568–3573, Online. Association for Computational Linguistics.

Peng Zhou, Wei Shi, Jun Tian, Zhenyu Qi, Bingchen Li, Hongwei Hao, and Bo Xu. 2016. Attention-based bidirectional long short-term memory networks for relation classification. In *Proceedings of the 54th Annual Meeting of the Association for Computational Linguistics (Volume 2: Short Papers)*, pages 207–212, Berlin, Germany. Association for Computational Linguistics.

A Distributions Emotion Spans and False Negatives

	Writer		Non-Writer	
Emotion	%	#	%	#
anger	.61	204	.39	132
disgust	.76	66	.24	21
fear	.61	135	.39	85
joy	.45	118	.55	147
no emotion	.16	43	.84	226
other	.50	59	.50	58
sadness	.59	249	.41	174
shame	.64	209	.36	116

Table 4: Frequency (absolute and relative) of writer and non-writer spans annotated with a given emotion.

	total	due to non-recogn. span	
Emotion	#	#	%
anger	28	7	.25
disgust	7	5	.71
fear	13	4	.31
joy	12	7	.58
no emotion	23	14	.61
other	19	4	.21
sadness	21	9	.43
shame	21	10	.48

Table 5: Number of false negative emotion predictions (relative and absolute) that were introduced due to the experiencer predictor not recognizing the span.

B Distributions Appraisal Spans and False Negatives

	Writer		Non-Writer	
Appraisal	%	#	%	#
suddenness	.62	333	.38	202
familiarity	.9	3	.91	30
pleasantness	.53	99	.47	87
understand	.58	642	.42	460
goal relev.	.47	40	.53	45
self resp.	.47	244	.53	273
other resp.	.50	256	.50	251
sit. resp.	.70	140	.30	59
effort	.33	25	.67	51
exert	.38	3	.62	5
attend	.44	18	.56	23
consider	.54	140	.46	119
outcome prob.	.54	211	.46	177
expect. discrep.	.60	380	.40	252
goal conduc.	.44	76	.56	96
urgency	.40	10	.60	15
self control	.39	136	.61	217
other control	.50	199	.50	203
sit. control	.67	135	.33	67
adj. check	.33	145	.67	301
int. check	.39	26	.61	41
ext. check	.21	9	.79	34

Table 6: Frequency (absolute and relative) of writer-/non-writer spans annotated with a given appraisal class.

	total	due to non-recogn. span	
Appraisal	#	#	%
suddenness	30	11	.37
familiarity	3	1	.33
pleasantness	5	3	.60
understand	28	28	1
goal relev.	7	2	.29
self resp.	25	23	.92
other resp.	28	13	.46
sit. resp.	6	3	.50
effort	6	3	.50
exert	2	1	.50
attend	5	2	.40
consider	15	5	.33
outcome prob.	20	13	.65
expect. discrep.	41	16	.39
goal conduc.	9	4	.44
urgency	3	1	.33
self control	23	19	.83
other control	33	12	.36
sit. control	6	3	.50
adj. check	36	20	.56
int. check	7	2	.29
ext. check	6	4	.67

Table 7: Number of false negative appraisal predictions (relative and absolute) that were introduced due to the experiencer predictor not recognizing the span.

Personalized Intended and Perceived Sarcasm Detection on Twitter

Joan Plepi* †‡ and **Magdalena Buski*** † and **Lucie Flek** †‡
Conversational AI and Social Analytics (CAISA) Lab
† Department of Mathematics and Computer Science, University of Marburg
‡ Department of Computer Science, University of Bonn
{plepi,flek}@bit.uni-bonn.de
magdalena.buski@gmx.de
* These authors contributed equally to this work

Abstract

Sarcasm detection is a challenging task for various NLP applications. It often requires additional context related to the conversation or participants involved to interpret the intended meaning. In this work, we introduce an extended reactive supervision method to collect sarcastic data from Twitter and improve the quality of the data that is extracted. Our new dataset contains around 35K labeled tweets sarcastic or non-sarcastic, as well as additional tweets regarding both conversational and author context. The experiments focus on two tasks, the binary classification task of sarcastic vs. non-sarcastic and intended vs. perceived sarcasm. We compare models using textual features of tweets and models utilizing additional author embeddings by using their historical tweets. Moreover, we show the importance of combining conversational features together with author ones.

1 Introduction

Sarcasm detection is one of the most challenging NLP tasks, having an implied negative sentiment but a positive surface sentiment (Băroiu and Trăusan-Matu, 2022). Initially, early sarcasm detection systems relied on lexical and syntactic cues (Carvalho et al., 2009; Davidov et al., 2010a; Tsur et al., 2010; González-Ibánez et al., 2011; Reyes et al., 2013). However, the intended and literal meaning of the text can be interpreted differently depending on additional contextual information and on the cultural imprint of the author as well as the audience of the utterance (Ackerman, 1982; Gibbs, 1986; Dews et al., 1995; Riloff et al., 2013; Wallace et al., 2014; Bamman and Smith, 2015; Hazarika et al., 2018). One such case is the political discourse on social media, where users often utilize sarcasm and irony to express their opinion. In datasets for sarcasm detection crawled from social media like Reddit, posts from political topics, usually dominate the other topics (Davis et al., 2018; Khodak et al., 2017), hence several models have attempted to model the topic of the tweet for sarcasm detection task (Kannangara, 2018; Ghosh et al., 2020). Therefore, the effectiveness of models, predicting whether an utterance is sarcastic or not, depends not only on the choice of the model but also on the availability and quality of a high amount of labeled data (Oprea and Magdy, 2020a). The collection of such is hampered by the aforementioned challenges.

Sarcasm can be categorized into three types based on the perception of the audience and the intent of the author. The first type of sarcastic utterance is one that is not intended as sarcastic by the author but is perceived as such by the audience. The second type is an utterance that is both intended as sarcastic by the author and perceived as such by the audience. Lastly, the third type is an utterance that is intended as sarcastic by the author, but it is not perceived as such by the audience. Prior works focus on three different methods of collecting sarcastic data, distant supervision method which uses hashtags on Twitter, manual annotation, and manual collection. However, all the previous methods were able to capture only one type of sarcasm, thus limiting their ability to train models that could detect both intended and perceived sarcasm (Joshi et al., 2016; Oprea and Magdy, 2020a; Băroiu and Trăusan-Matu, 2022).

Shmueli et al. (2020) introduces a new reactive supervision method to collect sarcastic data from Twitter. This method has two advantages that address some of the issues present in previous works by relying on cues from participants in online conversations. First, it contains both types of sarcasm intended and perceived, and also additional conversational context. Our manual analysis of the data collected with this method revealed a considerable number of false positive examples due to cue tweets indicating the need for clarification rather than pointing out sarcasm. To

Proceedings of the 3rd Workshop on Computational Linguistics for the Political and Social Sciences, pages 8–18
September 22, 2023.

address this issue, we propose an extension of the reactive supervision method that improves the rate of false positives, hence the quality of the sarcastic tweets. Moreover, we collect a dataset of 35k tweets that contain both perceived and intended sarcasm and non-sarcastic tweets. In addition, we enrich the dataset with additional contextual information regarding both conversation and authorship.

The key contributions of this paper are as follows:

(1) We collect a new dataset on Twitter by extending a semi-supervised method that uses reactive supervision and provides additional contextual information.

(2) We evaluate the models using binary classification for both sarcastic vs. non-sarcastic classes and perceived vs. intended sarcasm classes.

(3) We analyze the performance of two classes of models for sarcasm detection: (i) text-only-based models that rely solely on textual features and (ii) author-contextual-based models that use author representations based on historical tweets. In addition, we also combine textual and author features with conversational features.

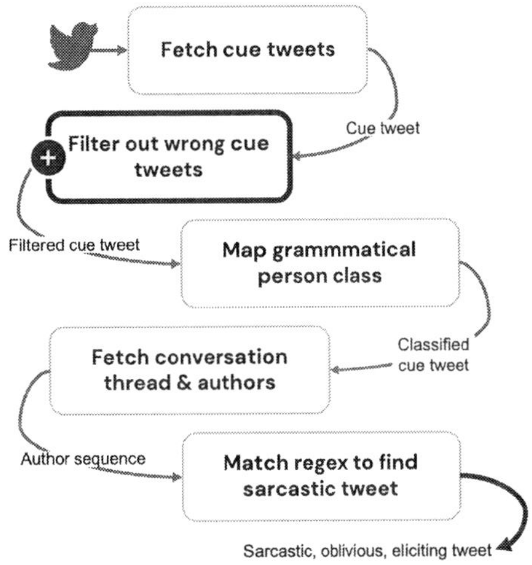

Figure 1: 5-step pipeline of enhanced reactive supervision.

2 Related Work

Collection and Labeling of Sarcastic Data Previous approaches to data collection for automatic sarcasm detection can be divided into two groups: distant supervision and manual annotation (Joshi et al., 2016; Băroiu and Trăusan-Matu, 2022). One approach requires annotators to manually label whether a given utterance is sarcastic or not (Filatova, 2012), while distant supervision focuses on automatically collecting large datasets of intended sarcasm. The automatic data collection uses specific keywords to query social networks (Davidov et al., 2010b; Barbieri et al., 2014; Ptácek et al., 2014; Khodak et al., 2017). Nevertheless, the subjectivity and sociocultural dependence of perceived sarcasm (Rockwell and Theriot, 2001; Dress et al., 2008) often lead to discrepancies between intended and perceived sarcasm. Recent approaches have addressed this issue by generating datasets for automatic sarcasm detection that reflect this discrepancy. For example, the iSarcasm dataset (Oprea and Magdy, 2020a) manually collects and labels sarcastic utterances by their authors, instead of relying on third-party annotators. However, this dataset only contains 777 sarcastic tweets and does not include perceived sarcasm. In contrast, the SPIRS dataset (Shmueli et al., 2020) utilizes reactive supervision to collect both intended and perceived sarcasm. The dataset consists of 30k tweets and relies on cues from participants in online conversations, therefore using context-aware annotations.

Models for Automatic Sarcasm Detection Various previous works emphasize the importance of contextual representations for sarcasm detection. One method uses author's behavioral trait features using different techniques (Bamman and Smith, 2015). Amir et al. 2016 proposed the usage of paragraph2vec (Le and Mikolov, 2014) over the historical utterance of users creating the user2vec model, placing similar users into nearby regions of the embedding space. On the other hand, (Zhang et al., 2016) build a deep learning model to combine text features with contextual tweets for sarcasm classification. In addition, several works have focused on different user features like behavior traits (Rajadesingan et al., 2015), user sentiment priors over entities (Khattri et al., 2015), style and personality features (Hazarika et al., 2018), or social network interactions (Plepi and Flek, 2021).

While we focus on combining different contextual text features, several studies have been dedicated to detecting sarcasm in a multimodal setting. Such works utilize information from different modalities, mainly images, and text features, and aim to capture cross-modal context for sarcasm classification (Pan et al., 2020; Xu et al., 2020; Wen et al., 2023).

Cue tweet indication	Gold	4-step	5-step
Sarcastic	318	24	109
Non-sarcastic	182	21	6
Total	500	45	115

Table 1: Comparison of the 4- and the 5-step data collection pipeline.

Person	Perspective	Cue tweet
1st	Intended	@user @user **I was being sarcastic**. That is what they tried to spin after the Nazi speech.
2nd	Perceived	@user I know **you are being sarcastic** btw. I just figure answering honestly is the best policy.
3rd	Perceived	@user @user Do you not see how many repeats there are? **He's being sarcastic**.

Table 2: Exemplary cue tweets per grammatical person class.

3 Proposed Method

3.1 Dataset Collection and Labeling

For the collection and labeling of intended and perceived sarcastic tweets, we focus on the reactive supervision method (Shmueli et al., 2020) using tweets from social media

The existing reactive supervision approach consists of four steps:

1. Fetching cue tweets q_n, querying for tweets containing "being sarcastic"
2. Mapping the cue tweets to a grammatical person class (1st, 2nd, 3rd) by examining the personal subject pronoun in the cue tweet
3. For a cue tweet q_i, fetching the corresponding conversation $C^i = \{c_n, ..., c_1\}$, where c_n is the main post, $c_1 = q_i$ and the corresponding tweet author sequence $A^i = \{a_n, a_{n-1}, ..., a_1\}$
4. Applying specific regular expressions on the author sequence to identify the sarcastic tweet. Unmatched sequences are discarded and matched are saved along with the cue tweet and the eliciting[1] and oblivious[2] tweets.

After manual analysis of random data points in the dataset (Shmueli et al., 2020), we found that the proposed approach can mistakenly label certain non-sarcastic tweets as sarcastic. We discovered several cue tweets containing "being sarcastic" which are noisy reactions from the audience, which express doubt, or ask for clarification for example: "*@user I can't tell if you are being sarcastic*".To create a dataset excluding those falsely classified tweets we propose an extension of the reactive supervision method. We add an additional filter (Figure 1), to remove tweets falsely identified as cue tweets using regular expressions, hence improving the quality of the extracted data. The filter contains a series of regular expressions to clear out the false positive cue tweets. We show a list of these regular expressions in Appendix A. In order to compare both methods, we collected 500 random cue tweets, which we labeled manually into three classes: sarcastic, non-sarcastic, and unknown (the user is asking for clarification, rather than pointing out sarcasm). Given the cue tweet and the conversation, we annotated the examples into three categories: sarcastic, non-sarcastic, and unknown. Fleiss' Kappa inter-annotator agreement between two annotators was almost a perfect agreement, with a kappa value of 0.94. Upon manual inspection and discussion, we found that the cases where the annotators were disagreeing were mainly between classes unknown and sarcastic (possible perceived sarcasm), where the user was expressing doubts if the previous tweet was sarcastic or not. Hence, we were able to resolve the disagreements through deeper inspection of the conversation thread. In Table 1 we show the number of tweets filtered out as sarcastic from both methods and also the false positive rate (we treat unknown and non-sarcastic as a single category). We observed that the number of filtered sarcastic tweets increased while, the rate of false positive examples decreased from 46.6% to 5%.

Pers.	Perspective	Sarcastic	Oblivious	Eliciting
1st	Intended	12574	12574	9023
2nd	Perceived	3295	0	519
3rd	Perceived	846	846	120
–	Non-sarc.	18535	4346	10639
Total		**35250**	**17766**	**20301**

Table 3: Break down by grammatical person class and perspective of our new dataset.

[1]Occurring if the sarcastic tweet is a reply and represents tweets which evoked the sarcastic reply (Shmueli et al., 2020)

[2]A reply to the sarcastic tweet that lacks awareness of sarcasm (Shmueli et al., 2020)

3.2 Data Statistics and Analysis

We applied our method (Figure 1) on a large scale to collect a dataset for sarcasm detection. For the collection of cue tweets, we queried for English tweets containing "being sarcastic", which are not retweets and were generated in the period from January until November 2022. For the collection of non-sarcastic tweets, we chose to fetch tweets randomly, querying for English tweets that have been generated from January until November 2022, are not retweets, and don't contain the words "sarcastic", "sarcasm" or the tags "#sarcasticquote", "#sarcasticquotes", "#sarcasticmemes", "#sarcastic", "#sarcasm". Finally, we gathered 17k English sarcastic tweets and 19k non-sarcastic tweets with corresponding additional conversational contexts such as oblivious or elicit tweets (a tweet that caused the sarcastic reply). In addition, we collected around 89M historical tweets for the users in our dataset in order to extend the dataset with additional author contextual information.

Statistics We collected 100K cue tweets for the new dataset. In Table 2 we present examples of the cue tweet for each grammatical person class. Next, we applied the exclusive filter, filtering out 26.6% of the cue tweets. After collecting the threads, and corresponding authors for the remaining cue tweets and matching those author sequences, we end up with 17k English sarcastic tweets, 10k eliciting, and 13k oblivious tweets. In addition, we collected 19k non-sarcastic tweets as well as 11k corresponding eliciting and 4k oblivious tweets. We summarize the new dataset grouped by grammatical person classes and perspectives in Table 3, and with the statistics of user history in Table 4.

In Table 5 we examine the distribution of different author sequence patterns of the sarcastic threads. We observed that 80% of the threads are equal to or smaller than 4 tweets per thread. In addition, it shows the most common author thread pattern per grammatical-person class, indicating that sarcastic tweets are often provoked by other authors (see eliciting tweets). Moreover, we notice the patterns used to detect perceived sarcasm, grouped in 2nd and 3rd person perspective cues. These cues capture conversations where other participants detect the presence of sarcasm.

During our analysis of the most common bi-grams in the dataset, we noticed that political or politician-related bi-grams predominated within the perceived sarcasm class (Figure 2). This finding reinforces the link between sarcasm and political discourse (Davis et al., 2018; Khodak et al., 2017), offering insights into the potential significance of the detection of (perceived) sarcasm in understanding the political stance and the presence of this linguistic phenomenon in online interactions.

Class/Perspective	# Authors	# Historical tweets
Sarcastic	**15884**	**45244265**
Intended	12245	33328130
Perceived	3686	12257193
Both	47	–
Non-sarcastic	**17340**	**43475563**
Both	**99**	–
Total	**33125**	88719828

Table 4: Break down of the number of tweet authors by class and perspective.

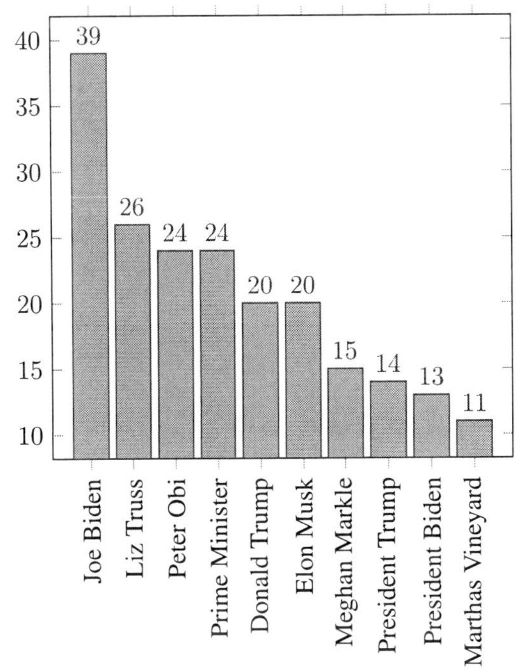

Figure 2: Top 10 most common bi-grams in as sarcastic perceived tweets.

Historical tweets The 35k sarcastic and non-sarcastic tweets of our new dataset have been composed by 33k different authors. Along with the new dataset we collected 89M historical tweets for those 32k authors (Table 4). The number of historical tweets per author varies between 1 (16 authors have 1 historical tweet) and 500 (upper bound) with an average tweet number of 471.46.

Person	Pattern	Count	% of person class
1st	*ABAC*	3368	27%
(intended)	*ABA*	2795	22%
	ABAB	1918	15%
	other	4493	36%
Subtotal		12574	
2nd	*AB*	2679	82%
(perceived)	*ABA*	476	14%
	other	140	4%
Subtotal		3295	
3rd	*ABC*	621	73%
(perceived)	*ABCA*	54	6%
	other	171	20%
Subtotal		846	
Total		16715	

Table 5: Most common thread pattern by person class. The colors represent cue, oblivious, sarcastic and eliciting tweets. The shown letters correspond to different authors in the thread. Equal letters encode equal authors, and the author sequences are shown in reverse order. The rightmost letter represents the end of the thread (cue tweet) while the leftmost represents the beginning of the thread.

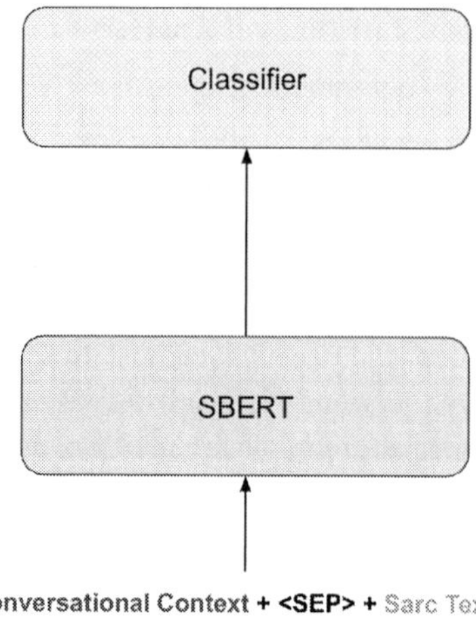

Figure 3: For the conversational context, we still use SBERT model as our base model. We only append the conversational context (namely oblivious and elicit tweet) to the original tweet to be classified and separated with special tokens.

4 Methodology

The models used for our experiments can be divided into two model groups: Text-only-based models and author-contextual-based models.

4.1 Text-only-based models

This model only uses a representation of the textual information in the sarcastic and non-sarcastic tweets as input. For this purpose, we fine-tuned the pre-trained Transformer encoder like SentenceBERT (Reimers and Gurevych, 2019) on the binary task of predicting the label sarcastic vs. non-sarcastic or perceived vs. intended, given only the tweet text. In this setup, we are also able to append the conversational context, namely oblivious and elicit tweet [3], in case those exist. We do so by appending the conversational context with the tweet that is to be classified, and we use special tokens to separate those (as in Figure 3).

4.2 Author Contextual Models

These models expand the textual features of tweets by adding representations of the authors of tweets as features. For encoding user representations, we used different models similar to Plepi et al. (2022a), namely: a) Priming, b) Average SentenceBERT for authors (A-SBERT), c) Authorship Attribution (AA) d) Graph Neural Networks (GNN).

[3] Cue tweets are not part of the conversational context.

Priming For our purpose, we randomly sample a number of tokens and append them as a prefix to the tweet text to classify. For each author a, we randomly sample a number of tokens from their historical tweets H^a (consisting of a sequence of historical tweets $\{h_1, h_2, ..., h_n\}$ and $|w_i|$ corresponding to the number of tokens/words in the tweets) until the maximum number of tokens is less than 200 or corresponds to the number of tokens in their historical tweets $\sum_{i=1}^{n} |w_i|$, if $\sum_{i=1}^{n} |w_i| < 200$. We append the sampled text to the beginning of the tweet text, which is to be classified during fine-tuning of SentenceBERT.

Average SentenceBERT for authors (A-SBERT) Given an author a and their historical tweets, H^a. We compute the author representation by averaging the SentenceBERT tweet embeddings h_i' of all $h_i \in H^a$, resulting in: $\bar{a} = \frac{1}{|H^a|} \sum_{k=1}^{|H^a|} h_i'$.

Authorship Attribution (AA) With this technique, we pre-train a neural network to predict the author of a given tweet, $p(a|t_i')$. We forward the SentenceBERT tweet embeddings t_i' into a two-layer feed-forward network parameterized from weight matrices $W_1 \in R^{\frac{d}{2} \times d}$ and $W_2 \in R^{n \times \frac{d}{2}}$, where d is 768 (dimension of the SentenceBERT tweet embeddings), and $n \equiv$ number of authors during the training. Then, we forward the output of the last linear layer to a softmax layer to get a

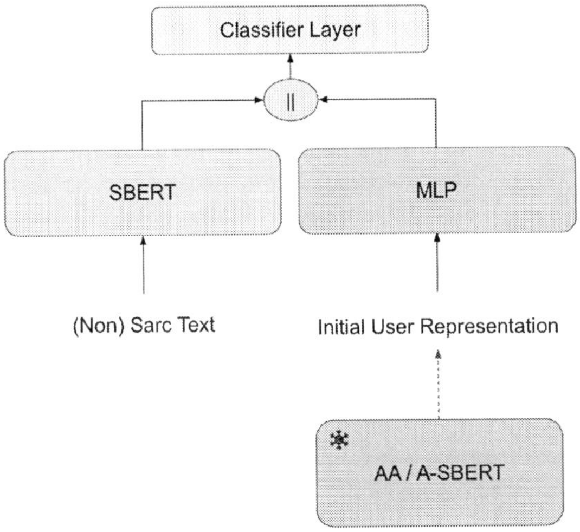

Figure 4: In this figure we show how we combine pre-computed user representation with SBERT. A-SBERT, and AA, are separate encoding methods, to extract initial user representations, utilizing their comments during the history. After computing those, we combine both user and text representations to classify. The encoding layer is frozen during training.

distribution over the authors. After training, we use the linear layers to extract a representation of the author. For each author a, we forward all their historical tweets H^a to the trained network, extracting the predictions, $Y = \{y_h | h \in H^a\}$. Next, we initialize a vector of size n, where $\bar{a}_i = | \{y | y \in Y \wedge y = i\} |$, for $i = (1, ..., n)$, representing the number of times each author is predicted for all tweets of a. We extend this representation by normalizing the vector, so that the sum of all predictions is equal to 1 and thus get another representation - the distribution of authors predicted.

A-SBERT, and AA, are separate encoding methods to extract initial user representations, utilizing their comments during the history. After computing those, we combine both user and text representations, as in Figure 4 to classify the text.

Graph Neural Network (GNN) In this model, we aim to model the social relations between users, and the relations between tweets and users. For this purpose, we build a heterogeneous graph $\mathcal{G} = (V, E)$, where $V = \{U \cup T\}$, which consists of two types of nodes: users and tweets (Plepi and Flek, 2021). In order to model both types of relations, we use two types of edges $E = \{e^U \cup e^T\}$, where e^U represents the social interaction between users [4], and e^T represents the relation between an author and his tweet. Finally, we use Graph Attention Networks (GATs, (Veličković et al., 2018)) to learn the representations of the nodes in the graph. In recent works, GNNs have shown improvements in the performance for various NLP tasks (Mishra et al., 2019a,b; Kacupaj et al., 2021; Sakketou et al., 2022; Plepi et al., 2022b).

We then combine the SentenceBERT model, fine-tuned on the binary task of predicting the label (sarcastic vs. non-sarcastic and intended vs. perceived), given the tweet with an additional layer concatenating the tweet with the author representation computed using Average SentenceBERT for authors or Authorship Attribution. For priming, we also use the SentenceBERT model but fine-tuned to the binary task of predicting the label (sarcastic vs. non-sarcastic and intended vs. perceived), given the sampled text from each author and the sarcastic/non-sarcastic tweet.

5 Experimental Setup

Our experiments are focused on two main tasks: sarcasm detection to predict if a tweet is sarcastic or not, and perspective classification to predict if a sarcastic tweet is intended or perceived. We utilized our new dataset, consisting of 35K tweets, to train our text-only-based models. On the other hand, to train the author-contextual-based models, we also included historical tweets to precompute user representations.

5.1 Implementation details

We split both datasets randomly along the tweet IDs. Splitting them into 80% training and 20% testing tweets. For all models, we use a dropout of 0.2, the Adam optimizer with a learning rate of $1e-4$ and weighted cross entropy loss. Each model was trained for a total of 10 epochs, with a batch size of 32, and was saved each time the performance on the validation set is topped. We pre-processed the data using the DistilRoBERTa (Sanh et al., 2019) Tokenizer[5]. We replaced mentions of users with $@user$, encoded emojies with text, removed URLs, non-ASCII characters and digits. The dataset and the code repository for reproducibility are available

[4]Interactions on Twitter include quoting, mentioning, or replying

[5]https://huggingface.co/sentence-transformers/all-distilroberta-v1

Dataset	Model	F1	Accuracy
$N = 34938$	SBERT	74.4	74.5
	Priming	77.5	77.7
	AA	79.3	79.3
	A-SBERT	80.1	80.1
	GNN	**82.0**	**82.2**

Table 6: Accuracy and macro F1 scores as percentages for sarcasm detection.

here https://github.com/caisa-lab/konvens2023-sarcasm-detection.git.

6 Results and Analysis

6.1 Sarcasm Detection

Our initial experiments focused on the task of sarcasm detection, and we show the results in Table 6. As also seen in previous works (Bamman and Smith, 2015; Amir et al., 2016; Plepi and Flek, 2021), author-contextual-based models outperform text-based models. The additional context from the author's representations enriches the text features and enhances its performance on the task of sarcasm detection.

Our results' analysis revealed that GNN based model is our best-performing one with an 82.2% F1-score. Modeling social network interactions as graphs proves to be an effective way to learn better representations for both text and users. Furthermore, author attribution performed slightly worse than A-SBERT, mainly due to sparsity in AA representation. Another limitation of AA is its scaling over more authors. Overall, GNN and A-SBERT proved to be the most effective in terms of both performance and computational costs, due to no additional training for computing the author representation.

6.2 Conversational context

In addition, we also incorporate conversational context, which includes oblivious and eliciting tweets into our models. [6] We observe an improvement in all our models, where the most significant one is for the text-only SBERT model, with 10.4%. Interestingly, the model that gains less from the conversational context is the GNN model with only 1.3% (Table 7). One reason for this might be due to the way in which the GNN model incorporates the additional context. In the GNN model, the oblivious and eliciting tweets are added as separate nodes in the graph, while for the other models, we incorporate the conversational context by concatenating with the text to be classified. The best-performing model in this setup is the author attribution-based model.

[6] Except priming due to the maximum length limitation that can be taken as an input to the SBERT model.

Dataset	Model	F1	Accuracy
$N = 34938$	o/e SBERT	84.9	84.9
	o/e A-SBERT	85.0	85.0
	o/e AA	**85.6**	**85.5**
	o/e GNN	83.0	83.5

Table 7: Accuracy and macro F1 scores as percentages for sarcasm detection. O/e indicates the usage of eliciting and oblivious tweets.

Dataset	Model	F1	Accuracy
$N = 16278$	SentenceBERT	68.5	79.2
	Priming	70.9	79.8
	A-SBERT	70.6	79.2
	AA	71.3	**82.2**
	GNN	**72.2**	80.8

Table 8: Accuracy and macro F1 scores as percentages for perspective classification.

6.3 Sarcasm Perspective Classification

Finally, we also experimented with the perspective classification task. Here, we face an imbalanced dataset, where 75.2% is intended sarcasm and 24.8% is perceived sarcasm. Our results for this task are shown in Table 8. We notice a lower improvement of at most only 3.0%, of author-contextual-based models over the SBERT model compared to sarcasm detection task, where the improvement was up to 7.6%. These results also align with the conclusion in (Oprea and Magdy, 2019; Plepi and Flek, 2021), on the perception classification task. Hence, we believe that modelling the representation of the author is less useful for the classification of perceived sarcasm. To increase the number of tweets classified as perceived, it could be of benefit to additionally model user embeddings for the audience of the tweet, predicting how individual users will react towards the tweet.

6.4 Error Analysis

Generally, we found that in the perception classification task, perceived tweets are harder to detect than intended sarcasm, which is in line with the results of (Oprea and Magdy, 2019; Plepi and Flek, 2021). This challenge is caused not only by the imbalance but also by the complexity of perceived sarcasm, and how the text is interpreted from the broad audience on Twitter. Table 9 presents the percent-

Model	F_I	F_P
SBERT	59.1	7.5
Priming	50.9	9.9
A-SBERT	49.2	11.4
AA	58.5	4.5
GNN	51.4	7.8
o/e SBERT	50.4	7.8
o/e A-SBERT	39.9	9.1
o/e AA	38.3	10.6
o/e GNN	50.6	8.2

Table 9: False predicted sarcastic perspectives as percentages in relation to gold labels for all models used. F_I is the percentage of perceived tweets falsely classified as intended; F_P, the percentage of intended tweets falsely classified as perceived. Number of test instances: 3343 tweets.

ages of misclassified examples for both perceived and intended sarcasm across different models. In the first part, we show the models without conversational context. Consistently across all models, one can observe a higher percentage of misclassified perceived sarcasm compared to intended sarcasm. Improving the quality and quantity of perceived sarcasm remains a challenging task, given its subjective nature that is often influenced by the audience's diverse social and cultural backgrounds, which may influence their interpretation of tweets on a certain topic. However, as the performance improves by adding the conversational context, it seems that the improvement comes mainly from the classifications of the perceived tweets. We notice a significant drop in the percentage for false classified perceived tweets as intended. These results show the importance of exploring the use of additional context that involves the audience to enhance the detection of perceived sarcasm.

7 Conclusions

In this work, we present an improvement of reactive supervision, in order to collect higher-quality data for the sarcasm detection task. Our manual analysis indicates a reduced number of false positives due to the reduction of noise in the sarcastic data, and removal of unclear cues. In addition, we also collect conversational and author context for our dataset in order to enhance the performance in the sarcasm detection task. Our findings show the importance of additional context in both the sarcasm detection task and the perception classification.

Limitations

Our dataset was collected only in the English language, and the dataset might be focused more on English speakers' sarcasm. In addition, the amount of perceived sarcasm that we collected is lower than the intended sarcasm. The main reason is the complexity of the perspective sarcasm, and the difficulty in solving cases that request additional clarification from the users. Future work can focus more on analyzing these cases by taking into account the topic where the potential sarcastic comment was made and also the communities in social media that may perceive such text as sarcastic. Moreover, it might be interesting to include an additional sarcastic type that is both intended and perceived. However, this type might be difficult to capture using distant supervision, and might need to be combined with additional manual annotation of the conversational thread where the cue tweet is happening. In our experiments, we used a pretrained model SBERT (Reimers and Gurevych, 2019); however, the results might slightly differ with the usage of bigger and more recent pretrained models. Finally, we did not focus on extracting different demographic features from the historical data of the users. Such features might improve the analysis and understanding of the perceived sarcasm (Oprea and Magdy, 2020b). In addition, one could explore adding feature with respect to the political topics, such as political bias in a conversation, in order to improve conversational features for the sarcasm detection task (Kannangara, 2018; Ghosh et al., 2020).

Ethical Considerations

Improving the performance of artificial agents by modeling the personal characteristics of online users' language requires careful consideration of a wide range of ethical concerns.

To ensure data privacy, all collected user history is kept separately on protected servers, linked to the raw text only through hashed anonymous IDs for each user. The collected dataset is solely limited to the purpose of this study for sarcasm detection, and no individual posts shall be republished (Hewson and Buchanan, 2013). Moreover, we utilize publicly available Twitter data in a purely observational (Norval and Henderson, 2017) and non-intrusive manner.

The use of models that incorporate contextual user information may carry the risk of invoking stereotyping and essentialism, as the models may lean toward labeling people rather than posts (Rudman and Glick, 2008). Therefore, it is crucial to remain mindful of these effects when interpreting the model results in its own end-application context.

References

Brian P. Ackerman. 1982. Contextual integration and utterance interpretation: The ability of children and adults to interpret sarcastic. *Child Development, Volume 53*, pages 1075–1083.

Silvio Amir, Byron C. Wallace, Hao Lyu, Paula Carvalho, and Mário J. Silva. 2016. Modelling context with user embeddings for sarcasm detection in social media. In *Proceedings of The 20th SIGNLL Conference on Computational Natural Language Learning*, pages 167–177, Berlin, Germany. Association for Computational Linguistics.

David Bamman and Noah Smith. 2015. Contextualized sarcasm detection on twitter. In *Proceedings of the International AAAI Conference on Web and Social Media*, volume 9.

Francesco Barbieri, Horacio Saggion, and Francesco Ronzano. 2014. Modelling sarcasm in Twitter, a novel approach. In *Proceedings of the 5th Workshop on Computational Approaches to Subjectivity, Sentiment and Social Media Analysis*, pages 50–58, Baltimore, Maryland. Association for Computational Linguistics.

Alexandru-Costin Băroiu and Stefan Trăusan-Matu. 2022. Automatic sarcasm detection: Systematic literature review. *Information* ***2022****, 13, 399.*

Paula Carvalho, Luís Sarmento, Mário J Silva, and Eugénio De Oliveira. 2009. Clues for detecting irony in user-generated contents: oh...!! it's" so easy";-. In *Proceedings of the 1st international CIKM workshop on Topic-sentiment analysis for mass opinion*, pages 53–56.

Dmitry Davidov, Oren Tsur, and Ari Rappoport. 2010a. Semi-supervised recognition of sarcasm in twitter and amazon. In *Proceedings of the fourteenth conference on computational natural language learning*, pages 107–116.

Dmitry Davidov, Oren Tsur, and Ari Rappoport. 2010b. Semi-supervised recognition of sarcasm in Twitter and Amazon. In *Proceedings of the Fourteenth Conference on Computational Natural Language Learning*, pages 107–116, Uppsala, Sweden. Association for Computational Linguistics.

Jenny L Davis, Tony P Love, and Gemma Killen. 2018. Seriously funny: The political work of humor on social media. *New Media & Society*, 20(10):3898–3916.

Shelly Dews, Joan Kaplan, and Ellen Winner. 1995. Why not say it directly? the social functions of irony. *Discourse processes*, 19(3):347–367.

Megan L. Dress, Roger J. Kreuz, Kristen E. Link, and Gina M. Caucci. 2008. Regional variation in the use of sarcasm. *Journal of Language and Social Psychology*, 27(1):71–85.

Elena Filatova. 2012. Irony and sarcasm: Corpus generation and analysis using crowdsourcing. In *Proceedings of the Eighth International Conference on Language Resources and Evaluation (LREC'12)*, pages 392–398, Istanbul, Turkey. European Language Resources Association (ELRA).

Debanjan Ghosh, Avijit Vajpayee, and Smaranda Muresan. 2020. A report on the 2020 sarcasm detection shared task. *arXiv preprint arXiv:2005.05814*.

Raymond W Gibbs. 1986. On the psycholinguistics of sarcasm. *Journal of experimental psychology: general*, 115(1):3.

Roberto González-Ibánez, Smaranda Muresan, and Nina Wacholder. 2011. Identifying sarcasm in twitter: a closer look. In *Proceedings of the 49th Annual Meeting of the Association for Computational Linguistics: Human Language Technologies*, pages 581–586.

Devamanyu Hazarika, Soujanya Poria, Sruthi Gorantla, Erik Cambria, Roger Zimmermann, and Rada Mihalcea. 2018. Cascade: Contextual sarcasm detection in online discussion forums. In *Proceedings of the 27th International Conference on Computational Linguistics*, pages 1837–1848.

Claire Hewson and Tom Buchanan. 2013. Ethics guidelines for internet-mediated research. The British Psychological Society.

Aditya Joshi, Pushpak Bhattacharyya, and Mark James Carman. 2016. Automatic sarcasm detection: A survey. *ACM Computing Surveys (CSUR)*, 50:1 – 22.

Endri Kacupaj, Joan Plepi, Kuldeep Singh, Harsh Thakkar, Jens Lehmann, and Maria Maleshkova. 2021. Conversational question answering over knowledge graphs with transformer and graph attention networks. In *Proceedings of the 16th Conference of the European Chapter of the Association for Computational Linguistics: Main Volume*, pages 850–862, Online. Association for Computational Linguistics.

Sandeepa Kannangara. 2018. Mining twitter for fine-grained political opinion polarity classification, ideology detection and sarcasm detection. In *Proceedings of the Eleventh ACM International Conference on Web Search and Data Mining*, pages 751–752.

Anupam Khattri, Aditya Joshi, Pushpak Bhattacharyya, and Mark Carman. 2015. Your sentiment precedes you: Using an author's historical tweets to predict sarcasm. In *Proceedings of the 6th workshop on computational approaches to subjectivity, sentiment and social media analysis*, pages 25–30.

Mikhail Khodak, Nikunj Saunshi, and Kiran Vodrahalli. 2017. A large self-annotated corpus for sarcasm. *arXiv preprint arXiv:1704.05579*.

Quoc Le and Tomas Mikolov. 2014. Distributed representations of sentences and documents. In *Proceedings of the 31st International Conference on International Conference on Machine Learning - Volume 32*, ICML'14, page II–1188–II–1196. JMLR.org.

Pushkar Mishra, Marco Del Tredici, Helen Yannakoudakis, and Ekaterina Shutova. 2019a. Abusive Language Detection with Graph Convolutional Networks. In *Proceedings of the 2019 Conference of the North American Chapter of the Association for Computational Linguistics: Human Language Technologies, Volume 1 (Long and Short Papers)*, Minneapolis, Minnesota.

Rohan Mishra, Pradyumn Prakhar Sinha, Ramit Sawhney, Debanjan Mahata, Puneet Mathur, and Rajiv Ratn Shah. 2019b. SNAP-BATNET: Cascading author profiling and social network graphs for suicide ideation detection on social media. In *Proceedings of the 2019 Conference of the North American Chapter of the Association for Computational Linguistics: Student Research Workshop*, pages 147–156, Minneapolis, Minnesota. Association for Computational Linguistics.

Chris Norval and Tristan Henderson. 2017. Contextual consent: Ethical mining of social media for health research. *CoRR*, abs/1701.07765.

Silviu Oprea and Walid Magdy. 2019. Exploring author context for detecting intended vs perceived sarcasm. In *Proceedings of the 57th Annual Meeting of the Association for Computational Linguistics*, pages 2854–2859, Florence, Italy. Association for Computational Linguistics.

Silviu Oprea and Walid Magdy. 2020a. iSarcasm: A dataset of intended sarcasm. In *Proceedings of the 58th Annual Meeting of the Association for Computational Linguistics*, pages 1279–1289, Online. Association for Computational Linguistics.

Silviu Vlad Oprea and Walid Magdy. 2020b. The effect of sociocultural variables on sarcasm communication online. *Proceedings of the ACM on Human-Computer Interaction*, 4(CSCW1):1–22.

Hongliang Pan, Zheng Lin, Peng Fu, Yatao Qi, and Weiping Wang. 2020. Modeling intra and intermodality incongruity for multi-modal sarcasm detection. In *Findings of the Association for Computational Linguistics: EMNLP 2020*, pages 1383–1392, Online. Association for Computational Linguistics.

Joan Plepi and Lucie Flek. 2021. Perceived and intended sarcasm detection with graph attention networks. In *Findings of the Association for Computational Linguistics: EMNLP 2021*, pages 4746–4753, Punta Cana, Dominican Republic. Association for Computational Linguistics.

Joan Plepi, Béla Neuendorf, and Lucie Flek. 2022a. Unifying data perspectivism and personalization: An application to social norms. In *Proceedings of the 2022 Conference on Empirical Methods in Natural Language Processing*, pages 7391–7402. Association for Computational Linguistics.

Joan Plepi, Flora Sakketou, Henri-Jacques Geiss, and Lucie Flek. 2022b. Temporal graph analysis of misinformation spreaders in social media. In *Proceedings of TextGraphs-16: Graph-based Methods for Natural Language Processing*, pages 89–104, Gyeongju, Republic of Korea. Association for Computational Linguistics.

Tomás Ptácek, Ivan Habernal, and Jun Hong. 2014. Sarcasm detection on czech and english twitter. In *COLING 2014*, pages 213–223.

Ashwin Rajadesingan, Reza Zafarani, and Huan Liu. 2015. Sarcasm detection on twitter: A behavioral modeling approach. In *Proceedings of the eighth ACM international conference on web search and data mining*, pages 97–106.

Nils Reimers and Iryna Gurevych. 2019. entence- bert: Sentence embeddings using siamese bert- networks. In *In Proceedings of the 2019 Conference on Empirical Methods in Natural Language Processing and the 9th International Joint Conference on Natural Language Processing (EMNLP-IJCNLP)*, pages 3982–3992. Association for Computational Linguistics.

Antonio Reyes, Paolo Rosso, and Tony Veale. 2013. A multidimensional approach for detecting irony in twitter. *Language resources and evaluation*, 47(1):239–268.

Ellen Riloff, Ashequl Qadir, Prafulla Surve, Lalindra De Silva, Nathan Gilbert, and Ruihong Huang. 2013. Sarcasm as contrast between a positive sentiment and negative situation. In *Proceedings of the 2013 conference on empirical methods in natural language processing*, pages 704–714.

Patricia Rockwell and Evelyn M. Theriot. 2001. Culture, gender, and gender mix in encoders of sarcasm: A self-assessment analysis. *Communication Research Reports*, 18(1):44–52.

Laurie A Rudman and Peter Glick. 2008. The social psychology of gender: How power and intimacy shape gender relations.

Flora Sakketou, Joan Plepi, Riccardo Cervero, Henri Jacques Geiss, Paolo Rosso, and Lucie Flek. 2022. FACTOID: A new dataset for identifying misinformation spreaders and political bias. In *Proceedings of the Thirteenth Language Resources and Evaluation Conference*, pages 3231–3241, Marseille, France. European Language Resources Association.

Victor Sanh, Lysandre Debut, Julien Chaumond, and Thomas Wolf. 2019. Distilbert, a distilled version of bert: smaller, faster, cheaper and lighter.

Boaz Shmueli, Lun-Wei Ku, and Soumya Ray. 2020. Reactive supervision: A new method for collecting sarcasm data. *Proceedings of the 2020 Conference on Empirical Methods in Natural Language Processing*, pages 2553–2559.

Oren Tsur, Dmitry Davidov, and Ari Rappoport. 2010. Icwsm—a great catchy name: Semi-supervised recognition of sarcastic sentences in online product reviews. In *Proceedings of the International AAAI Conference on Web and Social Media*, volume 4.

Petar Veličković, Guillem Cucurull, Arantxa Casanova, Adriana Romero, Pietro Liò, and Yoshua Bengio. 2018. Graph Attention Networks. *International Conference on Learning Representations*. Accepted as poster.

Byron C. Wallace, Do Kook Choe, Laura Kertz, and Eugene Charniak. 2014. Humans require context to infer ironic intent (so computers probably do, too). In *Proceedings of the 52nd Annual Meeting of the Association for Computational Linguistics (Volume 2: Short Papers)*, pages 512–516, Baltimore, Maryland. Association for Computational Linguistics.

Changsong Wen, Guoli Jia, and Jufeng Yang. 2023. Dip: Dual incongruity perceiving network for sarcasm detection. In *Proceedings of the IEEE/CVF Conference on Computer Vision and Pattern Recognition*, pages 2540–2550.

Nan Xu, Zhixiong Zeng, and Wenji Mao. 2020. Reasoning with multimodal sarcastic tweets via modeling cross-modality contrast and semantic association. In *Proceedings of the 58th Annual Meeting of the Association for Computational Linguistics*, pages 3777–3786, Online. Association for Computational Linguistics.

Meishan Zhang, Yue Zhang, and Guohong Fu. 2016. Tweet sarcasm detection using deep neural network. In *Proceedings of COLING 2016, the 26th International Conference on Computational Linguistics: technical papers*, pages 2449–2460.

Regular expressions
r"not being sarcastic"
r"not(\s*[A-Za-z,;'\\\/s@])* \s*sarcastic") r"(sarcastic)\s*(\?)+"
r"wasn't being sarcastic"
r"wasnt being sarcastic"
r"wasn't being sarcastic"
r"was not being sarcastic"
r"weren't being sarcastic"
r"weren't being sarcastic"
r"werent being sarcastic"
r"were not being sarcastic"
r"(sarcastic)\s*(\?)+"
r"sarcastic\sor"
r"hope(\s*[A-Za-z,;'\\s@])*\s*being sarcastic"
r"hope(\s*[A-Za-z,;'\\s@])*\s*being(\s* A-Za-z,;'\\s@)*\s*sarcastic"
r"hope you're being sarcastic"
r"pray(\s*[A-Za-z,;'\\s@])*\s*being sarcastic"
r"if(\s*[A-Za-z,;'\\s@])*\s*being sarcastic"
r"sarcastic[A-Za-z,;'\\s@]*\s*correct"
r"sarcastic\s*([A-Za-z,;'\\s@]\s)0,2 right"
r"are you being sarcastic"

Table 10: Compound regular expression used to filter tweets incorrectly identified as cue tweets.

A Regular Expressions

Table 10, shows a list of curated regular expressions that we used to filter out false positive cue tweets. The main target class that was fixed from the regular expressions, was the perceived sarcasm, where the number of false positive rate was significantly reduced.

SpeakGer: A meta-data enriched speech corpus of German state and federal parliaments

Kai-Robin Lange and **Carsten Jentsch**
Department of Statistics, TU Dortmund University, 44221 Dortmund, Germany
{kalange, jentsch} @statistik.tu-dortmund.de

Abstract

The application of natural language processing on political texts as well as speeches has become increasingly relevant in political sciences due to the ability to analyze large text corpora which cannot be read by a single person. But such text corpora often lack critical meta information, detailing for instance the party, age or constituency of the speaker, that can be used to provide an analysis tailored to more fine-grained research questions. To enable researchers to answer such questions with quantitative approaches such as natural language processing, we provide the SpeakGer data set, consisting of German parliament debates from all 16 federal states of Germany as well as the German Bundestag from 1947-2023, split into a total of 10,806,105 speeches. This data set includes rich meta data in form of information on both reactions from the audience towards the speech as well as information about the speaker's party, their age, their constituency and their party's political alignment, which enables a deeper analysis. We further provide three exploratory analyses, detailing topic shares of different parties throughout time, a descriptive analysis of the development of the age of an average speaker as well as a sentiment analysis of speeches of different parties with regards to the COVID-19 pandemic.

1 Introduction

In February of 2022, Germany's chancellor Scholz held a speech in the German Bundestag regarding the outbreak of the Russian-Ukrainian war of 2022. It was one of the most prolific speeches in a German parliament in the latest years due to its impact on Germany's foreign and defense policy, as it can be seen as the starting point for an increase in military spending and distancing towards the Russian government. But such decisions and speeches portrait the political stance of the speaker but not necessarily of the entire government or the speaker's party. We propose a data set with parliamentary debates from 16 German federal state parliaments as well as the German Bundestag over the time span of 76 years which is split into individual speeches with meta data to identify the current speaker. This meta data enables the analysis of topics, opinions and speech patterns of different politicians by party, political alignment, age, or constituency. We additionally identified comments from the audience, interrupting the speeches, to enable the analysis of crowd reactions to specific topics or speech patterns. We also labeled the speeches of session chairs: analyses can thus reduce the text corpus to only politically relevant speeches. As our data contains speeches from all 16 federal state parliaments, it can also be used to compare speeches across states to verify regional differences. We will publish the data set upon publication of this paper.

Further, we conduct an exploratory data analysis on the given corpus, using the "party" meta data to analyze party topic shares as well as the sentiment of the 7 Bundestag parties in COVID-19 related speeches. We then use the "age" indicator to analyze the developement of the average speaker age across time.

2 Related Work

In recent years, the interest in researching German political speeches by the means of Natural Language Processing has greatly increased. For instance, Lange et al. (2022a) identify important political change points in the German political discourse using RollingLDA (Rieger et al., 2021, 2022), a time-varying version of the topic model LDA (Blei et al., 2003), on a similar political data set of speeches of the German Bundestag. Another common research topic is the comparison of party positions (Ceron et al., 2022), estimation of political alignment or ideological clarity of German and European political parties by using document scaling techniques. Some follow a classical bag-of-

Proceedings of the 3rd Workshop on Computational Linguistics for the Political and Social Sciences, pages 19–28
September 22, 2023. ©2023 Association for Computational Linguistics

word approach (Jentsch et al., 2020, 2021; Slapin and Proksch, 2008; Proksch and Slapin, 2010; Lo et al., 2016), while others use topic models such as Top2Vec (Angelov, 2020) to scale the available speeches or party manifestos (Diaf and Fritsche, 2022). Such analyses have also been extended to the predecessors of the Federal Republic of Germany, as Walter et al. (2021) analyze political biases throughout the years using Reichstag as well as Bundestag data by using diachronic embeddings. Recent developments have also demonstrated the importance of claims and frames for the analysis of party positions, as Blokker et al. (2022) exemplified using a data set of party manifestos. This aforementioned research does however often focus on the federal political level but disregards politics on the state level and below. And even at state level such analyses can often only differentiate their findings by party by using party manifestos over parliamentary speeches, as the available data sets used do not provide the necessary meta data. Goet (2019) also argues that such meta information is important to, for instance, measure political polarity in a supervised manner. The SpeakGer data set is meant to enable such fine-grained political research by meta-data enrichment.

In recent years, several similar data sets have been released which however lack some properties that are needed for quantitative text analysis of German parliaments. For instance, Open Parliament TV provide an interface for qualitative researchers for speeches in the German Bundestag from 2013 to 2023, split into individual speeches. This data set does however lack the speeches from the federal state parliaments and all Bundestag speeches prior to 2013. The ParlSpeech data set (Rauh and Schwalbach, 2020) provides split speeches of the German Bundestag from 1991 to 2018, but does not include speeches prior to this or from the 16 state parliaments. Still, Rauh and Schwalbach (2020) include information, to which agenda item the current speech refers to, which our corpus does not as of the publication of this paper, due to the different agenda and document structures across the 17 parliaments and the differences in stenographic reporting across 76 years. Abrami et al. (2022) provide a similar data set which also includes parliamentary documents of the German Bundestag and the German federal state parliaments. This data set is also only provided in already pre-processed and part-of-speech-annotated form, while we publish unprocessed data to enable all researchers to apply pre-processing of their liking. We also split our data set by speeches and equip it with meta data about all speakers to enable a more fine-grained political analysis which includes meta-data such as the constituency, the party and the year of birth of all speakers while also allowing users to filter out speeches e.g. by session chairs and comments from the audience. Additionally, our data set contains data of the first 10 legislative periods of the federal state parliament of Berlin and the first 8 legislative periods of the federal state parliament of Baden-Württemberg.

3 Data collection

We primarily recieved our data from the websites of the respective parliaments. However, some parliaments do not publish the documents of all legislative periods on their website, even if they are available. Thus, we collected additional documents from the Parlamentsspiegel-website and looked for additional digitized documents in corresponding local museums. Still, not every legislative period of every German federal state parliament is digitized, as Bremen, Hamburg and Niedersachsen are missing digitized versions of the first legislative periods. However, representatives of all three federal state parliaments assured us that the remaining protocols are planned to be digitized as a part of a retro-digitization project. We therefore aim to update our data set as soon as the missing protocols are available to us. The source of each protocol gathered is detailed in Table 1. To enable a time-dependent analysis, we collected the exact dates for each plenary session of all 17 parliaments and integrated these dates into our meta data. We directly received this information from the respective parliament officials we contacted.

3.1 Text extraction and spelling correction

Out of the available 240 legislative periods, the protocols of a total of 106 periods are either available as text files or pdf-files from which text can be extracted. Some of the remaining documents are scanned pdf files in which each page of the protocol is only displayed as a picture with no possibility for direct text extraction. To extract the text from these documents, we use Google's tesseract (Kay, 2007), a model for Optimal Character Recognition (OCR), with the German language option (and a Fraktur-option for the first legislative period of the state

Table 1: Sources and links to all protocols that were analyzed. If the protocols of a parliament cannot be found in one place, we provide multiple sources for all possible legislative periods.

Parliament (English name)	Legislative period	Source
Baden-Württemberg (Baden-Wuerttemberg)	12-17	Landtag von Baden-Württemberg
	1-11	Württembergische Landesbibliothek
Bayern (Baveria)	1-18	Bayrischer Landtag
Berlin	12-19	Abgeordnetenhaus Berlin
	6-11	Zentral- und Landesbibliothek Berlin
	1-5	Zentral- und Landesbibliothek Berlin
Brandenburg	8-10	Landtag Brandenburg
	1-7	Parlamentsspiegel
Bremen	18-20	Bremische Bürgerschaft
	7-17	Parlamentsspiegel
Bundestag	1-20	Deutscher Bundestag
Hamburg	20-22	Hamburgerische Bürgschaft
	6-19	Parlamentsspiegel
Hessen	1-20	Hessischer Landtag
Mecklenburg-Vorpommern (Mecklenburg-Western Pomerania)	1-8	Landtag Mecklenburg-Vorpommern
Niedersachsen (Lower Saxony)	17-18	Landtag Niedersachsen
	8-16	Parlamentsspiegel
Nordrhein-Westfalen (North Rine Westfalia)	1-18	Landtag Nordrhein-Westfalen
Rheinland-Pfalz (Rhineland Palatinate)	1-18	Landtag Rheinland-Pfalz
Saarland	14-17	Landtag des Saarlandes
	7-13	Parlamentsspiegel
Sachsen (Saxony)	1-8	Sächsischer Landtag
Sachsen-Anhalt (Saxony-Anhalt)	6-8	Landtag von Sachsen-Anhalt
	1-5	Parlamentsspiegel
Schleswig-Holstein	1-20	Schleswig-Holsteiner Landtag
Thüringen (Thuringia)	4-7	Thüringer Landtag
	1-4	Parlamentsspiegel

Bayern). We improve tesseract's performance by binarizing each page to a pure black-white format using Otsu's threshold (Otsu, 1979) and by correcting a possible skew of each page using OpenCV (Bradski, 2000). We found tesseract to best capture the text of two-column documents in a sample of our data we used as an experiment.

Such an OCR model is however not able to detect a text perfectly, but will, especially for older and less clean fonts, yield "spelling"-errors. That is, despite not literally spelling the word, single letters of a word can be misinterpreted as a different letter, having a similar effect to a misspelled word. The term "Bravo!" is for instance often misclassified as "Bravol" by tesseract. We contemplated using a prediction-based spelling correction, e.g. a masked word prediction based on BERT (Devlin et al., 2019), but due to frequent mistakes in particularly old documents, this context-based prediction yielded sub-optimal results. To correct the errors that are caused by such OCR models, we therefore aim to instead use a lexicon-based approach by using Symspell's (Garbe, 2012) German language dictionary which we additionally provided with the last names of all members of parliament (mps) of all 16 federal state parliaments to stop the spelling correction from affecting our speech-splitting. We detect every word in every OCR scanned document that is not part of this dictionary and determine, whether there is a word in the dictionary that is sufficiently similar to the misspelled word with regards to their Levenshtein-distance (Levenshtein et al., 1966), that is the number of character transformations needed to turn one misspelled token into a correctly spelled token. This distance is chosen dynamically, depending on the word's length. For instance, a word with 7 characters is allowed to have a larger levenshtein-distance to it's "correct spelling" than a word with just two characters. We publish both the spell-checked versions as well as the original processed documents.

3.2 Speech splitting

To identify speeches, we first gathered crucial information about possible speakers by scraping meta data about the first name, last name, year of birth, party, constituency and Wikipedia-links of each speaker, if available. For this, we used the Wikipedia-pages of each federal state parliament, detailing all participating members of parliament during each legislative period. To simplify the interpretation of smaller and regional parties, we also include the political alignment of the parties according to their Wikipedia-pages (e.g. left-populist, social democratic, liberal or conservative). The regular expressions used to identify the start and end of a plenary session as well as splitting the speeches can be found in our GitHub-repository. We will also use said GitHub-repository to detail link and update on the publication of the data set. In the following paragraphs, we describe how they are designed as well as their purpose.

To split the speeches, we first determine, where the plenary session starts and when it ends to cut off the table of contents and a possible appendix to the pdf-file. To account for possible OCR mistakes, we use Regular Expressions to identify either a comment such as "(Beginn: ... Uhr)" marking the start of a session, or, if this cannot be detected, the first appearance of common speech patterns, such as a greeting like "Meine sehr verehrten Damen und Herren". We also incorporate common OCR errors for those phrases in our Regular Expressions, such as misinterpreting an "B" as an "ß". To find the end of the session, we look for either a comment marking the end of the session similar to "(Ende: ... Uhr)" or we end the session when we detect common speech patterns, which are used to close a session like "die Sitzung ist damit geschlossen" or "Ich schließe damit die Sitzung". If none such indicators are found, which usually only happens in old documents with bad quality scans, we heuristically cut the last/first 1000 lines of our document to remove the table of contents and appendix.

After detecting in which part of the document the speeches take place, we split the remaining text into pieces with the use of Regular Expressions and our meta data. All documents have common styles which can be used to identify comments and the start of a speech.

Speeches can be identified by a string search for each line by looking for the last name of said mp, followed by a colon. There are some variations of this, such as including the word "Abgeordneter" or a title before stating the name ("Abgeordneter Dr. Mustermann:"), or the party of the mp ("Mustermann (SPD):"), but the last name of the mp as well as the colon are always present across all analyzed parliaments. Thus, we detect a change in speakers by scanning the lines for the last names of all possible mps in this legislative period paired with a colon. For this we use the names from the mps of the parliament and legislative period that are analyzed, which were scraped from Wikipedia. If we detect the word "Präsident" or get another indication that the speech is held by the chair of the session, we mark it accordingly, as it will likely only cover the organization of the plenary session and rarely contains political statements or arguments.

As a comment, we define additional information provided by the stenographer about the organization of the session (such as information on pauses when the parliament votes on a bill) as well as interjections from the audience during a speech. Such comments can be identified, as they are surrounded by either square or round brackets. Some contain an interjection from a specific member of the parliament, which is detected if the last name of an mp is used in the comment, or about reactions of certain parties, which are detected if said party names are used in the comment. Otherwise, the meta data regarding the speaker is set to "unknown" for such comments. We consider a speech that is interrupted by such a comment to be two separate speeches, before and after the comment, held by the same speaker. This is done to enable the analysis of interactions between comments and speeches such that the effect of a comment on the speech or vice versa can be analyzed.

4 Descriptive Analysis

In total, the SpeakGer data set contains 17,784,802 texts across the 16 German federal state parliaments as well as the German Bundestag, which include a total of 5,510,951 comments, 1,467,746 speeches of session chairs and 10,806,105 speeches of other mps. The total number of documents (in thousands), split into comments, speeches of the session chair and other speeches, separated by parliament are displayed in Table 2.

4.1 Topic shares per party

To determine topic shares per party over time, we use RollingLDA (Rieger et al., 2021), a rolling window approach to topic modeling that creates coherently interpretable topics modeled over time that are allowed to adapt to a changing vocabulary. We thus receive a topic model each year from 1950 to 2022. The years 1947 to 1950 are used to fit the initial model while later years update the model that came beforehand. For this, we consider $K = 30$ topics to give the topic model the opportunity to separate a wide range of political aspects in different topics but still enabling a clear analysis in the scope of this paper. We additionally set the parameters $\alpha = \gamma = \frac{1}{K}$ and the memory-parameter to 4, thus enabling the model to "remember" the previous 4 years to create topics in the current year. We fit our model on the data of all federal state parliaments simultaneously but only use speeches that were not classified as comments to prevent topics simply representing crowd reactions like applause.

The topic shares for each topic over time, separated by party are displayed in Figure 1. For this figure, we used the ggplot-package (Wickham, 2016) for the R programming language (R Core Team, 2022). For better visibility, we limited the plots to topic shares up to 15%, which only has minor implications for most topic. Only the topic share of the Baverian party CSU is off the charts for most of topic 10 and 11, as these cover topics extensively covered in the Baverian parliament. In the figure, the topics' top words over the entire time period are used to title the respective topics graphs. These overall top words most often are not the top words at all times, but still decently represent said topic as a whole. Speeches that are part of documents with particular bad scan quality often contain a lot of misspelled words, which leads to topics that are characterized by commonly misspelled words – this can be seen by observing the top words "dar", "dan", "ale" (which are likely misspelled versions of the words "das" and "alle") of the topics 8 and 15. This filtering aspect of the topic model allows us to focus on the other, relevant topics without the need to account for misspelled words - also due to the properties of RollingLDA, these topics "rotate out" as soon as the OCR errors disappear.

Due to the fact that we perform a topic analysis on documents from all 16 federal state parliaments, several German states have a specific topic designated to them, which can be interpreted as the talk about local affairs. Despite talking about different places, some of these topics overlap, possibly due to similar actions that need to be taken – the city states Berlin, Bremen and Hamburg have a joint topic dealing with city state affairs (Topic 18). We can further inspect the respective topics of these states to gather information about the most important discussion in said parliament at the time. To further analyze the contents of each parliament though, a detailed topic analysis can be performed on only those documents that belong to said parliament. Apart from these topics, which specifically define misspelled words or German states, topics 9, 14, 16, 19, 22, 24, 25, 26, 27 and 28 also cover more general topics that are of interest in every federal state, for instance education, climate change and state-finances. The rest of the topics cover parliament-specific vocabulary like "drucksachen" or "gesetzesentwurf" in topics 11 and 2 respectively.

The topics of political interest confirm several political assumptions to parties that can be made by observing the parties in the Bundestag and considering their party manifestos on a federal level. For instance, we can observe the green party Die Grünen, having the highest topic shares of all parties in topics 16 and 24 covering climate change and agriculture respectively. The party CSU that is only present in the federal state Bavaria, which contains a lot of rural areas, also talks a lot about agriculture while talking the least of all parties about renewable energies and climate change. Conversely, the liberal party FDP, whose party manifestos focus on new technology, have a high topic share in the topic about climate change and renewable energy, while barely talking about agriculture.

For the right-wing party AfD, we observe a high topic share in the topics 19 and 28. Starting from 2020, topic 19 covers the COVID-19 pandemic during which the AfD was very vocal about opposing the lockdowns and other restrictions of the government to prevent the spread of the virus. Topic 28 covers the refugee crisis in Germany starting in 2014, which has been one of the AfD's biggest topics since it was founded in 2014. In 2022, topic 28 transformed about a topic about the Russian-

Table 2: Total number of speeches in thousands in each parliament, divided by party of speaker and whether the speech is a comment or given by the chair of the session. As the party Die Linke is the successor of the parties SED and PDS, we look at the speeches of said parties combined.

Parliament	Chair	Comment	AfD	CDU	CSU	FDP	Grünen	SPD	Linke
Bundestag	378	1168	26	644	144	282	167	605	116
Baden-Württemberg	18	555	14	319	0	106	97	238	0
Bayern	110	312	2	0	263	14	30	115	0
Berlin	38	263	13	144	0	48	49	172	46
Brandenburg	39	75	9	34	0	4	9	83	37
Bremen	37	254	0	91	0	29	33	162	9
Hamburg	69	337	4	120	0	32	7	168	14
Hessen	110	390	7	247	0	74	95	220	24
Mecklenburg-Vorpommern	55	334	22	120	0	15	11	119	113
Niedersachsen	109	226	0	181	0	57	68	152	7
Nordrhein-Westfalen	133	503	8	201	0	73	72	271	5
Rheinland-Pfalz	56	253	7	110	0	29	24	132	0
Saarland	34	122	1	78	0	9	9	76	6
Sachsen	67	129	11	97	0	11	18	35	50
Sachsen-Anhalt	49	106	14	67	0	10	17	32	35
Schleswig-Holstein	87	327	0	157	0	68	29	170	2
Thüringen	62	152	9	69	0	11	8	28	41

Ukrainian war with major parts of the major German parties AfD and Die Linke supporting Russia in the conflict. This is also reflected in our topic models, as both these parties have the highest share of all parties in this topics.

Interestingly, the two biggest parties of Germany, the SPD and CDU barely dominate the shares in any topic. This is likely because these two parties are considered the most centrist parties, that cover a broad range of political topics without extensively focusing on a specific topic.

Overall, the behavior of the major 7 German parties on the state level reflects their behavior on the federal level in the Bundestag. This analysis however only demonstrates this while looking at all federal states combined, to investigate whether this applies only "on average" or in all parliaments, said parliaments need to be evaluated individually.

4.2 Sentiment Analysis

As a further descriptive analysis of our data set, we perform a party-based sentiment analysis across each parliament to see if any party's speeches are particularly positive or negative in speeches regarding the COVID-19 pandemic. As there is no training data set available, we perform an unsupervised sentiment analysis. For this we use Lex2Sent (Lange et al., 2022b), an unsupervised sentiment analysis tool that uses Doc2Vec (Le and Mikolov, 2014) to enhance a lexicon-based sentiment analysis. This approach allows us to specify, how a positive or negative sentiment can be determined for political speeches compared to regular web documents as it is based on a sentiment lexicon specifically catered for this task. Lex2Sent further improves the classical lexicon-approach by measuring the distance of a document to both the positive and negative half of a lexicon using Doc2Vec, which is trained on resampled documents of the original corpus. This resampling leads to a bagging-effect which boosts the performance of this analysis. To enable a political analysis using Lex2Sent, we use the sentiment dictionary for German political language as a lexicon-base for Lex2Sent (Rauh, 2018).

In Figure 2, we display the average sentiment polarity, calculated by Lex2Sent, for each party in 2020 to 2022. The larger the sentiment polarity, the more positive a speech is estimated, with negative values indicating rather negative speeches. We can see that the average sentiment across all parties is rather negative, which is not surprising given the topic at hand. Terms such as "Pandemie" are generally considered to be negative and the speeches thus generally have a negative undertone. What is more interesting is the comparison of the parties' sentiment. For instance, speeches of the right-wing

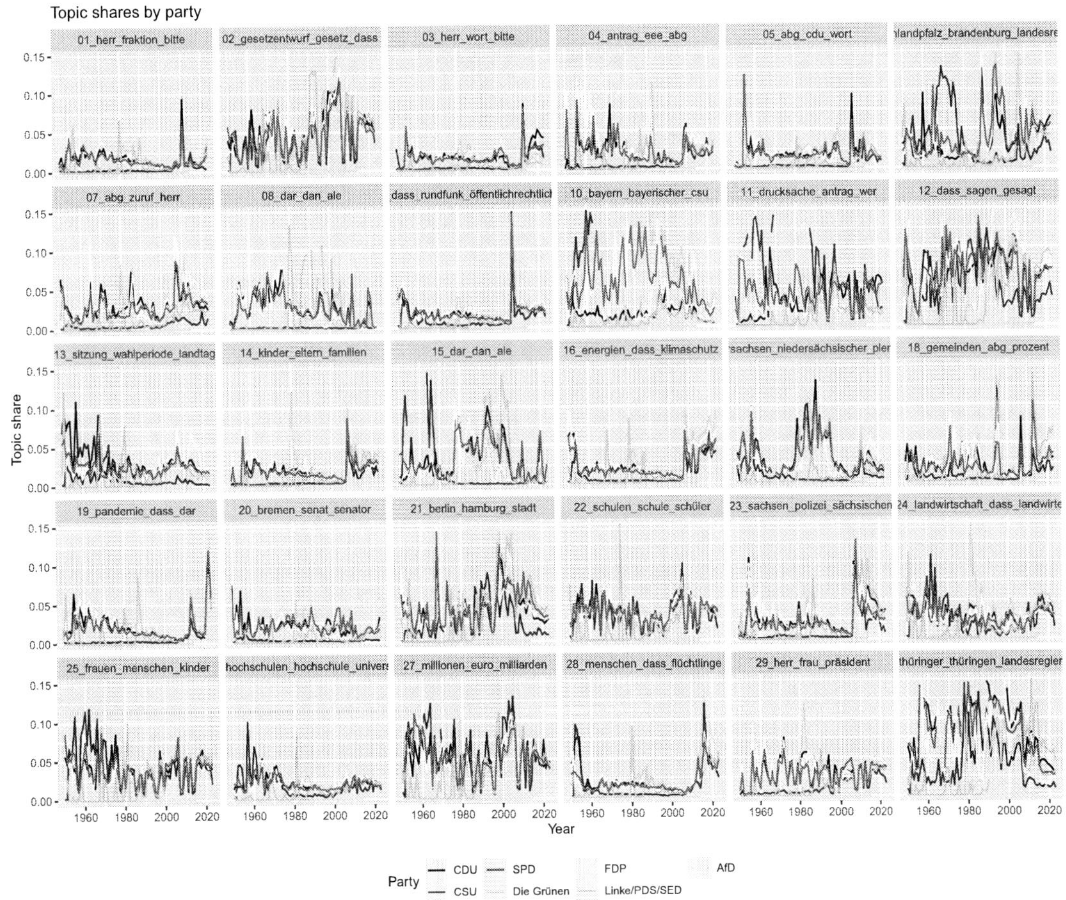

Figure 1: Topic shares of the current 7 Bundestag-parties from 1950 to 2022 in the 16 German federal state parliaments. As the party Die Linke is the successor of the parties SED and PDS, we look at the speeches of said parties combined.

party AfD, which heavily protested the COVID-19 lockdowns and restrictions, are considered to be the most negative in ten of the twelve observed quarters by the model.

In the last two quarters of 2022, the left-wing party Die Linke shows a more negative average sentiment compared to all other parties including the AfD. This is despite them generally delivering positive speeches until this point. One reason for this might be change of party doctrine following Russia's invasion of Ukraine. As mentioned before, major parts of Die Linke are considered to be Russian-favored. The debates resulting from the war outbreak might have thus caused the party to become more confrontational with other parties as a whole. This explanation should however be taken with caution, as the number of speeches concerning COVID-19 has greatly decreased in the last two quarters of 2022 and the observed negative sentiment could this be result of this low sample size.

The Bavarian party CSU also shifted its sentiment over time. As seen in Figure 2, the CSU starts off, having the most positive average sentiment in their speeches concerning COVID-19. During this time, the CSU were party of the government in both the Bundestag and the Bavarian state parliament. During this time the party, and especially their party leader Markus Söder, advocated in favor of hard lockdowns and restrictions. The CSU was thus very in-line with actions taken by the government to handle the pandemic. We see a shift in sentiment starting during the election campaign in the third quarter of 2021, worsening after the elections in 2021. This might be result of the CSU itself not being part of the German federal government anymore and thus not being so compliant with the actions of the government any more.

The same cannot be said for the CSU's sister party CDU however, as the conservative party's sentiment remains rather average across time. The same goes for Die Grüne, the FDP and the SPD.

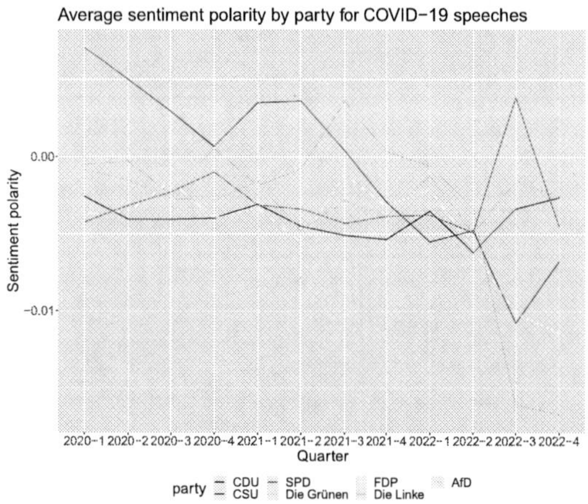

Figure 2: Average sentiment polarites of COVID-19 related speeches of the 7 Bundestag parties in all 17 state and federal parliaments of Germany from 2020 to 2022. The scores were calculated using Lex2Sent, where a negative value indicates a negative speech.

4.3 The age of speakers

In this subsection, we focus on the age of the speakers across Germany. The average age of all registered speakers in the SpeakGer data set from 1947 to 2022 is displayed in Figure 3. We can see that the average age of speakers started to decrease from 54.82 in 1963 to 48.17 in 1973. While the average age remained similar until 1991, the average speaker age started increasing after the German Reunification in 1990. Ultimately, the average speaker age continued to increase, reaching its maximum of 55.38 in 2022. This is partly due to the increasing age of CDU-speakers. While speakers of Germany's largest conservative party averaged at 54.37 years of age in 2018, this increased to an average of 60.04 years in 2021.

5 Summary

We propose the SpeakGer corpus, a comprehensive text data set detailing the long history of German parliamentary debates across 16 federal state parliaments as well as the German Bundestag, split into statements of the session chair, comments and interjections as well as speeches of members of the parliament. Each individual speech is equipped with rich meta data, such as the date of the speech, the

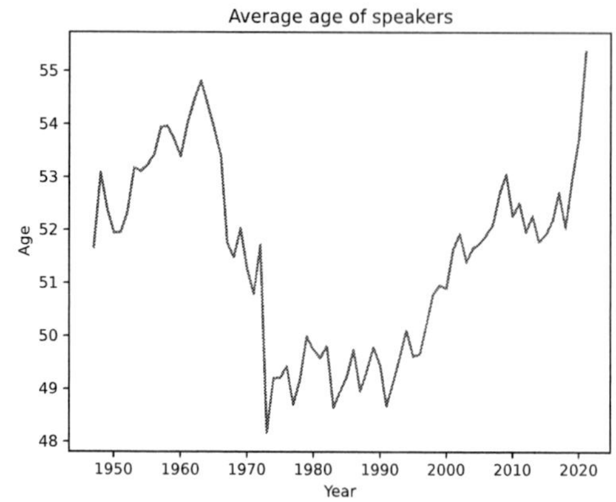

Figure 3: Average age of speakers in German parliaments from 1947 to 2022.

party of the speaker and the political alignment of said party, the speaker's age and the speaker's constituency. In total, the SpeakGer data set contains 10,806,105 speeches. This enables researchers to perform fine-grained political analyses of the data set, in which different parties, age-groups and states can be compared. As an exemplary usage of the data set, we performed unsupervised sentiment analysis as well as time-dependent topic modeling to our data and demonstrate how even simple analyses can provide interesting results with the help of meta data. Our results indicate that regional alterations of Bundestag parties often follow the lead of the federal party, despite regional differences, as the sentiment and topics align with the behavior of the parties on a federal level. For instance, the left-wing party Die Linke appears to follow a more confrontational approach to speeches in federal state parliaments after the outbreak of the Russian-Ukrainian war, even in seemingly unrelated topics such as COVID-19 and despite being part of regional state governments themselves. This is however only a preliminary result of our exploratory analysis and should be inspected further.

In future research, we aim to, among other possible research ideas, further use the SpeakGer data set proposed to inspect, validate and broaden our preliminary results on the differences between regional and federal versions of the same party. As we only focused on the "party" information in our exploratory research in this paper, in future research, we intend to use the remaining meta data, such as the age of the speaker or the speaker's constituency to perform analyses that take spatial and regional aspects into account.

Ethical considerations

We provide this data set with best intentions to enable researchers to gain a new perspective on German politics. We only use publicly available information to equip our corpus with meta data. We however cannot be certain that the data will not be misused to push political agendas by for instance framing a specific party. We do believe that the benefits of such a publicly available data set outweigh the possible negative aspects, as such malicious framing is commonly done without using a data set of federal state parliament speeches.

Limitations

As a result of sub-optimal document-scans in earlier legislative periods in almost all federal state parliaments, not all speeches and speakers could be correctly identified. In addition to this, old scans of the state Nordrhein-Westfalen contain not just one plenary session but multiple, which also had to be manually split. This session splitting might be sub-optimal due to the poor quality scans. While we contacted all federal state parliaments about the specific dates for all plenary sessions and most states were able to provide a complete list of all correct dates, the states Berlin, Niedersachsen and Schleswig-Holstein could only provide us with an incomplete list. Thanks to publicly available information on Wikipedia, we were able to estimate the dates for the missing plenary sessions of these states, which are however subject to some noise. Lastly, as a result of the meta-based splitting of speeches, we are not able to detect speeches of guests of the parliament, such as Wolodomyr Selensky speaking in the German Bundestag on March 17th 2023, as these guests' names are not part of our meta data containing only information about the mps of the parliament. We aim to improve on these aspects of the data set as soon as better OCR methods and the results of the retro-digitization project of the German federal state parliaments are released.

Acknowledgments

This paper is part of a project of the Dortmund Center for data-based Media Analysis (DoCMA) at TU Dortmund University. The work was supported by the Mercator Research Center Ruhr (MERCUR) with project number Pe-2019-0044. In addition, the authors gratefully acknowledge the computing time provided on the Linux HPC cluster at TU Dortmund University (LiDO3), partially funded in the course of the Large-Scale Equipment Initiative by the German Research Foundation (DFG) as project 271512359.

References

Giuseppe Abrami, Mevlüt Bagci, Leon Hammerla, and Alexander Mehler. 2022. German parliamentary corpus (gerparcor). In *Proceedings of the Language Resources and Evaluation Conference*, pages 1900–1906, Marseille, France. European Language Resources Association.

Dimo Angelov. 2020. Top2Vec: Distributed Representations of Topics.

David M. Blei, Andrew Y. Ng, and Michael I. Jordan. 2003. Latent Dirichlet Allocation. *Journal of Machine Learning Research*, 3:993–1022.

Nico Blokker, Tanise Ceron, André Blessing, Erenay Dayanik, Sebastian Haunss, Jonas Kuhn, Gabriella Lapesa, and Sebastian Padó. 2022. Why Justifications of Claims Matter for Understanding Party Positions.

G. Bradski. 2000. The OpenCV Library. *Dr. Dobb's Journal of Software Tools*.

Tanise Ceron, Nico Blokker, and Sebastian Padó. 2022. Optimizing text representations to capture (dis)similarity between political parties.

Jacob Devlin, Ming-Wei Chang, Kenton Lee, and Kristina Toutanova. 2019. BERT: Pre-training of Deep Bidirectional Transformers for Language Understanding.

Sami Diaf and Ulrich Fritsche. 2022. TopicShoal: Scaling Partisanship Using Semantic Search. In *Proceedings of the 18th Conference on Natural Language Processing (KONVENS 2022)*, pages 167–174, Potsdam, Germany. KONVENS 2022 Organizers.

Wolf Garbe. 2012. SymSpell.

Niels D. Goet. 2019. Measuring Polarization with Text Analysis: Evidence from the UK House of Commons, 1811–2015. *Political Analysis*, 27(4):518–539.

Carsten Jentsch, Eun Ryung Lee, and Enno Mammen. 2020. Time-dependent Poisson reduced rank models for political text data analysis. *Computational Statistics & Data Analysis*, 142:106813.

Carsten Jentsch, Eun Ryung Lee, and Enno Mammen. 2021. Poisson reduced-rank models with an application to political text data. *Biometrika*, 108(2):455–468.

Anthony Kay. 2007. Tesseract: An open-source optical character recognition engine.

Kai-Robin Lange, Jonas Rieger, Niklas Benner, and Carsten Jentsch. 2022a. Zeitenwenden: Detecting changes in the German political discourse. pages 47–53.

Kai-Robin Lange, Jonas Rieger, and Carsten Jentsch. 2022b. Lex2Sent: A bagging approach to unsupervised sentiment analysis.

Quoc V. Le and Tomas Mikolov. 2014. Distributed Representations of Sentences and Documents.

Vladimir I Levenshtein et al. 1966. Binary codes capable of correcting deletions, insertions, and reversals. In *Soviet physics doklady*, volume 10, pages 707–710. Soviet Union.

James Lo, Sven-Oliver Proksch, and Jonathan B. Slapin. 2016. Ideological Clarity in Multiparty Competition: A New Measure and Test Using Election Manifestos. *British Journal of Political Science*, 46(3):591–610.

Nobuyuki Otsu. 1979. A threshold selection method from gray-level histograms. *IEEE Transactions on Systems, Man, and Cybernetics*, 9(1):62–66.

Sven-Oliver Proksch and Jonathan B. Slapin. 2010. Position taking in European Parliament speeches. *British Journal of Political Science*, 40(3):587–611.

R Core Team. 2022. *R: A Language and Environment for Statistical Computing*. R Foundation for Statistical Computing, Vienna, Austria.

Christian Rauh. 2018. Validating a sentiment dictionary for German political language—a workbench note. *Journal of Information Technology & Politics*, 15(4):319–343.

Christian Rauh and Jan Schwalbach. 2020. The ParlSpeech V2 data set: Full-text corpora of 6.3 million parliamentary speeches in the key legislative chambers of nine representative democracies.

Jonas Rieger, Carsten Jentsch, and Jörg Rahnenführer. 2021. RollingLDA: An update algorithm of Latent Dirichlet Allocation to construct consistent time series from textual data. In *Findings Proceedings of the 2021 EMNLP-Conference*, pages 2337–2347. ACL.

Jonas Rieger, Kai-Robin Lange, Jonathan Flossdorf, and Carsten Jentsch. 2022. Dynamic change detection in topics based on rolling LDAs. In *Proceedings of the Text2Story'22 Workshop*, volume 3117 of *CEUR-WS*, pages 5–13.

Jonathan B. Slapin and Sven-Oliver Proksch. 2008. A Scaling Model for Estimating Time-Series Party Positions from Texts. *American Journal of Political Science*, 52(3):705–722.

Tobias Walter, Celina Kirschner, Steffen Eger, Goran Glavaš, Anne Lauscher, and Simone Paolo Ponzetto. 2021. Diachronic Analysis of German Parliamentary Proceedings: Ideological Shifts through the Lens of Political Biases.

Hadley Wickham. 2016. *ggplot2: Elegant Graphics for Data Analysis*. Springer-Verlag New York.

Multilabel Legal Element Classification on German Parliamentary Debates in a Low-Ressource Setting

Martin Hock ÷
Technische Universität Dresden
martin.hock@tu-dresden.de

Christopher Klamm ÷
University of Mannheim
klamm@uni-mannheim.de

Abstract

Parliamentary debates provide a broad overview of (legal) pieces of evidence for supporting or opposing the use of force by a state. If a state backs its practice by referring to a legal concept or the legal elements of that concept, the existence of a rule of customary international law (CIL) may be assumed. Traditionally, however, parliamentary debates have rarely been used as a source of CIL. We address this research gap with a joint approach that combines methods from political science, legal studies and natural language processing in order to ascertain the existence of CIL regarding the legal concepts of humanitarian intervention and responsibility to protect. We introduce a new framework and dataset to tackle the task of automatic *legal elements* classification LegalECGPD to analyse the use of force in german parliamentary debates. We performed multiple experiments in low-resource settings, showing the need of in-domain expertise and the existing limitations of supervised approaches when faced with tasks necessitating the interpretation of rich contextual information. Our resources are available under an open-source license for further research.

1 Introduction

The use of force by states is unlawful. The Charter of the United Nations (UNC, the most important treaty of international law) prohibits every threat of or use of force (Art. 2 (4) UNC). There are two undisputed exceptions to the prohibition of the use of force: self-defence (art. 51 UNC) and authorization by the Security Council of the United Nations (arts. 39 and 42 UNC). Two further concepts - humanitarian intervention (HI) and responsibility to protect (R2P) - are legally disputed. Arguments supporting the lawfulness of the latter concepts are often based at least partly on customary international law (CIL) (Gray, 2018, p. 40-64). CIL consists of state practice that is accompanied by a sense of legal obligation, the so-called opinio iuris (Lepard, 2010, p. 6-7). State practice and opinio iuris can be found in all branches of the state (International Law Commission, 2018, conclusion 5). All legal concepts are composed of *legal elements*[1], *these are the requirements that have to be fulfilled in order to achieve legal consequences and effects* (Wienbracke, 2013, p. 25-39). This highlights the importance of the legal elements. Legal elements, however, are highly context specific and cannot be assumed by a given word order. They are always composed of the requirements for legal consequences and effects in a given legal rule and vary from rule to rule. In order to prove the existence of opinio iuris the arguments brought forward to substantiate a legal concept are an important factor: if a state backs its practice by referring to a legal concept in general or to the legal elements of that concept the existence of opinio iuris and thus CIL can be assumed (Lepard, 2010, p. 6-7). The legal elements can be found inter alia in parliamentary debates. For example, Ludger Volmer during the KOSOVO debate[2]:

> *" Es kann keinen Zweifel darin geben, daß es überfällig war, den boshaftesten Despoten in Europa [Element 1], der Krieg gegen sein eigenes Staatsvolk führt, es entwurzelt, in die Wälder treibt und ermorden läßt, [Element 2] in seine Schranken zu verweisen, um eine humanitäre Katastrophe noch größeren Ausmaßes zu verhindern. [Element 3]".*

Scholarship on international law largely ignores parliamentary debates as a source of opinio iuris and thus CIL (a notable exceptions is Henckaerts et al. (2005)). It nevertheless refers to national laws that are enacted and the circumstances of their enactment that need to be taken into account when ascertaining opinio iuris (International Law Commission, 2018, conclusion 6). Part of these circumstances are the parliamentary debates that are

÷ contribution details in app. F

[1] German: Tatbestandsmerkmale

[2] https://dserver.bundestag.de/btp/13/13248.pdf

Proceedings of the 3rd Workshop on Computational Linguistics for the Political and Social Sciences, pages 29–45
September 22, 2023.

conducted in connection with the legislation. In the case of Germany it is highly important to study parliamentary debates since according to the German constitution, parliament is the only body that may legally decide on the use force in international affairs. If parliamentary debates are considered explicitly in international law scholarship the methodological difficulties of including large amounts of text are stressed (see for example Payandeh and Aust (2018, 638) and Bajrami (2022, 160)). We close this gap and treat parliamentary debates as a source of CIL. We provide a new framework for annotating legal elements in parliamentary debates and an annotation of four debates with this new framework, creating our novel "**Legal** **E**lement **C**lassification on **G**erman **P**arliamentary **D**ebates" LegalECGPD dataset. Additional complexity when analysing parliamentary debates is added by the large amount of text in the debates. Legal expertise beyond word search is needed since legal arguments are often ambiguous (i.e. a single sentence can be applied to more than one legal element). Furthermore, the legal concept referred to by a speaker is often not made explicit in parliamentary debates. For example, Minister of Defence Volker Rühe in the KOSOVO debate[3]:

> *"Es geht aber um die Abwehr einer humanitären Katastrophe."*

Implicit in this claim is the legal concept of HI. It is not, however, explicitly mentioned. Nevertheless, the legal element of humanitarian catastrophe is stated. In order to deal with these ambiguities and the lack of explicit references to legal concepts the present system goes beyond word search and shows the need for a more comprehensive approach. From an international law point of view the paper asks weather legal elements can be found in parliamentary debates and thus substantiate the claim that opinio iuris regarding HI and R2P exists. Furthermore, it is asked whether the applied methods of Natural Language Processing (NLP) are sufficiently precise in order to automate the subsumption of parliamentary debates under legal elements.

Advantages in NLP show the possibilities of applying new contextualized language models (Devlin et al. (2019); Reimers and Gurevych (2019); Brown et al. (2020); Lewis et al. (2020); BigScience et al. (2022), and many more) to deal with the automatic identification of supporting and opposing argumentative sentences within natural language (Cabrio and Villata, 2018; Lawrence and Reed, 2019; Reimers et al., 2019; Schaefer and Stede, 2020; Toledo-Ronen et al., 2020; Chakrabarty et al., 2019; Wang et al., 2020; Vecchi et al., 2021; Lapesa et al., 2023). These two fields of research are to be combined in order to enable the analysis of legal elements regarding the validity of legal concepts. This helps international law scholarship to ascertain the opinio iuris of states via the legislature and substantiate the claim to validity of a given legal concept faster and on a broader empirical basis. Analyzing arguments in legal texts, adapting annotation schemes to the legal domain and the overall creation of domain-adapted models is an actively studied NLP area (Haigh, 2018; Yamada et al., 2019; Poudyal et al., 2020; Zhong et al., 2020; Xu et al., 2020; Zhang et al., 2022; Grundler et al., 2022; Chalkidis et al., 2022; Bergam et al., 2022; Niklaus et al., 2023b; Habernal et al., 2023). At the same time, focusing on legal arguments on the intersection between international law and NLP on political texts tends to be rather underexposed in the existing literature. Parliamentary debates can be considered a cross-domain use case inasmuch as they treat questions of international law in an genuinely political setting. As of yet, there are no sufficiently fine-grained analyses regarding legal elements in the context of HI and R2P discussed in debates.

The contributions of our work address several points: First, (1) we introduce a new insight-driven task on the legal element classification in a cross-domain environment. Second, (2) we provide a theoretical-based framework to annotate parliamentary debates and a novel corpus LegalECGPD based on it with 476 sentences (including four debates with 16.836 lines, 324 identified legal elements for 238 sentences), concluded by a legal expert. Furthermore, (3) we present an expert-based analysis of this new corpus giving comprehensive interpretation of the label distribution found. Afterwards, (4) we performed four different state-of-the art deep learning setups in our low-resource setting with transformer-based contextualized sentence embedding and domain-adaptation. Finally, (5) we did a comprehensive error analysis showing multiple limitations of the used models. We conclude that due to the overall moderate performance an expert supported approach is still needed, which points to the need for legal experts in such complex settings.

[3] https://dserver.bundestag.de/btp/13/13248.pdf

2 Related Work

Our work is related to (a) data-driven methods in legal studies as well as international relations scholarship and (b) legal text analysis in NLP.

2.1 Data-driven methods in legal studies

Over the last years the use of data-driven methods in international legal scholarship with several strands of research (Holtermann and Madsen, 2016, p. 11-18; Holtermann and Madsen, 2015) has emerged (Tyler, 2017; Davies, 2020; Dyevre, 2021) leading to the claim of an "empirical turn in international legal scholarship" (Shaffer and Ginsburg, 2012). Empirical legal research aims to identify facts and evidence in order to better understand the topics law regulates and to generate knowledge about the functioning of a given legal system through systematic research supported by quantitative and qualitative data (Eisenberg, 2011, p. 1720; Boom et al., 2018, p. 8; van Dijck et al., 2018). This is where NLP can be used to advance the research agenda. Empirical international legal research has focused on several subfields of international law (Alschner et al., 2017; Ginsburg and Shaffer, 2009), (Posner and de Figueiredo, 2005), (Evangelista and Tannenwald, 2017) and decisions by international courts (Aletras et al., 2016; Medvedeva et al., 2020) or debates in the UN Security Council (Glaser et al., 2022; Patz et al., 2022). In doing so, attention has been given to inter alia big-data analysis or the representation of judicial networks (Coupette, 2019). Research has started to employ machine learning and NLP on subfields of international law (Nay, 2018; Eckhard et al., 2020; Dyevre, 2021; Alschner, 2020)[4]. Nevertheless, there are gaps in the research. Even though questions of customary international law have been singled out as being able to benefit from empirical and digital methods, not much research has been conducted (Megiddo, 2019). Questions regarding the prohibition on the use of force as well as parliamentary debates have been mostly excluded in international law scholarship (a notable exception is Lewis et al. (2019)) Analysis of parliamentary debates and the use of force using empirical methods are conducted in political science and international relations scholarship (Vignoli (2020); Wagner (2020); Hock (2021)) but largely excluded from legal scholarship. Thus, the present work is set on the interdisciplinary boundaries between international legal scholarship, international relations scholarship and NLP.

2.2 Legal Elements Classification in Natural Language Processing

We introduced that *legal elements* prove the existence of legal concepts. Therefore, we can conceptualize these elements close to the concept of *arguments supporting or opposing (as premises or reasons)* (Lawrence and Reed, 2019) the existence of an *implicitly or explicitly claimed legal concept (claim)*.

Automated argument mining, a rapidly emerging subfield of Natural Language Processing (NLP), finds wide application in the automatic detection, verification, and characterisation of arguments (Lippi and Torroni, 2016; Cabrio and Villata, 2018; Stede and Schneider, 2018; Lawrence and Reed, 2019; Vecchi et al., 2021; Lapesa et al., 2023). The benefits of new contextualized models for argument mining have been exhibited in the recent research (Reimers et al., 2019; Wang et al., 2020; Habernal et al., 2023).

More and more studies are now focusing on legal texts. This trend is driven by two factors: creating automated systems to process legal text can reduce the repetitive and time-consuming tasks of legal practitioners and scholars. Moreover, these systems can offer a reliable reference to those not familiar with the legal domain (Zhong et al., 2020).

The existing body of research has made available legal corpora that serve as the subject of various classification tasks, thereby giving rise to new datasets (Zhang et al., 2022). Chalkidis et al. (2023) have offered a multinational English legal corpus consisting of 11 sub-corpora that encompass legislation and case law from six English-speaking legal systems, namely, the EU, the Council of Europe, Canada, the US, the UK, and India. A recent release by Niklaus et al. (2023b) includes a multilingual legal corpus spanning 24 languages (including German, English, Spanish, and others) from 17 jurisdictions.

Specific to argumentation mining, Poudyal et al. (2020) have made available an annotated corpus composed of decisions from the European Court of Human Rights (ECHR), building on the previously annotated corpus provided by Mochales and Moens (2011). Grundler et al. (2022) released a corpus

[4] For a recent data set on argument mining and the European Court of Human Rights see Poudyal et al. (2020); see also Altwicker (2019) and Barczentewicz (2021) for an overview of the methodological challenges for international law scholarship.

for argument mining, composed of decisions of the Court of Justice of the European Union. Other examples include Japanese judgement documents (Yamada et al., 2019) and case holdings on legal decisions (Zheng et al., 2021). Habernal et al. (2023) recently introduced a labeled corpus for argument mining based on the English corpus of the European Court of Human Rights.

Legal language is often categorized as a "sub-language". Like other specialized domains such as medical texts, legal texts (laws, pleadings, contract) possess distinctive properties such as specialized vocabulary, formal syntax, and semantics rooted in extensive domain-specific knowledge. This leads to unique properties in comparison to generic corpora (Haigh, 2018). A base model like BERT (Devlin et al., 2019) often falls short in specialized domains (Beltagy et al., 2019). In this regard, Chalkidis et al. (2020) suggested LegalBERT, pre-trained on multiple legal corpora such as `EURLEX` and `LEGISLATION.GOV.UK`. Another study by Zheng et al. (2021) employed the complete English Harvard Law case corpus to pre-train CaseLaw-BERT. Legal language models have been also pre-trained for Italian (Licari and Comandè, 2022), Romanian (Masala et al., 2021), and Spanish (Gutiérrez-Fandiño et al., 2021) as well. Furthermore, Niklaus et al. (2023b) trained a multilingual Legal-XLM and evaluated it on the newly introduced LEXTREME (Niklaus et al., 2023a), a legal benchmark. Habernal et al. (2023) performed continuous pre-training on the ECHR corpus using the RoBERTa-Large model for argument mining.

Moreover, argument mining in political debates, particularly in (German) parliamentary debates, remains rather unexplored. Limited research has been conducted in this area, including works by Menini et al. (2018), who annotated speeches by Nixon and Kennedy during the 1960 Presidential campaign, Visser et al. (2021), who annotated the 2016 US presidential debates, and Hüning et al. (2022), who used messages from an online survey about a Local Rent Control Initiative for argument mining. Another noteworthy contribution is by Mestre et al. (2021), who built a corpus consisting of labeled sentence pairs from the 2020 US political election debates. Recently, Mancini et al. (2022) released a multi-modal corpus, where the text input is enriched by and aligned to the audio input.

Unlike existing research, our legal context is situated in the cross-domain of parliamentary debates *(political texts)*, limiting the usability of existing methods due to the differing use of language. This demonstrates that a clear separation between legal texts and other types of texts does not always represent reality. Therefore, the cross-domain task of legal element recognition on German parliamentary debates is not covered by the existing datasets and models, which means that we can not use existing corpora or models to adapt them to our use case. Instead, we need to provide a *new corpus* that represents legal element types in the context of *German parliamentary debates* more comprehensively.

3 Legal Background

In this paper we address several unique types of legal elements derived from the legal concepts of HI and R2P. Both share the same argumentative basis: gravest violations of human rights may serve as a justification for the use of force by third states. They lack, however, a clear-cut distinction from each other as well as clear dogmatic legal grounding. Both have often been based on CIL as well as expansive interpretations of the UNC. By the end of the 19th century HI was mostly considered lawful if there was a just cause for intervention. In principle, if a state conducted gross abuses against its population, any other state that was willing to intervene militarily in order to stop these abuses had the right to do so (Neff, 2005, p. 217-218). Thus, the two legal elements of a humanitarian catastrophe and the protection of locals were needed. With the signing of the UNC, the idea of HI became superseded by art. 2 (4). While there have been some uses of force under the justification of HI between 1945 and the early 1990s, the claim to the legality of HI remained weak (Dave, 2009, p. 37-38; Gray, 2018, p. 40-44). The failure to prevent the genocide in Rwanda in 1994 and NATO's intervention without an authorization by the Security Council under the framework of HI in Kosovo in 1999 lead to renewed debate regarding the lawfulness of HI (Crossley, 2018, p. 418-420; Thakur, 2016). These discussions culminated in the development of R2P. R2P was brought forward by the International Commission on Intervention and State Sovereignty and argued for two major changes. Contrary to HI, R2P's main focus is not the right to intervene but the protection of the population. Additionally, sovereignty is seen as conditional to the protection of a population from suffering serious harm. If a state is

Label	Legal Element	Definition	Example
HUMA	**Humanitarian catastrophe**	The code is used if the speaker refers to a humanitarian catastrophe taking place or being imminent (major human rights violations that amount to war crimes, genocide, ethnic cleansing and crimes against humanity) that makes the use of force necessary.	The situation in this country is a humanitarian catastrophe, people starve and suffer, therefore we must use force to stop the aggressor.
PROT	**Protection of local civilians**	This code applies if the speaker considers that the need to protect the local civilians from major human rights violations, that amount to war crimes, genocide, ethnic cleansing and crimes against humanity makes the use of force necessary.	We have to use our country's military to protect the civilians in this country.
FAIL	**Failure to Protect by home state**	This code applies if the speaker considers that the home state has failed to protect its population from war crimes, genocide, ethnic cleansing and crimes against humanity makes the use of force necessary.	This country is not protecting its people from the crimes against humanity occurring, thus we need to use our military.
LAST	**Last Resort**	This code applies if the speaker considers to the use of force as a last resort and that all peaceful means (such as diplomacy) are exhausted.	We have tried every diplomatic means available but to no avail, there is no choice but to use force.
PROP	**Proportionality of the use of force to the threat**	This code applies if a speaker sees the way force is used in a proportional manner (including that civilians are protected as far as possible or receive special treatment to help with the suffering.)	When we use force we take every possible precaution to protect the civilians from our attacks.
REAS	**Reasonable prospect of success**	This code applies if the speaker argues that a reasonable prospect of success is given.	Using the military is always risky but we are sure that we will succeed.
AUTH	**Rightful authority given**	This code applies if the speaker argues that a rightful or legitimate authority for the use of force is given (this includes but is not limited to references to the Security Council).	We have every right to use force and our actions are covered by the Security Council.
INTE	**Right intention**	This code applies if the speaker refers to having the right intention of the use of force. This might be the case, for example, if speakers refer to a moral cause for going to war as being given.	This is not a war for our national interest it is a moral duty.

Table 1: Framework adapted from codebook from Hock (2021), drawing on work from Wagner (2020).

not willing or not able to protect its population, the responsibility for doing so shifts to the international community (Bellamy, 2014, p. 1-3; Saba and Akbarzadeh, 2018, p. 244-245). In order for the responsibility to pass on to the international community, several criteria have to be fulfilled: a just cause has to be given, the use of force has to be conducted with the right intention as a last resort, proportional to the threat, and with reasonable chance of success. The authority to authorize an intervention under R2P should generally lie with the Security Council (ICISS, 2001, p. XI-XIII). The 2005 World Summit Outcome[5] endorsed the R2P in principle. It also stressed the sovereignty of states and the importance of an authorization by the Security Council. This brought R2P closer in line with traditional understandings of the UNC. R2P could be invoked in cases of war crimes, genocide, ethnic cleansing, and crimes against humanity but only if a state manifestly failed to protect its population. Nevertheless, a definite and exhaustive list of criteria needed for a situation of R2P was not brought forward. Following from the above, several legal elements that are shared between HI and R2P can be distilled: humanitarian catastrophe, protection of locals, failure to protect by the home state, right intention, last resort, proportionality of the use of force to the threat, reasonable chance of success, rightful authority given. R2P remains controversial amongst states and the international community (Crossley, 2018). Thus, the analysis of customary international law and state's opinions regarding HI and R2P remains highly relevant.

[5]UN Doc. A/Res/60/1 (24. October 2005) para. 138-140

4 Dataset for Legal Elements Classification

We claimed that a new dataset is needed to cover the task of classifying legal elements in parliamentary debates. In this section, we will give details on the creation of our "LegalECPD-dataset". (1) Inspired by Hock (2021), drawing on work from Wagner (2020), we introduce an adapted framework to annotate the different facets of legal elements regarding HI and R2P. (2) We then show the annotation process of four debates (KOSOVO (BTP 13/248), LIBYA (BTP 17/095), SYRIA-A (BTP 18/042), SYRIA-B (BTP 18/044). Moreover, (3) we analyze the generated dataset LegalECGPD of the identified 324 legal elements in 238 sentences in terms of the distribution and characteristics of the debates.

Dataset Creation. We base our work on four parliamentary debates regarding the authorization to

set	*ratio*	*sentences #*	Huma	Prot	Fail	Last	Prop	Reas	Auth	Inte	labels #
			multilabel								
full	100%	**238**	51	52	20	44	8	32	39	78	*324*
stratified-debate split											
train	*70%*	**165**	31	38	13	30	5	23	27	52	*219*
dev	*10%*	**25**	6	8	3	3	1	3	7	8	*39*
test	*20%*	**48**	14	6	4	11	2	6	5	18	*66*
cross-debate split											
train	KOSOVO, SYRIA-A	**191**	46	43	13	36	7	29	24	64	*262*
dev	LIBYA	**20**	4	3	4	4	0	1	10	3	*29*
test	SYRIA-B	**28**	1	6	3	4	1	2	5	11	*33*

Table 2: Summary of our legal elements dataset, detailing the *sample counts* and *multilabel distributions* for two data splitting strategies: the **stratified-debate split** (ensuring balanced representation of the four debates in each set) and the **cross-debate split** (allocating two debates for training, and one each for development and testing).

use force[6]. Parliamentary debates are especially interesting for two reasons. Firstly, they are a means to ascertain the opinio iuris of a state. Secondly, while they cover questions of international law, they do so as part of a political speech, not as for example a legal analysis. Thus, legal concepts will be mentioned but intertwined with genuinely political arguments. It is safe to assume that the legal elements mentioned may be vague or ambiguous due to the political nature of the texts. In order to analyse the legal basis of these concepts we take the cases of the war in Kosovo, the war in Libya and the war against ISIS (Syria-A and Syria-B) as examples. The datasets draws on all German debates authorizing to use of force for the first time (the ISIS debates are strongly connected in the sense that Syria-A is the debate that continues to the vote in Syria-B. The latter is thus considered as to fall into these criteria as well). This is based on the observation that the war in Kosovo was a catalyst for the creation of R2P. The war against Libya as well as the war against ISIS can be considered as examples in which R2P featured prominently - even though in both cases other legal justifications, such as authorization by the Security Council and self-defence played a more important role. *No further debates* that fulfil the criteria of authorizing the use of force for the first time in a situation in which either HI or R2P might apply exist. For example, while there are more parliamentary debates on the use of force in Kosovo, the situation has changed from an international law perspective. After the Kosovo War the debate turned towards the presence of foreign forces in the Kosovo and the fulfillment of inter alia Security Council resolution 1244[7]. Thus, an expansion of the dataset on the ground of the above mentioned criteria is not possible.

Annotation. Our coding framework is adapted from the coding scheme of Hock (2021), which draws on the work of Wagner (2020). We adapt the coding scheme to better cover the concepts of HI and R2P. This includes merging and expanding several codes that aimed for grasping different facets of legal theory into codes adapted to cover legal elements. For example "just cause", "just war", and "right intention, warfare as morally justified" have been merged to "right intention". The codes "failure to protect by home state" and "proportionality of the use of force to the threat" have been included in our coding framework. Furthermore, codes that focused exclusively on questions of legal theory, such as for example "just war" or "state of exception makes legality less important" have been deleted. Our aim is to include all legal elements made for the legal framework of HI and R2P. We used the presented annotation scheme and defined categories (”codebook”). Our codebook itself consists of seven domain-specific categories. We did our study with one legal domain expert. Our legal

[6]https://dserver.bundestag.de/btp/{ID}.pdf (ID=13/13248|17/17095|18/18042|18/18044)

[7]UN Doc. S/Res/1244 (1999)

expert is a 30-35 years old (male) with a strong academic background in international law and more than three years experience in this domain. He checked more than $15k$ sentences of all debates.

Statistics and Analysis. The resulting dataset (Tab. 2) contains 324 legal elements in 238 sentences (only 1-2% of all sentences in the debates included legal elements). While there are many similarities (App. D), such as the large amount of right intention and protection of local civilians in all debates - as was expected since we are analysing the same legal exception to the prohibition of the use of force - there are several noteworthy aspects. The element of humanitarian catastrophe is most widely used in the debate on Kosovo. This illustrates the point that HI was re-discovered as a legal doctrine with the war in Kosovo. The shift towards the R2P explains the relative decline in the usage of humanitarian catastrophe. This is connected with the element of right intention being used most frequently in the Kosovo debate as well. Since the use of force in support of human rights was a rather novel occurrence in the Kosovo war, this finding is not surprising. Syria-A features protection of local civilians prominently, Syria-B right intention. Regardless of several outliers, the distribution pattern is comparable over cases. From an international law perspective, it is regrettable that only around 1.5 per cent of all lines contained legal elements. Normatively, this questions whether a strong base for opinio iuris can be found in parliamentary debates at all. Further research is necessary to determine the relative strength of the arguments made. Thus, the lack of relevant lines could be due to a strong belief that the legal basis is clear and unequivocal. Speakers may not have referred towards legal elements because they took their existence for granted.

5 Automatic Approach for Legal Elements Classification

In this section, we analyse the performance of NLP methods on legal element classification on German parliamentary debates. We focuses on the concrete type of the legal element, performing a multi-label classification task in a few-shot setting.

Task. We model the *classification of legal elements* as a sentence-level multi-label classification task. Given a sentence s composed of words w_i, where $i \in \{1, ..., n\}$, the goal is to assign a list of legal elements $e = (e_0, ..., e_m)$ to the sentence. For example[8]:

> *"Es kann keinen Zweifel darin geben, daß es überfällig war, den boshaftesten Despoten in Europa [right intention], der Krieg gegen sein eigenes Staatsvolk führt, es entwurzelt, in die Wälder treibt und ermorden läßt, [failure to protect] in seine Schranken zu verweisen, um eine humanitäre Katastrophe noch größeren Ausmaßes zu verhindern. [humanitarian catastrophe]"* $\xrightarrow{e}$ **Inte, Fail, Huma**

Dataset. We use our novel LegalECGPD dataset and create two different dataset splits (Tab. 2): *stratified random split* and *cross-debate split*. In the *stratified random split*, we randomly but stratified the dataset, allocating 70% for train, 10% for development, and 20% for test. This ensured a balanced representation of our different debates across the subsets. In the *cross-debate split*, designed for cross-debate evaluation, we divided the data based on the perspectives captured in the debates. Two debates were included in the train set, one in the development set, and the remaining one in the test set. This approach facilitated the exploration of distinct perspectives across different debates, enabling a comprehensive evaluation of the model's performance in a cross-debate scenario.

Models. We base our analyses on freely available traditional and state-of-the-art NLP methods. We intend to demonstrate the performance of existing models to provide a basis for further research. We applied four types of models (A) dictionary-base **(DB)**, (B) feature-based **(FB)**, (C) transformer-based fine-tuning **(FT)** and (D) domain-adapted sentence-transformer **(DASent)**:

(A) Dictionary-based (DB): We apply *dictionary-based models* with two pre-defined lexicons: an expert-curated one with domain knowledge (App. B.1) and a generated lexicon via Pointwise Mutual Information (PMI) (Church and Hanks, 1989) for statistical associations. These models offer a simple and efficient baseline.

(B) Feature-based (FB): Furthermore, we test *feature-based models*, extracting specific features from data for classifications. We used TF-IDF to measure word importance (Sparck Jones, 1988) and GermanBERT embeddings (Chan et al., 2020) to represent data and capture semantic relationships. We use a multi-layer perceptron (Rumelhart et al., 1986) as classification head incorporating the features for classification (App. B.2)

[8]https://dserver.bundestag.de/btp/13/13248.pdf

(C) Transformer-based Fine-tuning (FT): We also test a transformer-based GermanBERT (Chan et al., 2020) with fine-tuning on our task-specific dataset (App. B.3). This approach leverages prior knowledge from the BERT base model.

(D) Domain-Sent-Transformer (DASent): Finally, we apply SetFit (Tunstall et al., 2022) that adapts sentence-transformer models to our domain by training on `LegalECGPD` (App. B.4). SetFit employs contrastive learning for fine-tuning. This technique distinguishes between similar and dissimilar sentence pairs to capture semantic relationships. The adapted model generates domain-specific sentence embeddings for classification and is "efficient [...] for few-shot fine tuning." (ib.)

Results. Our results (Tab. 3 and App. 6) show that domain adaptation using sentence embeddings outperforms other approaches (**DASent**, .63 F1-Micro, $\pm$.01 std). Specifically, the task-specific fine-tuning method **(FT)** shows comparable performance (.61 F1-Micro, $\pm$.01 std) to the domain-adaptation technique, albeit slightly lower. On the other hand, the baseline models, including the dict-based **(DB)** and feature-based models **(FB)**, demonstrate inferior performance. These findings emphasize the effectiveness of leveraging domain-specific knowledge encoded within sentence embeddings for improved performance in the given task.

Model	**F1micro**	*Pre*	*Rec*	**F1macro**	*Pre*	*Rec*
DB-Expert	.16	*.75*	*.06*	.09	*.19*	*.06*
DB-PMI	.17	*.24*	*.14*	.16	*.19*	*.18*
FB-TFIDF	.43	*.58*	*.35*	.31	*.45*	*.25*
FB-BERT	.55	*.64*	*.55*	.45	*.58*	*.43*
FT-BERT	.61	***.72***	*.53*	.48	*.60*	*.44*
DASent (SetFit)	**.63**	*.57*	***.70***	**.63**	***.65***	***.71***

Table 3: Results on our *stratified random test set*.

Model	**F1micro**	*Pre*	*Rec*	**F1macro**	*Pre*	*Rec*
DB-Expert	.00	*.00*	*.00*	.00	*.00*	*.00*
DB-PMI	.19	*.25*	*.16*	.14	*.18*	*.14*
FB-TFIDF	.37	*.50*	*.29*	.22	*.33*	*.19*
FB-BERT	.38	*.38*	*.38*	.36	*.40*	*.38*
FT-BERT	.47	***.64***	*.37*	.34	*.44*	*.33*
DASent (SetFit)	**.57**	*.47*	***.71***	**.43**	***.43***	***.56***

Table 4: Results on our *cross-debate test set* `SYRIA-B`.

Additionally, when considering the more challenging dataset that involved cross-debate evaluation, our results (Tab. 4 and app. 6) continue to showcase the effectiveness of domain adaptation using sentence embeddings (**DASent**, .57 F1-Micro $\pm$.01 std).

Error Analysis. Our results of the best performing model `DASent` show that the most interesting task is connected to the label `INTE`, covering the legal element of right intention. Here, we have seen several divergences between the coder and the model. This is due to the fact that `INTE` covers arguments that are deeply intertwined with moral judgments. Furthermore, in these cases, connections between different parts of the argument are often implicit and highly dependent on context as well as prior knowledge. They represent fringe cases that are difficult to evaluate even with domain expertise (translations DE $\rightarrow$EN in app. E).

"Nennen Sie mir einen weltweit, der sich mehr darum bemüht, dass dieser politische Prozess zustande kommt." (id 173)

Here, the model labeled the argument as `LAST`, the domain expert as `Last` and `INTE`. While it is clear that the argument centers partly around the use of force as being an action of last resort, the argument is also morally based. This is due to the fact that the speaker claims to be the one who is the most concerned with keeping the peace. Another example is:

"Es kann keinen Zweifel darin geben, daß es überfällig war, den boshaftesten Despoten in Europa, der Krieg gegen sein eigenes Staatsvolk führt, es entwurzelt, in die Wälder treibt und ermorden läßt, in seine Schranken zu verweisen, um eine humanitäre Katastrophe noch größeren Ausmaßes zu verhindern." (id 138)

Here, the moral judgment is made via the classification of the political leader as evil despot instead of simply as enemy. Implicit in the understanding of the leader as evil despot (as well as explicit in the further parts of the text) is the humanitarian catastrophe and the failure to protect. Thus, the domain expert has labeled this as `HUMA`, `FAIL`, and `INTE` while the model did label it as `HUMA` and `PROT`. Arguably, the label `PROT` could be used as well, nevertheless, `FAIL` is the more fitting label. Moral judgments are also contained in the following argument:

"Wenn wir diese schrecklichen Szenen als Fernsehzuschauer in Westeuropa einfach konsumieren würden, ohne zu handeln, dann würden wir letztlich mit einer rostigen Rasierklinge unser Gesicht zerschneiden und unser eigenes Gesicht entstellen." (id 72)

Here, the reference towards a rusty razor cutting one's own face can be understood as a moral judgement claim. It was thus labeled as `INTE` by the domain expert. The model labeled it as `PROT`. Here, however, the argument refers towards the self-image and their own understanding of moral and ethical considerations and not towards the protection of civilians as such. Another example is:

"Wir können nicht tatenlos zusehen, wenn sich regionale Faustrechte entwickeln und Menschenrechte in Regionen so verletzt werden, daß es zu humanitären Katastrophen kommen kann, weil das Gewaltmonopol der Vereinten Nationen nicht ausgeübt werden kann." (id 114)

In this last example the model labeled it as HUMA and PROT. The domain expert labeled it as HUMA and INTE. Here, the notion of taking the law into one's own hand leads to the argument centering around legality and the moral role of the law. Nevertheless, there is merit to the label PROT. It remains to be said that there are far-reaching consequences if the existence of a rule of CIL that considers HI and R2P to be lawful were ascertained. Ultimately, warfare might occur more often (Orford, 2003).

6 Conclusion

International legal concepts are in most cases based on treaty law or CIL. CIL consists of state practice and opinio iuris. We claim that opinio iuris can be found in parliamentary debates. A legal concept consists of legal elements. Thus, in order to prove the existence of opinio iuris one has to find legal elements in parliamentary debates. We tried to ascertain the existence of opinio iuris regarding HI and R2P by analysing legal elements in parliamentary debates. Our use case offers a cross-domain approach inasmuch as it combines two domains that usually are treated separately, i.e. legal elements in genuinely political texts. This presents a novel task for NLP methods. We offer a new dataset and a contribution to the fields of NLP as well as empirical legal scholarship. Our experiments have shown several results. There is a surprisingly low amount of legal elements mentioned in parliamentary debates. The distribution of legal elements follows expected patters inasmuch as all cases cover the same legal concepts. Nevertheless, it became evident that the used NLP models do not provide sufficient accuracy (yet) in such a few-shot multilabel setting. Thus, domain specific knowledge is needed. Our provided framework enables future research and our data set is available under an open-source license[9].

7 Future Work

Possible future work on this project could benefit from several different extensions. From the viewpoint of NLP and its methods three major expansions would be beneficial: First, improving the granularity of annotation to extend it to a span- and token-level would potentially yield greater detail and precision in data labeling. Furthermore, the reliability and diversity of annotations could be bolstered by expanding the number of legal experts involved in annotating legal elements. This approach may augment the range and depth of perspectives, thereby enhancing the overall quality and balance of the dataset. Second, building on the recently introduced models for multilingual legal language, there is an opportunity to develop a cross-domain language model specifically tailored for analyzing legal language in political debates. Lastly, conducting a more in-depth study to interpret the domain features that the model uses to classify legal elements would be beneficial. This could involve a legal expert-guided analysis of the typical underlying features that should be deployed, and further expanding the model to concentrate more on these conceptual features. The ultimate objective is to develop a model that is guided more by defined legal concepts than merely by linguistic characteristics, potentially leading to more accurate and relevant interpretation and classification of legal elements. From the viewpoint of international law two further extensions would be of value to further work. In order to further ascertain the CIL-base of HI and R2P it would be beneficial to study other parliamentary democracies besides Germany since the more states support a legal concepts based on CIL the more substantial is the claim towards the legality of that concept. Furthermore, the present methods could be applied to legal concepts besides HI and R2P in the area of international law and the use of force, such as for example expansive understandings of the right to self-defence. This would provide international law scholarship and international political decision making with an empirically grounded substantiation of the legality of the use of force within the context of legally contested situations.

8 Limitations

The present paper shows several problems when dealing with international law empirically. We showed the challenging aspects of classification in a low resource setting. Unfortunately due to specific use case we can not simply scale up the amount of data. As discussed our dataset covers the use case for the legal domain. Furthermore, le-

[9] github.com/chkla/LegalECGPD

gal norms have a inherent ambiguity regarding the situation they are applicable to. More often than not, a legal argument is multi-faceted and highly complex with often implicit and highly context-based references as well as moral judgments. Only rarely will a speaker invoke clearly which legal norm he might be referring to. Furthermore, the legal concepts of HI and R2P remain difficult to define. Consequently, a statement made in a debate may count towards more than one legal element. Thus only a limited amount of the argumentative depth of a legal argument can be covered with the present methods. This points towards a general problem of empirical legal sciences that needs to be answered in further research.

9 Ethics Statement

When developing a model to predict legal element types in parliamentary debates, several ethical considerations must be addressed. *Firstly*, the accuracy and reliability of the model are critical; moderate results might indicate that the model may not capture the nuances and complexities of legal concepts within debates. Involving legal experts in the training and evaluation process can help to refine the model, ensuring that it properly reflects legal terminologies and concepts. However, expert involvement should be balanced to avoid biases that may inadvertently be introduced by the experts. Incorporating the fact that only one expert was involved adds another layer of ethical consideration. Relying on a single expert could introduce a lack of diversity in perspectives and potentially skew the model towards the biases and opinions of that particular individual. Legal interpretation often requires a range of perspectives to account for the complexities and subtleties of language and context. With just one expert, there is a risk that the model may not be as robust or as representative as it could be with the input from multiple experts with diverse backgrounds and areas of expertise. Nevertheless, even the inclusion of more than one legal expert might not lead to significantly better results. Legal questions are always based on interpretation. This interpretation cannot be fully objective, even though the methodology of legal science aims to reduce the subjectivity involved in interpretation. Thus, standard solutions such as taking the average of several experts might improve performance but do not in each and every case lead to better results. Additionally, domain expertise is scarce. It is therefore difficult to include more than one expert *Secondly*, the transparency and explainability of the model are essential, particularly in the legal domain where the decisions and analyses can have far-reaching consequences. Adding to this aspect concerning the transparency and explainability of the model, it is crucial to consider that error analysis typically reveals only a fraction of the possible errors. This limitation in understanding the full scope of the model's errors is a vital ethical concern. It means that the model could have underlying issues that are not immediately apparent, and these unidentified issues could lead to incorrect or misleading predictions. *Thirdly*, one must consider the potential misuse of the model. If the model is not highly accurate, relying on its predictions without human verification could lead to misinterpretations of legal elements in debates, which in turn could have policy implications or affect legal interpretations and decisions.

References

Nikolaos Aletras, Dimitrios Tsarapatsanis, Daniel Preoţiuc-Pietro, and Vasileios Lampos. 2016. Predicting judicial decisions of the European Court of Human Rights: a Natural Language Processing perspective. *PeerJ Computer Science*, 2:e93.

Wolfgang Alschner. 2020. Sense and Similarity: Automating Legal Text Comparison. In Ryan Whalen, editor, *Computational Legal Studies: The Promise and Challenge of Data-Driven Legal Research*, pages 9–28. Edward Elgar.

Wolfgang Alschner, Joost Pauwelyn, and Sergio Puig. 2017. The Data-Driven Future of International Economic Law. *Journal of International Economic Law*, 20(2):217–231.

Tilmann Altwicker. 2019. International Legal Scholarship and the Challenge of Digitalization. *Chinese Journal of International Law*, 18(2):217–246.

Shpetim Bajrami. 2022. *Selbstverteidigung gegen nichtstaatliche Akteure*. Mohr Siebeck.

Mikolaj Barczentewicz. 2021. Teaching Technology to (Future) Lawyers. *Erasmus Law Review*, 15(1).

Alex J. Bellamy. 2014. *The Responsibility to Protect*. Oxford University Press.

Iz Beltagy, Kyle Lo, and Arman Cohan. 2019. SciBERT: A pretrained language model for scientific text. In *Proceedings of the 2019 Conference on Empirical Methods in Natural Language Processing and the 9th International Joint Conference on Natural Language Processing (EMNLP-IJCNLP)*, pages 3615–3620, Hong Kong, China. Association for Computational Linguistics.

Noah Bergam, Emily Allaway, and Kathleen Mckeown. 2022. Legal and political stance detection of SCOTUS language. In *Proceedings of the Natural Legal Language Processing Workshop 2022*, pages 265–275, Abu Dhabi, United Arab Emirates (Hybrid). Association for Computational Linguistics.

BigScience, Teven Le Scao, Angela Fan, Christopher Akiki, Ellie Pavlick, Suzana Ilić, Daniel Hesslow, Roman Castagné, Alexandra Sasha Luccioni, François Yvon, Matthias Gallé, Jonathan Tow, Alexander M. Rush, Stella Biderman, Albert Webson, Pawan Sasanka Ammanamanchi, Thomas Wang, Benoît Sagot, Niklas Muennighoff, Albert Villanova del Moral, Olatunji Ruwase, Rachel Bawden, Stas Bekman, Angelina McMillan-Major, Iz Beltagy, Huu Nguyen, Lucile Saulnier, Samson Tan, Pedro Ortiz Suarez, Victor Sanh, Hugo Laurençon, Yacine Jernite, Julien Launay, Margaret Mitchell, Colin Raffel, Aaron Gokaslan, Adi Simhi, Aitor Soroa, Alham Fikri Aji, Amit Alfassy, Anna Rogers, Ariel Kreisberg Nitzav, Canwen Xu, Chenghao Mou, Chris Emezue, Christopher Klamm, Colin Leong, Daniel van Strien, David Ifeoluwa Adelani, Dragomir Radev, Eduardo González Ponferrada, Efrat Levkovizh, Ethan Kim, Eyal Bar Natan, Francesco De Toni, Gérard Dupont, Germán Kruszewski, Giada Pistilli, Hady Elsahar, Hamza Benyamina, Hieu Tran, Ian Yu, Idris Abdulmumin, Isaac Johnson, Itziar Gonzalez-Dios, Javier de la Rosa, Jenny Chim, Jesse Dodge, Jian Zhu, Jonathan Chang, Jörg Frohberg, Joseph Tobing, Joydeep Bhattacharjee, Khalid Almubarak, Kimbo Chen, Kyle Lo, Leandro Von Werra, Leon Weber, Long Phan, Loubna Ben allal, Ludovic Tanguy, Manan Dey, Manuel Romero Muñoz, Maraim Masoud, María Grandury, Mario Šaško, Max Huang, Maximin Coavoux, Mayank Singh, Mike Tian-Jian Jiang, Minh Chien Vu, Mohammad A. Jauhar, Mustafa Ghaleb, Nishant Subramani, Nora Kassner, Nurulaqilla Khamis, Olivier Nguyen, Omar Espejel, Ona de Gibert, Paulo Villegas, Peter Henderson, Pierre Colombo, Priscilla Amuok, Quentin Lhoest, Rheza Harliman, Rishi Bommasani, Roberto Luis López, Rui Ribeiro, Salomey Osei, Sampo Pyysalo, Sebastian Nagel, Shamik Bose, Shamsuddeen Hassan Muhammad, Shanya Sharma, Shayne Longpre, Somaieh Nikpoor, Stanislav Silberberg, Suhas Pai, Sydney Zink, Tiago Timponi Torrent, Timo Schick, Tristan Thrush, Valentin Danchev, Vassilina Nikoulina, Veronika Laippala, Violette Lepercq, Vrinda Prabhu, Zaid Alyafeai, Zeerak Talat, Arun Raja, Benjamin Heinzerling, Chenglei Si, Davut Emre Taşar, Elizabeth Salesky, Sabrina J. Mielke, Wilson Y. Lee, Abheesht Sharma, Andrea Santilli, Antoine Chaffin, Arnaud Stiegler, Debajyoti Datta, Eliza Szczechla, Gunjan Chhablani, Han Wang, Harshit Pandey, Hendrik Strobelt, Jason Alan Fries, Jos Rozen, Leo Gao, Lintang Sutawika, M Saiful Bari, Maged S. Al-shaibani, Matteo Manica, Nihal Nayak, Ryan Teehan, Samuel Albanie, Sheng Shen, Srulik Ben-David, Stephen H. Bach, Taewoon Kim, Tali Bers, Thibault Fevry, Trishala Neeraj, Urmish Thakker, Vikas Raunak, Xiangru Tang, Zheng-Xin Yong, Zhiqing Sun, Shaked Brody, Yallow Uri, Hadar Tojarieh, Adam Roberts, Hyung Won Chung, Jaesung Tae, Jason Phang, Ofir Press, Conglong Li, Deepak Narayanan, Hatim Bourfoune, Jared Casper, Jeff Rasley, Max Ryabinin, Mayank Mishra, Minjia Zhang, Mohammad Shoeybi, Myriam Peyrounette, Nicolas Patry, Nouamane Tazi, Omar Sanseviero, Patrick von Platen, Pierre Cornette, Pierre François Lavallée, Rémi Lacroix, Samyam Rajbhandari, Sanchit Gandhi, Shaden Smith, Stéphane Requena, Suraj Patil, Tim Dettmers, Ahmed Baruwa, Amanpreet Singh, Anastasia Cheveleva, Anne-Laure Ligozat, Arjun Subramonian, Aurélie Névéol, Charles Lovering, Dan Garrette, Deepak Tunuguntla, Ehud Reiter, Ekaterina Taktasheva, Ekaterina Voloshina, Eli Bogdanov, Genta Indra Winata, Hailey Schoelkopf, Jan-Christoph Kalo, Jekaterina Novikova, Jessica Zosa Forde, Jordan Clive, Jungo Kasai, Ken Kawamura, Liam Hazan, Marine Carpuat, Miruna Clinciu, Najoung Kim, Newton Cheng, Oleg Serikov, Omer Antverg, Oskar van der Wal, Rui Zhang, Ruochen Zhang, Sebastian Gehrmann, Shachar Mirkin, Shani Pais, Tatiana Shavrina, Thomas Scialom, Tian Yun, Tomasz Limisiewicz, Verena Rieser, Vitaly Protasov, Vladislav Mikhailov, Yada Pruksachatkun, Yonatan Belinkov, Zachary Bamberger, Zdeněk Kasner, Alice Rueda, Amanda Pestana, Amir Feizpour, Ammar Khan, Amy Faranak, Ana Santos, Anthony Hevia, Antigona Unldreaj, Arash Aghagol, Arezoo Abdollahi, Aycha Tammour, Azadeh HajiHosseini, Bahareh Behroozi, Benjamin Ajibade, Bharat Saxena, Carlos Muñoz Ferrandis, Daniel McDuff, Danish Contractor, David Lansky, Davis David, Douwe Kiela, Duong A. Nguyen, Edward Tan, Emi Baylor, Ezinwanne Ozoani, Fatima Mirza, Frankline Ononiwu, Habib Rezanejad, Hessie Jones, Indrani Bhattacharya, Irene Solaiman, Irina Sedenko, Isar Nejadgholi, Jesse Passmore, Josh Seltzer, Julio Bonis Sanz, Livia Dutra, Mairon Samagaio, Maraim Elbadri, Margot Mieskes, Marissa Gerchick, Martha Akinlolu, Michael McKenna, Mike Qiu, Muhammed Ghauri, Mykola Burynok, Nafis Abrar, Nazneen Rajani, Nour Elkott, Nour Fahmy, Olanrewaju Samuel, Ran An, Rasmus Kromann, Ryan Hao, Samira Alizadeh, Sarmad Shubber, Silas Wang, Sourav Roy, Sylvain Viguier, Thanh Le, Tobi Oyebade, Trieu Le, Yoyo Yang, Zach Nguyen, Abhinav Ramesh Kashyap, Alfredo Palasciano, Alison Callahan, Anima Shukla, Antonio Miranda-Escalada, Ayush Singh, Benjamin Beilharz, Bo Wang, Caio Brito, Chenxi Zhou, Chirag Jain, Chuxin Xu, Clémentine Fourrier, Daniel León Periñán, Daniel Molano, Dian Yu, Enrique Manjavacas, Fabio Barth, Florian Fuhrimann, Gabriel Altay, Giyaseddin Bayrak, Gully Burns, Helena U. Vrabec, Imane Bello, Ishani Dash, Jihyun Kang, John Giorgi, Jonas Golde, Jose David Posada, Karthik Rangasai Sivaraman, Lokesh Bulchandani, Lu Liu, Luisa Shinzato, Madeleine Hahn de Bykhovetz, Maiko Takeuchi, Marc Pàmies, Maria A Castillo, Marianna Nezhurina, Mario Sänger, Matthias Samwald, Michael Cullan, Michael Weinberg, Michiel De Wolf, Mina Mihaljcic, Minna Liu, Moritz Freidank, Myungsun Kang, Natasha Seelam, Nathan Dahlberg, Nicholas Michio Broad, Nikolaus Muellner, Pascale

Fung, Patrick Haller, Ramya Chandrasekhar, Renata Eisenberg, Robert Martin, Rodrigo Canalli, Rosaline Su, Ruisi Su, Samuel Cahyawijaya, Samuele Garda, Shlok S Deshmukh, Shubhanshu Mishra, Sid Kiblawi, Simon Ott, Sinee Sang-aroonsiri, Srishti Kumar, Stefan Schweter, Sushil Bharati, Tanmay Laud, Théo Gigant, Tomoya Kainuma, Wojciech Kusa, Yanis Labrak, Yash Shailesh Bajaj, Yash Venkatraman, Yifan Xu, Yingxin Xu, Yu Xu, Zhe Tan, Zhongli Xie, Zifan Ye, Mathilde Bras, Younes Belkada, and Thomas Wolf. 2022. Bloom: A 176b-parameter open-access multilingual language model.

Willem Boom, Pieter Desmet, and Peter Mascini. 2018. Empirical legal research: charting the terrain. In Willem Boom, Pieter Desmet, and Peter Mascini, editors, *Empirical Legal Research in Action. Reflections on Methods and their Applications*, pages 1–22.

Tom Brown, Benjamin Mann, Nick Ryder, Melanie Subbiah, Jared D Kaplan, Prafulla Dhariwal, Arvind Neelakantan, Pranav Shyam, Girish Sastry, Amanda Askell, Sandhini Agarwal, Ariel Herbert-Voss, Gretchen Krueger, Tom Henighan, Rewon Child, Aditya Ramesh, Daniel Ziegler, Jeffrey Wu, Clemens Winter, Chris Hesse, Mark Chen, Eric Sigler, Mateusz Litwin, Scott Gray, Benjamin Chess, Jack Clark, Christopher Berner, Sam McCandlish, Alec Radford, Ilya Sutskever, and Dario Amodei. 2020. Language models are few-shot learners. In *Advances in Neural Information Processing Systems*, volume 33, pages 1877–1901. Curran Associates, Inc.

Elena Cabrio and Serena Villata. 2018. Five years of argument mining: a data-driven analysis. In *Proceedings of the Twenty-Seventh International Joint Conference on Artificial Intelligence, IJCAI 2018, July 13-19, 2018, Stockholm, Sweden*, pages 5427–5433. ijcai.org.

Tuhin Chakrabarty, Christopher Hidey, Smaranda Muresan, Kathy McKeown, and Alyssa Hwang. 2019. AMPERSAND: Argument mining for PERSuAsive oNline discussions. In *Proceedings of the 2019 Conference on Empirical Methods in Natural Language Processing and the 9th International Joint Conference on Natural Language Processing (EMNLP-IJCNLP)*, pages 2933–2943, Hong Kong, China. Association for Computational Linguistics.

Ilias Chalkidis, Manos Fergadiotis, Prodromos Malakasiotis, Nikolaos Aletras, and Ion Androutsopoulos. 2020. LEGAL-BERT: The muppets straight out of law school. In *Findings of the Association for Computational Linguistics: EMNLP 2020*, pages 2898–2904, Online. Association for Computational Linguistics.

Ilias Chalkidis, Nicolas Garneau, Catalina Goanta, Daniel Katz, and Anders Søgaard. 2023. LeXFiles and LegalLAMA: Facilitating English multinational legal language model development. In *Proceedings of the 61st Annual Meeting of the Association for Computational Linguistics (Volume 1: Long Papers)*, pages 15513–15535, Toronto, Canada. Association for Computational Linguistics.

Ilias Chalkidis, Abhik Jana, Dirk Hartung, Michael Bommarito, Ion Androutsopoulos, Daniel Katz, and Nikolaos Aletras. 2022. LexGLUE: A benchmark dataset for legal language understanding in English. In *Proceedings of the 60th Annual Meeting of the Association for Computational Linguistics (Volume 1: Long Papers)*, pages 4310–4330, Dublin, Ireland. Association for Computational Linguistics.

Branden Chan, Stefan Schweter, and Timo Möller. 2020. German's next language model. In *Proceedings of the 28th International Conference on Computational Linguistics*, pages 6788–6796, Barcelona, Spain (Online). International Committee on Computational Linguistics.

Kenneth Ward Church and Patrick Hanks. 1989. Word association norms, mutual information, and lexicography. In *27th Annual Meeting of the Association for Computational Linguistics*, pages 76–83, Vancouver, British Columbia, Canada. Association for Computational Linguistics.

Corinna Coupette. 2019. *Juristische Netzwerkforschung*. Mohr Siebeck GmbH and Co. KG.

Noele Crossley. 2018. Is R2P still controversial? Continuity and change in the debate on 'humanitarian intervention'. *Cambridge Review of International Affairs*, 31(5):415–436.

Benjamin Dave. 2009. LAST RESORT: BRIDGING PROTECTION AND PREVENTION. *International Journal on World Peace*, 26(4):37–62.

Gareth Davies. 2020. The Relationship between Empirical Legal Studies and Doctrinal Legal Research. *Erasmus Law Review*, 13(2):3–12.

Jacob Devlin, Ming-Wei Chang, Kenton Lee, and Kristina Toutanova. 2019. BERT: Pre-training of deep bidirectional transformers for language understanding. In *Proceedings of the 2019 Conference of the North American Chapter of the Association for Computational Linguistics: Human Language Technologies, Volume 1 (Long and Short Papers)*, pages 4171–4186, Minneapolis, Minnesota. Association for Computational Linguistics.

Gijs van Dijck, Shahar Sverdlov, and Gabriela Buck. 2018. Empirical Legal Research in Europe: Prevalence, Obstacles, and Interventions. *Erasmus Law Review*, 11(2):105–119.

Arthur Dyevre. 2021. Text-mining for Lawyers: How Machine Learning Techniques Can Advance our Understanding of Legal Discourse. *Erasmus Law Review*, 15(1):7–23.

Steffen Eckhard, Ronny Patz, and Mirco Schönfeld. 2020. Keine Spur von Sprachlosigkeit im Sicherheitsrat. *Vereinte Nationen*, 68(5):219.

Theodore Eisenberg. 2011. The Origins, Nature, and Promise of Empirical Legal Studies and a Response to Concerns. *University of Illinois Law Review*, (5):1713–1738.

Matthew Evangelista and Nina Tannenwald, editors. 2017. *Do the Geneva Conventions Matter?* Oxford University Press.

Tom Ginsburg and Gregory C. Shaffer. 2009. How Does International Law Work: What Empirical Research Shows. In Peter Cane and Herbert Kritzer, editors, *The Oxford Handbook of Empirical Legal Research*, pages 753–748. Oxford University Press.

Luis Glaser, Ronny Patz, and Manfred Stede. 2022. UNSC-NE: A Named Entity Extension to the UN Security Council Debates Corpus. *Journal for Language Technology and Computational Linguistics*, 35(2):51–67.

Christine Gray. 2018. *International Law and the Use of Force*. Oxford University Press.

Giulia Grundler, Piera Santin, Andrea Galassi, Federico Galli, Francesco Godano, Francesca Lagioia, Elena Palmieri, Federico Ruggeri, Giovanni Sartor, and Paolo Torroni. 2022. Detecting arguments in CJEU decisions on fiscal state aid. In *Proceedings of the 9th Workshop on Argument Mining*, pages 143–157, Online and in Gyeongju, Republic of Korea. International Conference on Computational Linguistics.

Asier Gutiérrez-Fandiño, Jordi Armengol-Estapé, Aitor Gonzalez-Agirre, and Marta Villegas. 2021. Spanish legalese language model and corpora. *ArXiv preprint*, abs/2110.12201.

Ivan Habernal, Daniel Faber, Nicola Recchia, Sebastian Bretthauer, Iryna Gurevych, Indra Spiecker genannt Döhmann, and Christoph Burchard. 2023. Mining legal arguments in court decisions. *Artificial Intelligence and Law*.

Rupert Haigh. 2018. *Legal English*. Routledge, Abingdon, Oxon; New York, NY.

Jean-Marie Henckaerts, Louise Doswald-Beck, Carolin Alvermann, Knut Dörmann, and Baptiste Rolle. 2005. *Customary International Humanitarian Law*. Cambridge University Press.

Martin Hock. 2021. The Influence of Strategic Culture on Legal Justifications. *Erasmus Law Review*, 14(2):68–81.

Jakob V. H. Holtermann and Mikael Madsen. 2015. European New Legal Realism and International Law: How to Make International Law Intelligible. *Leiden Journal of International Law*, 28(2):211–230.

Jakob V. H. Holtermann and Mikael Madsen. 2016. What is Empirical in Empirical Studies of Law? A European New Legal Realist Conception. *iCourts Working Paper Series*, 77.

Hendrik Hüning, Lydia Mechtenberg, and Stephanie Wang. 2022. Detecting arguments and their positions in experimental communication data. *SSRN Electronic Journal*.

ICISS. 2001. *The Responsibility to Protect. Report of the International Commission on Intervention and State Sovereignty*. International Development Research Centre, Ottawa, ON, Canada.

International Law Commission. 2018. *Draft conclusions on identification of customary international law, with commentaries*. United Nations.

Gabriella Lapesa, Eva Maria Vecchi, Serena Villata, and Henning Wachsmuth. 2023. Mining, assessing, and improving arguments in NLP and the social sciences. In *Proceedings of the 17th Conference of the European Chapter of the Association for Computational Linguistics: Tutorial Abstracts*, pages 1–6, Dubrovnik, Croatia. Association for Computational Linguistics.

John Lawrence and Chris Reed. 2019. Argument mining: A survey. *Computational Linguistics*, 45(4):765–818.

Brian D. Lepard. 2010. *Customary International Law*. Cambridge University Press, Cambridge.

Dustin A. Lewis, Naz K. Modirzadeh, and Gabriella Blum. 2019. Quantum of Silence: Inaction and Jus ad Bellum. In *Harvard Law School Program on International Law and Armed Conflict*.

Mike Lewis, Yinhan Liu, Naman Goyal, Marjan Ghazvininejad, Abdelrahman Mohamed, Omer Levy, Veselin Stoyanov, and Luke Zettlemoyer. 2020. BART: Denoising sequence-to-sequence pre-training for natural language generation, translation, and comprehension. In *Proceedings of the 58th Annual Meeting of the Association for Computational Linguistics*, pages 7871–7880, Online. Association for Computational Linguistics.

Daniele Licari and Giovanni Comandè. 2022. ITALIAN-LEGAL-BERT: A Pre-trained Transformer Language Model for Italian Law. In *Companion Proceedings of the 23rd International Conference on Knowledge Engineering and Knowledge Management*, volume 3256 of *CEUR Workshop Proceedings*, Bozen-Bolzano, Italy. CEUR. ISSN: 1613-0073.

Marco Lippi and Paolo Torroni. 2016. Argumentation Mining. *ACM Transactions on Internet Technology*, 16(2):1–25.

Eleonora Mancini, Federico Ruggeri, Andrea Galassi, and Paolo Torroni. 2022. Multimodal argument mining: A case study in political debates. In *Proceedings of the 9th Workshop on Argument Mining*, pages 158–170, Online and in Gyeongju, Republic of Korea. International Conference on Computational Linguistics.

Mihai Masala, Radu Cristian Alexandru Iacob, Ana Sabina Uban, Marina Cidota, Horia Velicu, Traian Rebedea, and Marius Popescu. 2021. jurBERT: A Romanian BERT model for legal judgement prediction. In *Proceedings of the Natural Legal Language Processing Workshop 2021*, pages 86–94, Punta Cana, Dominican Republic. Association for Computational Linguistics.

Masha Medvedeva, Michel Vols, and Martijn Wieling. 2020. Using machine learning to predict decisions of the European Court of Human Rights. *Artificial Intelligence and Law*, 28(2):237–266.

Tamar Megiddo. 2019. Knowledge Production, Big Data and Data-Driven Customary International Law. *SSRN Electronic Journal*.

Stefano Menini, Elena Cabrio, Sara Tonelli, and Serena Villata. 2018. Never retreat, never retract: Argumentation analysis for political speeches. *Proceedings of the AAAI Conference on Artificial Intelligence*, 32.

Rafael Mestre, Razvan Milicin, Stuart E. Middleton, Matt Ryan, Jiatong Zhu, and Timothy J. Norman. 2021. M-arg: Multimodal argument mining dataset for political debates with audio and transcripts. In *Proceedings of the 8th Workshop on Argument Mining*, pages 78–88, Punta Cana, Dominican Republic. Association for Computational Linguistics.

Raquel Mochales and Marie-Francine Moens. 2011. Argumentation mining. *Artificial Intelligence and Law*, 19:1–22.

John Nay. 2018. Natural Language Processing and Machine Learning for Law and Policy Texts. *SSRN Electronic Journal*.

Stephen C. Neff. 2005. *War and the Law of Nations*. Cambridge University Press.

Joel Niklaus, Veton Matoshi, Pooja Rani, Andrea Galassi, Matthias Stürmer, and Ilias Chalkidis. 2023a. Lextreme: A multi-lingual and multi-task benchmark for the legal domain. *ArXiv preprint*, abs/2301.13126.

Joel Niklaus, Veton Matoshi, Matthias Stürmer, Ilias Chalkidis, and Daniel E. Ho. 2023b. Multilegalpile: A 689gb multilingual legal corpus. *ArXiv preprint*, abs/2306.02069.

Anne Orford. 2003. *Reading Humanitarian Intervention. Human Rights and the Use of Force in International Law*. Cambridge University Press.

Ronny Patz, Manfred Stede, and Luis Glaser. 2022. Die Wahl der Worte im Sicherheitsrat. *Vereinte Nationen*, 70(6):260.

Mehrdad Payandeh and Helmut Philipp Aust. 2018. Praxis und Protest im Völkerrecht. *JuristenZeitung*, 73(13):633.

Eric A. Posner and Miguel F. P. de Figueiredo. 2005. Is the International Court of Justice Biased? *The Journal of Legal Studies*, 34(2):599–630.

Prakash Poudyal, Jaromir Savelka, Aagje Ieven, Marie Francine Moens, Teresa Goncalves, and Paulo Quaresma. 2020. ECHR: Legal corpus for argument mining. In *Proceedings of the 7th Workshop on Argument Mining*, pages 67–75, Online. Association for Computational Linguistics.

Nils Reimers and Iryna Gurevych. 2019. Sentence-BERT: Sentence embeddings using Siamese BERT-networks. In *Proceedings of the 2019 Conference on Empirical Methods in Natural Language Processing and the 9th International Joint Conference on Natural Language Processing (EMNLP-IJCNLP)*, pages 3982–3992, Hong Kong, China. Association for Computational Linguistics.

Nils Reimers, Benjamin Schiller, Tilman Beck, Johannes Daxenberger, Christian Stab, and Iryna Gurevych. 2019. Classification and clustering of arguments with contextualized word embeddings. In *Proceedings of the 57th Annual Meeting of the Association for Computational Linguistics*, pages 567–578, Florence, Italy. Association for Computational Linguistics.

David E Rumelhart, Geoffrey E Hinton, and Ronald J Williams. 1986. Learning representations by back-propagating errors. *Nature*, 323(6088):533–536.

Arif Saba and Shahram Akbarzadeh. 2018. The Responsibility to Protect and the Use of Force: An Assessment of the Just Cause and Last Resort Criteria in the Case of Libya. *International Peacekeeping*, 25(2):242–265.

Robin Schaefer and Manfred Stede. 2020. Annotation and detection of arguments in tweets. In *Proceedings of the 7th Workshop on Argument Mining*, pages 53–58, Online. Association for Computational Linguistics.

Gregory Shaffer and Tom Ginsburg. 2012. The Empirical Turn in International Legal Scholarship. *American Journal of International Law*, 106(1):1–46.

Karen Sparck Jones. 1988. A Statistical Interpretation of Term Specificity and Its Application in Retrieval. In *Document Retrieval Systems*, pages 132–142. Taylor Graham Publishing, GBR.

Manfred Stede and Jodi Schneider. 2018. Argumentation Mining. *Synthesis Lectures on Human Language Technologies*, 11(2):1–191.

Ramesh Thakur. 2016. Rwanda, Kosovo, and the International Commission on Intervention and State Sovereignty. In Alex J. Bellamy and Tim Dunne, editors, *The Oxford Handbook on the Responsibility to Protect*, pages 94–113. Oxford University Press.

Orith Toledo-Ronen, Matan Orbach, Yonatan Bilu, Artem Spector, and Noam Slonim. 2020. Multilingual argument mining: Datasets and analysis. In *Findings of the Association for Computational Linguistics: EMNLP 2020*, pages 303–317, Online. Association for Computational Linguistics.

Lewis Tunstall, Nils Reimers, Unso Eun Seo Jo, Luke Bates, Daniel Korat, Moshe Wasserblat, and Oren Pereg. 2022. Efficient Few-Shot Learning Without Prompts. *ArXiv preprint*, abs/2209.11055.

Tom R. Tyler. 2017. Methodology in Legal Research. *Utrecht Law Review*, 13(3):130.

Eva Maria Vecchi, Neele Falk, Iman Jundi, and Gabriella Lapesa. 2021. Towards argument mining for social good: A survey. In *Proceedings of the 59th Annual Meeting of the Association for Computational Linguistics and the 11th International Joint Conference on Natural Language Processing (Volume 1: Long Papers)*, pages 1338–1352, Online. Association for Computational Linguistics.

Valerio Vignoli. 2020. Where are the doves? Explaining party support for military operations abroad in Italy. *West European Politics*, 43(7):1455–1479.

Jacky Visser, John Lawrence, Chris Reed, Jean Wagemans, and Douglas Walton. 2021. Annotating argument schemes. *Argumentation*, 35:101–139.

Wolfgang Wagner. 2020. *The Democratic Politics of Military Interventions*. Oxford University Press.

Hao Wang, Zhen Huang, Yong Dou, and Yu Hong. 2020. Argumentation mining on essays at multi scales. In *Proceedings of the 28th International Conference on Computational Linguistics*, pages 5480–5493, Barcelona, Spain (Online). International Committee on Computational Linguistics.

Mike Wienbracke. 2013. *Juristische Methodenlehre*. C.F. Müller, Heidelberg ; München ; Landsberg ; Frechen ; Hamburg.

Thomas Wolf, Lysandre Debut, Victor Sanh, Julien Chaumond, Clement Delangue, Anthony Moi, Pierric Cistac, Tim Rault, Remi Louf, Morgan Funtowicz, Joe Davison, Sam Shleifer, Patrick von Platen, Clara Ma, Yacine Jernite, Julien Plu, Canwen Xu, Teven Le Scao, Sylvain Gugger, Mariama Drame, Quentin Lhoest, and Alexander Rush. 2020. Transformers: State-of-the-art natural language processing. In *Proceedings of the 2020 Conference on Empirical Methods in Natural Language Processing: System Demonstrations*, pages 38–45, Online. Association for Computational Linguistics.

Huihui Xu, Jaromír Šavelka, and Kevin D. Ashley. 2020. Using argument mining for legal text summarization. In *Frontiers in Artificial Intelligence and Applications*, volume 334: Legal Knowledge and Information Systems.

Hiroaki Yamada, Simone Teufel, and Takenobu Tokunaga. 2019. Building a corpus of legal argumentation in Japanese judgement documents: towards structure-based summarisation. *Artificial Intelligence and Law*, 27(2):141–170.

Gechuan Zhang, Paul Nulty, and David Lillis. 2022. A decade of legal argumentation mining: Datasets and approaches. In *Natural Language Processing and Information Systems*, pages 240–252, Cham. Springer International Publishing.

Lucia Zheng, Neel Guha, Brandon R. Anderson, Peter Henderson, and Daniel E. Ho. 2021. When does pretraining help? assessing self-supervised learning for law and the casehold dataset of 53,000+ legal holdings. In *Proceedings of the Eighteenth International Conference on Artificial Intelligence and Law*, ICAIL '21, page 159–168, New York, NY, USA. Association for Computing Machinery.

Haoxi Zhong, Chaojun Xiao, Cunchao Tu, Tianyang Zhang, Zhiyuan Liu, and Maosong Sun. 2020. How does NLP benefit legal system: A summary of legal artificial intelligence. In *Proceedings of the 58th Annual Meeting of the Association for Computational Linguistics*, pages 5218–5230, Online. Association for Computational Linguistics.

A Appendix

B Models

In this section, we provide further details regarding the models employed in our experimental setting:

B.1 Expert-Based Dictionary

We created an *expert-based dictionary*, drawing upon the wealth of knowledge from our domain expert. In the following table, we present the various terms and expressions contained within our dictionary (Tab. 5).

B.2 Feature-based Classification with MLP heads

We take the sentence embedding from the pre-trained models to perform a classification using a small *Multi-Layer Perceptron* (MLP) with 32 hidden layers (alpha=1e-5, random_state=$\{42, 111, 133\}$). We place these methods as classification headers over the TFIDF and GermanBERT embeddings (Chan et al., 2020)[10] to perform legal element classification.

[10]https://huggingface.co/deepset/gbert-base

labels	words
Huma	"humanitäre", "katastrophe", "gewalt", "massaker", "notlage"
Pro	"gewalt", "massaker", "notlage", "vertreibung", "flüchtlinge", "mord", "kriegsverbrechen", "opfer"
Fail	"angriffe", "bevölkerung", "regierung", "präsident", "bürgerkrieg", "vertreibung", "kriegsverbrechen", "volk", "säuberungen", "staatsterror"
Last	"letztes", "äußerstes", "mittel", "ultima", "ratio", "lösung", "politisch", "allein", "gewalt", "militärisch"
Prop	"begrenzt", "vertretbar", "proportional", "luftschlag", "erforderlich", "phasen", "angemessen", "gleichwertig"
Reas	"erfolg", "aussicht", "vertretbar", "lösung", "glaubhaft", "wirkung", "realistisch", "chance", "erreichbar", "ziel"
Auth	"sicherheitsrat", "resolution", "autorisierung", "staatengemeinschaft", "un", "vereinte nationen", "generalsekretär", "nato", "mandat", "eu"
Inte	"moral", "freiheit", "demokratie", "menschenrechte", "friede", "friedlich", "diplomatisch", "lösung", "tyrann", "stabilität"

Table 5: Dictionary.

B.3 Transformer-based Fine-Tuning

We use pre-trained models trained on monolingual GermanBERT (Chan et al., 2020). We fine-tuned the model with the HuggingFace *transformers* library (Wolf et al., 2020) on the random split (epochs=20, lr=1e-5, epsilon=2e-08 and batch=8) and the debates split (epochs=15, lr=5e-5, epsilon=1e-08 and batch=8) with three different seeds $\{42, 111, 133\}$ and selected the best performing model based on the evaluation loss.

B.4 Domain-Sent-Embeddings (DASent)

We used the framework SetFit in our experiments (Tunstall et al., 2022). We trained the domain-adapted sentence embeddings with SetFit for 10 epochs and 20 iterations (on three different seeds with batch_size=16, learning_rate=2e-5, warmup_proportion=0.1). SetFit employs a method known as contrastive learning in the fine-tuning process of the sentence transformer (Reimers and Gurevych, 2019). Contrastive learning is a natural language processing method in which the model learns to distinguish between a pair of sentences that are similar (positive pair) and a pair that are dissimilar (negative pair). The model learns to bring positive pairs closer in the embedding space while simultaneously pushing negative pairs further apart. This results in a better differentiation between positive and negative pairs. Contrastive learning is capable of capturing meaningful semantic relationships between texts, which significantly improves the model's performance. This is especially beneficial when dealing with small datasets. After this step, the fine-tuned model generates sentence embeddings that are used to train a classification head (Tunstall et al., 2022).

C Negative Example

Find below an example that does not contain any legal elements. This example serves to illustrate the kind of content that is not relevant for legal element classification. A negative example for classification is the following statement made by Karsten D. Voigt in the Kosovo debate[11]:

> *"Es gebührt auch dem bisherigen Kanzler und dem künftigen Kanzler, den bisherigen und künftigen Ministern, die durch diese Art des Zusammenwirkens einen Beitrag zur politischen Kultur in Deutschland geleistet haben, nachdrücklich Dank."* $\rightarrow$ **Element 1, Element 2, Element3**

No legally relevant statement has been given in this sentence.

D Dataset Characteristics

The following figure provides an overview of the label distribution across all debates, offering insights into the overall composition of the dataset (Fig. 1).

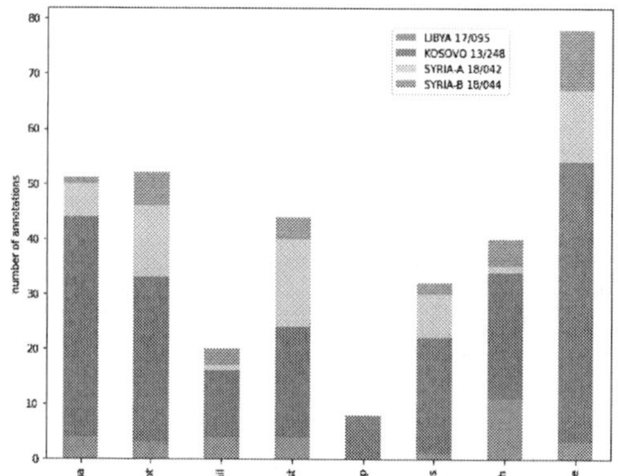

Figure 1: Dataset characteristics, showing the *overall label distribution* (see Tab. 1) for all debates.

E Translation

The translation (DE$\rightarrow$EN) has been conducted by the authors:

(**DE**, *id 138*) "Es kann keinen Zweifel darin geben, daß es überfällig war, den boshaftesten Despoten in Europa, der Krieg gegen sein eigenes

[11]https://dserver.bundestag.de/btp/13/13248.pdf

Model	Set	HL	CE	HUMA Pre	HUMA Rec	HUMA F1	PROT Pre	PROT Rec	PROT F1	FAIL Pre	FAIL Rec	FAIL F1	LAST Pre	LAST Rec	LAST F1	PROP Pre	PROP Rec	PROP F1	REAS Pre	REAS Rec	REAS F1	AUTH Pre	AUTH Rec	AUTH F1	INTE Pre	INTE Rec	INTE F1
													Stratified Random Split														
DB-Expert	dev	.20 ± .00	8.00 ± .00	.00 ± .00	.00 ± .00	.00 ± .00	.00 ± .00	.00 ± .00	.00 ± .00	.00 ± .00	.00 ± .00	.00 ± .00	.00 ± .00	.00 ± .00	.00 ± .00	.00 ± .00	.00 ± .00	.00 ± .00	.00 ± .00	.00 ± .00	.00 ± .00	.00 ± .00	.00 ± .00	.00 ± .00	.00 ± .00	.00 ± .00	.00 ± .00
DB-Expert	test	.16 ± .00	7.42 ± .00	1.0 ± .00	.36 ± .00	.53 ± .00	.00 ± .00	.00 ± .00	.00 ± .00	.00 ± .00	.00 ± .00	.00 ± .00	.50 ± .00	.09 ± .00	.15 ± .00	.00 ± .00	.00 .00	.00 ± .00	.00 ± .00	.00 ± .00	.00 ± .00	.00 ± .00	.00 ± .00	.00 ± .00	.00 ± .00	.00 ± .00	.00 ± .00
DB-PMI	dev	.23 ± .00	6.92 ± .00	.50 ± .00	.33 ± .00	.40 ± .00	.50 ± .00	.12 ± .00	.20 ± .00	.33 ± .00	.67 ± .00	.44 ± .00	.17 ± .00	.33 ± .00	.22 ± .00	.17 ± .00	1.0 ± .00	.29 ± .00	.50 ± .00	.33 ± .00	.40 ± .00	.75 ± .00	.43 ± .00	.55 ± .00	1.0 ± .00	.12 ± .00	.22 ± .00
DB-PMI	test	.22 ± .00	7.33 ± .00	.00 ± .00	.00 ± .00	.00 ± .00	.00 ± .00	.00 ± .00	.00 ± .00	.00 ± .00	.00 ± .00	.00 ± .00	.60 ± .00	.27 ± .00	.37 ± .00	.17 ± .00	.50 ± .00	.25 ± .00	.25 ± .00	.33 ± .00	.29 ± .00	.20 ± .00	.20 ± .00	.20 ± .00	.29 ± .00	.11 ± .00	.16 ± .00
FB-TFIDF	dev	.17 ± .00	6.44 ± .20	.50 ± .00	.17 ± .00	.25 ± .00	.69 ± .04	.29 ± .06	.41 ± .06	1.0 ± .00	.33 ± .00	.50 ± .00	.61 ± .08	.67 ± .00	.63 ± .04	.00 ± .00	.00 ± .00	.00 ± .00	.83 ± .24	.33 ± .00	.47 ± .05	1.0 ± .00	.38 ± .07	.55 ± .07	.48 ± .11	.25 ± .1	.33 ± .11
FB-TFIDF	test	.16 ± .00	5.91 ± .18	.87 ± .05	.60 ± .03	.70 ± .01	.10 ± .02	.17 ± .00	.13 ± .01	.00 ± .00	.00 ± .00	.00 ± .00	.62 ± .05	.30 ± .04	.41 ± .05	.00 ± .00	.00 ± .00	.00 ± .00	.58 ± .31	.17 ± .00	.25 ± .04	.43 ± .05	.40 ± .00	.41 ± .02	1.0 ± .00	.41 ± .05	.58 ± .05
FB-GermanBERT	dev	.21 ± .01	5.92 ± .11	.50 ± .00	.17 ± .00	.25 ± .00	.63 ± .04	.50 ± .00	.54 ± .02	1.0 ± .00	.33 ± .00	.50 ± .00	.67 ± .00	.67 ± .00	.67 ± .00	.00 ± .00	.00 ± .00	.00 ± .00	1.0 ± .00	.33 ± .00	.50 ± .00	1.0 ± .00	.29 ± .00	.44 ± .00	.50 ± .00	.25 ± .00	.33 ± .00
FB-GermanBERT	test	.14 ± .00	5.10 ± .31	.81 ± .07	.57 ± .00	.67 ± .02	.24 ± .05	.56 ± .08	.34 ± .04	.44 ± .08	.42 ± .12	.43 ± .10	.64 ± .10	.21 ± .04	.32 ± .06	.00 ± .00	.00 ± .00	.00 ± .00	.59 ± .07	.39 ± .08	.46 ± .06	.70 ± .07	.87 ± .09	.77 ± .03	.91 ± .07	.69 ± .07	.78 ± .03
FT-GermanBERT	dev	.13 ± .01	5.64 ± .14	1.0 ± .00	.22 ± .08	.36 ± .10	.71 ± .06	.42 ± .12	.52 ± .11	.67 ± .47	.22 ± .16	.33 ± .24	.83 ± .24	.55 ± .16	.67 ± .19	.00 ± .00	.00 .00	.00 ± .00	.89 ± .16	.56 ± .16	.66 ± .12	1.0 ± .00	.52 ± .07	.68 ± .08	.78 ± .02	.46 ± .08	.58 ± .03
FT-GermanBERT	test	.12 ± .00	5.12 ± .07	.92 ± .01	.81 ± .07	.86 ± .04	.33 ± .09	.44 ± .16	.37 ± .11	.83 ± .24	.42 ± .12	.52 ± .11	.66 ± .00	.36 ± .15	.45 ± .13	.00 ± .00	.00 ± .00	.00 ± .00	.55 ± .42	.17 ± .14	.24 ± .18	.57 ± .00	.80 ± .00	.67 ± .00	.93 ± .06	.56 ± .14	.70 ± .09
DASent (SetFit)	dev	.13 ± .01	4.45 ± .10	.72 ± .21	.33 ± .00	.45 ± .04	.74 ± .02	.71 ± .06	.72 ± .04	.56 ± .08	.67 ± .00	.60 ± .04	.35 ± .07	.67 ± .00	.45 ± .06	.00 ± .00	.00 ± .00	.00 ± .00	.60 ± .00	1.0 ± .00	.75 ± .00	.91 ± .06	.95 ± .07	.93 ± .06	.64 ± .05	.71 ± .06	.67 ± .00
DASent (SetFit)	test	.14 ± .003	4.22 ± .11	.84 ± .03	.86 ± .00	.85 ± .01	.21 ± .01	.67 ± .00	.32 ± .01	.62 ± .03	.67 ± .12	.63 ± .04	.76 ± .01	.58 ± .04	.65 ± .03	.00 ± .00	.00 ± .00	.00 ± .00	.55 ± .03	.67 ± .00	.60 ± .02	.44 ± .03	.93 ± .09	.59 ± .04	.78 ± .03	.67 ± .05	.72 ± .04
													Cross-Debate Split														
DB-Expert	LIBYA	.19 ± .00	8.00 ± .00	.00 ± .00	.00 ± .00	.00 ± .00	.00 ± .00	.00 ± .00	.00 ± .00	.00 ± .00	.00 ± .00	.00 ± .00	.00 ± .00	.00 ± .00	.00 ± .00	.00 ± .00	.00 .00	.00 ± .00	.00 ± .00	.00 ± .00	.00 ± .00	.00 ± .00	.00 ± .00	.00 ± .00	.00 ± .00	.00 ± .00	.00 ± .00
DB-Expert	SYRIA-B	.16 ± .00	8.00 ± .00	.00 ± .00	.00 ± .00	.00 ± .00	.00 ± .00	.00 ± .00	.00 ± .00	.00 ± .00	.00 ± .00	.00 ± .00	.00 ± .00	.00 ± .00	.00 ± .00	.00 ± .00	.00 ± .00	.00 ± .00	.00 ± .00	.00 ± .00	.00 ± .00	.00 ± .00	.00 ± .00	.00 ± .00	.00 ± .00	.00 ± .00	.00 ± .00
DB-PMI	LIBYA	.19 ± .00	7.65 ± .00	.00 ± .00	.00 ± .00	.00 ± .00	.00 ± .00	.00 ± .00	.00 ± .00	.00 ± .00	.00 ± .00	.00 ± .00	.00 ± .00	.00 ± .00	.00 ± .00	.00 ± .00	.00 ± .00	.00 ± .00	.00 ± .00	.00 ± .00	.00 ± .00	.50 ± .00	.20 ± .00	.29 ± .00	.00 ± .00	.00 ± .00	.00 ± .00
DB-PMI	SYRIA-B	.19 ± .00	6.81 ± .00	.00 ± .00	.00 ± .00	.00 ± .00	.00 ± .00	.00 ± .00	.00 ± .00	.00 ± .00	.00 ± .00	.00 ± .00	.00 ± .00	.00 ± .00	.00 ± .00	.00 ± .00	.00 ± .00	.00 ± .00	.33 ± .00	.50 ± .00	.40 ± .00	.67 ± .00	.40 ± .00	.50 ± .00	.40 ± .00	.18 ± .00	.25 ± .00
FB-TFIDF	LIBYA	.23 ± .01	7.30 ± .00	.00 ± .00	.00 ± .00	.00 ± .00	.00 ± .00	.00 ± .00	.00 ± .00	.00 ± .00	.00 ± .00	.00 ± .00	.39 ± .08	.25 ± .00	.30 ± .02	.00 ± .00	.00 ± .00	.00 ± .00	.00 ± .00	.00 ± .00	.00 ± .00	.00 ± .00	.00 ± .00	.00 ± .00	.14 ± .00	.33 ± .00	.20 ± .00
FB-TFIDF	SYRIA-B	.15 ± .00	6.32 ± .20	.00 ± .00	.00 ± .00	.00 ± .00	.75 ± .00	.50 ± .00	.60 ± .00	.00 ± .00	.00 ± .00	.00 ± .00	.47 ± .05	.50 ± .00	.48 ± .03	.00 ± .00	.00 ± .00	.00 ± .00	.00 ± .00	.00 ± .00	.00 ± .00	1.0 ± .00	.20 ± .00	.33 ± .00	.39 ± .09	.30 ± .11	.34 ± .10
FB-GermanBERT	LIBYA	.21 ± .01	5.98 ± .37	.44 ± .08	.25 ± .00	.32 ± .02	.00 ± .00	.00 ± .00	.00 ± .00	1.0 ± .00	.25 ± .00	.40 ± .00	.39 ± .28	.25 ± .20	.30 ± .23	.00 ± .00	.00 ± .00	.00 ± .00	.25 ± .00	1.0 ± .00	.40 ± .00	.69 ± .04	.23 ± .05	.35 ± .06	.20 ± .00	.33 ± .00	.25 ± .00
FB-GermanBERT	SYRIA-B	.17 ± .01	5.59 ± .44	.44 ± .08	1.0 ± .00	.61 ± .08	.35 ± .05	.50 ± .00	.41 ± .04	.00 ± .00	.00 ± .00	.00 ± .00	.33 ± .00	.25 ± .00	.29 ± .00	.00 ± .00	.00 .00	.00 ± .00	1.0 ± .00	.83 ± .24	.89 ± .16	.67 ± .00	.40 ± .00	.50 ± .00	.44 ± .05	.45 ± .07	.45 ± .05
FT-GermanBERT	LIBYA	.16 ± .02	6.62 ± .27	.44 ± .31	.33 ± .24	.38 ± .27	.10 ± .11	.11 ± .16	.10 ± .13	.00 ± .00	.00 ± .00	.00 ± .00	.44 ± .42	.17 ± .12	.23 ± .17	.00 ± .00	.00 ± .00	.00 ± .00	.00 ± .00	.00 ± .00	.00 ± .00	.72 ± .04	.27 ± .05	.39 ± .06	1.0 ± .00	.67 ± .00	.80 ± .00
FT-GermanBERT	SYRIA-B	.12 ± .01	5.94 ± .33	.61 ± .28	1.0 ± .00	.72 ± .21	.76 ± .17	.61 ± .08	.67 ± .10	.00 ± .00	.00 ± .00	.00 ± .00	.67 ± .47	.17 ± .12	.27 ± .19	.00 ± .00	.00 ± .00	.00 ± .00	.00 ± .00	.00 ± .00	.00 ± .00	1.0 ± .00	.40 ± .00	.57 ± .00	.52 ± .08	.45 ± .07	.48 ± .06
DASent (SetFit)	LIBYA	.14 ± .01	4.12 ± .13	.78 ± .16	.75 ± .00	.76 ± .08	.30 ± .02	.67 ± .00	.41 ± .02	1.0 ± .00	.33 ± .12	.49 ± .13	.36 ± .02	.67 ± .12	.47 ± .05	.00 ± .00	.00 ± .00	.00 ± .00	.67 ± .24	1.0 ± .00	.78 ± .16	.93 ± .05	.87 ± .05	.90 ± .04	.48 ± .03	1.0 ± .00	.64 ± .03
DASent (SetFit)	SYRIA-B	.16 ± .01	3.99 ± .11	.22 ± .02	1.0 ± .00	.36 ± .05	.53 ± .02	1.0 ± .00	.69 ± .02	.00 ± .00	.00 ± .00	.00 ± .00	.33 ± .00	.50 ± .00	.40 ± .00	.00 ± .00	.00 ± .00	.00 ± .00	.83 ± .24	.50 ± .00	.61 ± .08	1.0 ± .00	.60 ± .00	.75 ± .00	.51 ± .05	.88 ± .04	.64 ± .04

Table 6: Performance comparison of our applied models for legal element classification on German parliamentary debates using our two different dataset splits: *Stratified Random Split* and *Cross-Debate Split* (**H**amming **L**oss, **C**overage **E**rror, **Pre**cision, **Rec**all, **F1**-Macro and ± **std**).

Staatsvolk führt, es entwurzelt, in die Wälder treibt und ermorden läßt, in seine Schranken zu verweisen, um eine humanitäre Katastrophe noch größeren Ausmaßes zu verhindern.".

(**EN**, *id 138*) *There can be no doubt, that it was due to put checks on the most evil despot in Europe who wages war against his own people, displaces them, and drives them into the woods in order to avoid a humanitarian catastrophe of even larger extent.*

(**DE**, *id 173*) "Nennen Sie mir einen weltweit, der sich mehr darum bemüht, dass dieser politische Prozess zustande kommt"

(**EN**, *id 173*) *Show me one person in the world, who is more concerned that this political process will take place.*

(**DE**, *id 72*) "Wenn wir diese schrecklichen Szenen als Fernsehzuschauer in Westeuropa einfach konsumieren würden, ohne zu handeln, dann würden wir letztlich mit einer rostigen Rasierklinge unser Gesicht zerschneiden und unser eigenes Gesicht entstellen."

(**EN**, *id 72*) *If we were to simply consume these horrible scenes on the TV screen in Western Europe without acting it would equal to cutting our own face with a rusty razor and disfiguring our own face.*

(**DE**, *id 114*) "Wir können nicht tatenlos zusehen, wenn sich regionale Faustrechte entwickeln und Menschenrechte in Regionen so verletzt werden, daß es zu humanitären Katastrophen kommen kann, weil das Gewaltmonopol der Vereinten Nationen nicht ausgeübt werden kann."

(**EN**, *id 114*) *We cannot stand-by idly when regionally the law is taken into their own hands and in certain regions human rights are violated that much that a humanitarian catastrophe takes place because the monopoly of violence of the United Nations cannot be enforced.*

F Contributions

This collaborative project combines expertise from the fields of political science, law, and natural language processing. The first author produced the underlying taxonomy and theoretical foundation of the project, as well as facilitating the annotation of legal elements in political debates (Section 3). A key part of the project was a collaboration between the authors (Sections 1-2 and 6-9). Furthermore, the coding was done by the first author (Section 4). The second author prepared the dataset for annotation and led the annotation process (Section 4). In addition, the second author designed and implemented various natural language processing tools to automatically predict legal elements in political debates (Section 5). In the subsequent phase, the first author did an error analysis of the predictions generated by the model (Section 5). The remaining aspects of the project were performed in collaboration with each other.

Bubble up – A Fine-tuning Approach for Style Transfer to Community-specific Subreddit Language

Alessandra Zarcone
Technische Hochschule Augsburg
Fakultät für Informatik
Augsburg, Germany
alessandra.zarcone@hs-augsburg.de

Fabian Kopf
Technische Hochschule Augsburg
Fakultät für Informatik
Augsburg, Germany
fabian.kopf@hs-augsburg.de

Abstract

Different online communities (social media bubbles) can be identified with their use of language. We looked at different social media bubbles and explored the task of translating between the language of one bubble into another while maintaining the intended meaning. We collected a dataset of Reddit comments from 20 different Subreddits and for a smaller subset of them we obtained style-neutral versions generated by a large language model. Then we used the dataset to fine-tune different (smaller) language models to learn style transfers between social media bubbles. We evaluated the models on unseen data from four unseen social media bubbles to assess to what extent they had learned the style transfer task and compared their performance with the zero-shot performance of a larger, non-fine tuned, language model. We show that with a small amount of fine-tuning the smaller models achieve satisfactory performance, making them more attractive than a larger, more resource-intensive model.

1 Introduction

Language on social media is not just a way to exchange information but it is a mean to effectively create a community identity, with each virtual community having their own, identifiable language (Baym, 2003; Gnach, 2017; Rheingold, 2000). For example, in some communities of investors it is common to use the term "HODL" to mean *hold* to describe holding a share (Duggan, 2023). Beyond the vocabulary, also the use of emojis and hashtags or the type of grammar can help identify the language of a social media community or bubble and can at the same time make it difficult for outsiders to understand what it is being said (Smith and Sturges, 1969).

We explore the task of translating between the language of one bubble into the language of another while maintaining the intended meaning of the original sentence (see Hovy, 1987 for a discussion of semantics vs. style). We define the task in the following way: given sentence A and sentence B, the task is to transfer the style of sentence B to sentence A while maintaining the original meaning of sentence A.

We demonstrate how to perform style transfers from neutral, non-style-marked English to a community-specific style (namely, the style or community-specific language of a Subreddit discussion forum). Our fine-tuning approach does not use a large amount of parallel data to specialize to a specific type of style transfer, but rather aims at working with a small amount of resources to learn the general task of style transfer from one social media bubble to another.

The task of transferring between the styles of different social media bubbles can provide interesting insights into what it means to perform a style transfer in the social media domain, where the style itself carries information about membership within a certain community. At the same time, looking at how style transfers can be automatically performed can contribute to the future detection of automatically-translated posts, which in turn can be used with malicious intents, for example to spread rumours or fake news.

We provide the dataset we collected and employed in this study as well as an evaluation of the datasets. The dataset itself provides a resource for future studies on the different styles used by different social media bubbles. We present our style transfer models, which we evaluate with regard to their ability to effectively perform the style transfer as well as their ability to maintain the original sentence meaning. The fine-tuned models can achieve satisfactory performance with a small amount of fine-tuning, which makes them more attractive than using a larger, more resource-intensive zero-shot approach.

Proceedings of the 3rd Workshop on Computational Linguistics for the Political and Social Sciences, pages 46–58
September 22, 2023.

Subreddit	Category	Participants
antiwork	politics	2.5M
atheism	religion	2.8M
Conservative	politics	1.0M
conspiracy	conspiracy theories	1.9M
dankmemes	memes	5.9M
gaybros	LGBT	380 000
leagueoflegends	computer games	6.3M
lgbt	LGBT	1.0M
Libertarian	politics	511 800
linguistics	science	297 800
MensRights	politics	348 200
news	news	26M
offbeat	news	690 500
politicalcompassmemes	memes	572 800
politics	politics	8.3M
teenager	memes	5.9M
TrueReddit	news	519 900
TwoXChromosomes	gender	13.5M
wallstreetbets	finance	13.8M
world news	news	31.5M

Table 1: The 20 Subreddits considered for our data collection.

2 Previous Work

Style transfer with parallel corpora The task of style transfer can be addressed by using parallel corpora, where to each sentence in the source style corresponds a sentence in the target style with the same meaning. Parallel corpora are employed for example to train sequence-to-sequence models to transfer an informal style to a more formal style (Rao and Tetreault, 2018), or to make a text more polite (Danescu-Niculescu-Mizil et al., 2013), or to transfer from Shakespeare's English to modern English (Xu et al., 2012).

Style transfer without parallel corpora It is not always possible or practical to collect a parallel corpus to train a style transfer model, which in the end would be specialized mostly on one specific style transfer. Thus more recent approaches have attempted at performing style transfer without resorting to parallel corpora, addressing the need to keep style and meaning separated (Shen et al., 2017; Bao et al., 2019; John et al., 2019), for example approximating the text content using bag-of-word vectors and aiming at predicting it (John et al., 2019), or training transformer models which could be fine-tuned to produce a network for each specific style transfer (Goyal et al., 2021). Luo et al. (2019) used pseudoparallel datasets with different styles and unrelated content and employed two different models to optimize the semantic similarity of source and target content and the style similarity between source and target styles. Generative models work particularly well for this: Riley et al.'s (2021) TextSETTR for example extracts a style vector using the T5 sequence-to-sequence model (Raffel et al., 2020) and then use it to condition the decoder during style transfer. For more style transfer approaches employing generative models see also Li et al. (2018); Lample et al. (2018, 2019); Krishna et al. (2020); Reid and Zhong (2021).

Prompt-based style transfer Large generative transformer models such as GPT3.5 (Brown et al., 2020) or GPTNeoX (Black et al., 2022) allow for zero-shot text style transfer. Reif et al. (2022) frame style transfer as sentence rewriting with natural language instruction, using prompts such as *"Here is some text: That is an ugly dress. Here is a rewrite of the text, which is more positive:"*. The text-davinci-003 GPT-3.5 model would for example rewrite it as *"That dress has an interesting style"*. Reif et al. (2022) also propose to provide several examples of style transfer as part of the prompt to obtain better results. Suzgun et al. (2022) additionally suggest generating multiple target candidates and ranking them regarding similarity to target content, strength of target style and fluency, showing that this approach is more suitable to smaller pretrained language models and thus a more resource-effective approach.

3 The Reddit Comments Dataset

3.1 Data collection

We collected community-specific language data from Reddit. Reddit is a social network which is used by its users to discuss a wide range of topic. Users can post text, links, images or videos, which can be commented and / or rated by the other users. The discussions on Reddit are organized in the so-called Subreddits, which specialize in different topics and interests and arguably constitute some sort of social media bubble. We observed that the stylistic homogeneity within each Subreddit may vary: Subreddits dealing with more general topics, the writing style of the user is typically not marked, whereas Subreddits that deal with special topics and have a specific, delimited circle of users (in particular, Subreddits on political topics), the style is more homogeneous and more easily identifiable.

We chose 20 Subreddits of varying degree of popularity - the list of Subreddits along with their topic and number of participants is provided in Table 1. The rationale we followed was to select Subreddits with a variety of different topics, showing a wide style variance between each other but a homogeneous style within each other - that is, showing a clearly-identifiable "language". This was based on our own impression, which we validated with the dataset evalauation (see below, section 3.5). We also aimed at providing some sort of balance between Subreddits of opposite positions (e.g. *TwoXChromosomes* for *MensRights*, *Libertarian* for *Conservative*).

The text in the Subreddits is easily accessible thanks to the Reddit API[1] as well as the Pushshift API provided by Baumgartner et al. (2020). We collected comments to the posts using the Subreddit Comment Downloader[2]. We selected comments which were between 10 and 512 tokens long, which were not `[removed]` or `[deleted]` and which did not contain any url.

3.2 Perplexity-based selection

In order to ensure that the crawled data was showing enough style-specific features to be meaningful for a style-transfer task, we aimed at selecting comments with easily-identifiable style features. We assumed that a large language model such as GPT-2 would yield higher perplexity values for more stylistically-marked comments, which deviate the most from standard language. For our training and evaluation set, we selected the 150 comments with highest GPT-2 perplexity for each Subreddit.

3.3 Creation of style-neutral versions

For our training and evaluation, we also needed style-neutral versions of the Reddit comments. Comparable available datasets were proposed by Rao and Tetreault (2018), Wu et al. (2020), Atwell et al. (2022), Logacheva et al. (2022), Liu et al. (2020) included human-generated style-transferred sentences . Due to time and resource limitations, we used synthetic data generation in order to obtain style-neutral versions of the comments. Arguably, a translation from style-marked to style-neutral is an easier task than a translation in the opposite direction or between different styles, because it requires generating text of a more standard variety, which can be more easily produced by a generic language model. We thus expect that a large language model (LLM) would be particularly effective at this when the neutral style is used as a target style (see also Josifoski et al., 2023 for an example of synthetic data use leveraging the asymmmetry in task difficulty).

We follow the zero-shot approach in Reif et al. (2022). The style-neutral versions were generated using the text-davinci-003 version of the GPT-3.5 Model.

We made a first attempt with a prompt similar to the one used by Reif et al. (2022) for their style transfer to formal style:

"Here is some text {[...]} Here is a rewrite of the text, which is more formal: {"

With the text-davinci-003 model, however, the results obtained with these prompts were not really style-neutral but rather too pompous, as in the following example:

"Here is some text: {Just saying, no brag or anything, but I make $35/hr off construction knowledge. I started low but got good at it.} Here is a rewrite of the text, which is more formal: {"

⇒ *"I humbly state that I am able to earn $35 per hour through my expertise in construction. Initially, I began at a lower rate, but I have since developed a high level of proficiency}".*

We thus changed the prompt to require a "more neutral" continuation, leading to better style-neutral versions:

⇒ *"I have experience in construction and I make $35/hr. I started out with a lower rate, but I have become more skilled over time.}".*

3.4 Dataset description

The dataset includes more than 49K comments from the 20 Subreddits, their token length and perplexity scores, along with the name of the Subreddit, a timestamp and a link to the original comment. For two smaller subsets of the dataset (training set and evaluation set), neutral-style versions were provided for 150 comments in each Subreddit (the 150 high-perplexity ones). This was in line with our goal of limiting the use of the largest language model, which we used to obtain the style-neutral versions and to create a small dataset for fine-tuning. The training set contains comments from 16 Subreddits, the evaluation set from 4 Subreddits. The dataset is publicly available on Zenodo: `https://doi.org/10.5281/zenodo.8023142` (Kopf, 2023).

[1] `https://www.reddit.com/dev/api/`

[2] `https://github.com/pistocop/subreddit-comments-dl`

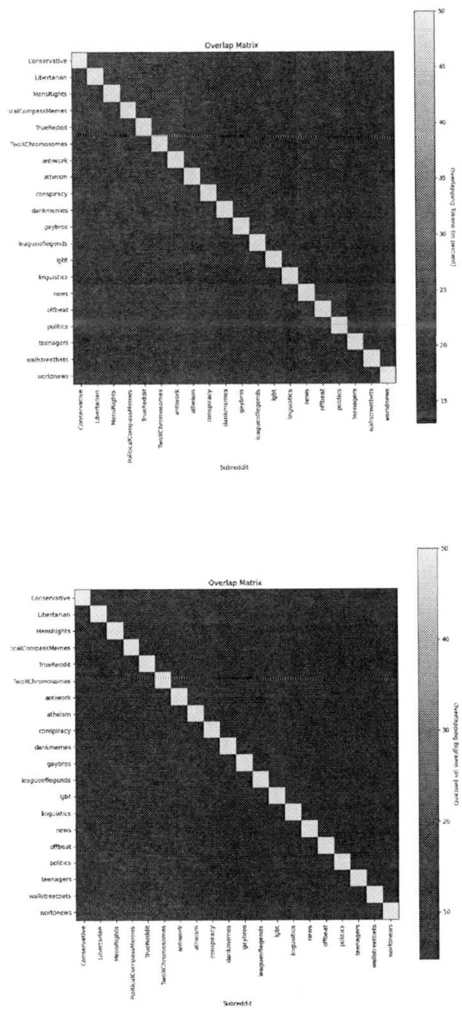

Figure 1: Lexical overlap (unigrams, top, and bigrams, bottom) between the high-perplexity comments for different Subreddit pairs.

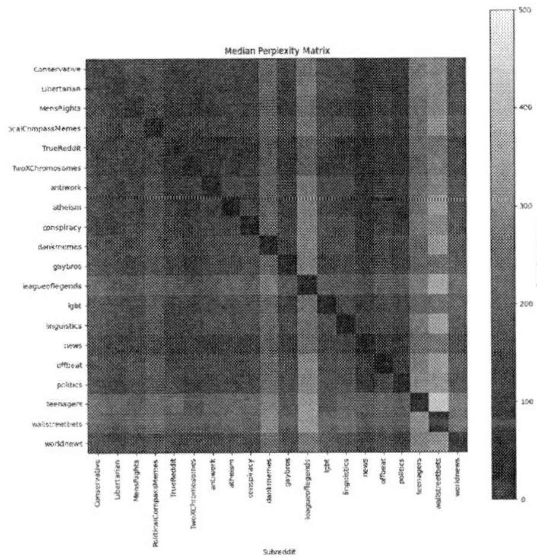

Figure 2: Median perplexity from fine-tuned GPT-2 language models between different Subreddits for the high-perplexity comments (high perplexity for the generic language model). On the y-axis are the fine-tuned language models, on the x-axis the comments of the Subreddit, for which the scores were computed.

3.5 Dataset Evaluation

Lexical Overlap In order to evaluate if the different Subreddits differ with regard to their lexical choices, we compared the percentage of shared lemmas and shared lemmatized bigrams between all possible Subreddit pairs for the high-perplexity comments (perplexity > 100). The lexical overlap scores (visualized in Figure 1) show that in particular the high-perplexity comments are not only clearly different from the standard language, but are also easily distinguishable from the other Subreddits, making them particularly suitable for our training and evaluation.

Perplexity Perplexity scores were also employed to evaluate differences between the Subreddits beyond lexical overlap. We thus fine-tuned a GPT-2 model for each Subreddit and used it to compute perplexity scores for the comments in the other Subreddits. We expect the model for a specific Subreddit to be "surprised" when exposed to the style of a different Subreddit.

The perplexity scores are rather homogeneous with the exception of the Subreddits "leagoflegend", "teenagers" and "wallstreetbets", whose comments yield high perplexity scores in all style-specific language models - with the obvious exception of the style-specific model fine-tuned on the comments from this Subreddit.

Neutral-style versions We compared our dataset with the GYAFC dataset (Rao and Tetreault, 2018), a large human-labelled parallel datasets often used to evaluate formal/informal style transfer systems, in order do evaluate how the quality of our LLM-generated neutral-style versions compared with the quality of human-generated data. We used BERTScore (Zhang et al., 2019) and chrF++ (Popović, 2015, 2017) to compare our dataset with GYAFC with regard to the semantic similarity between style-specific and neutral version. While the BERTScore and chrF++ for the neutral-versions generated with the "more formal" and "more neutral" prompt are marginally lower than the human-

Data	F1-Score	Precision	Recall	chrF++	Perplexity
more formal	0.79	0.79	0.78	44.97	36.73
more neutral	0.79	0.79	0.78	45.15	34.63
more neutral, high perplexity	0.89	0.90	0.88	37.16	123.77
GYAFC (Rao and Tetreault, 2018)	0.81	0.82	0.81	45.74	99.21

Table 2: Comparison between the two prompting techniques and with the neutral-prompt versions of the high-perplexity comments. We compared our LLM-generated data to the GYAFC dataset (Rao and Tetreault, 2018) - whose formal versions were generated by human annotators - using the same evaluation metrics for better comparison.

Model	Version	Parameters
BART	bart-base (Lewis et al., 2020)	110M
T5	t5-base, flan-t5-base, (Raffel et al., 2020)	250M
GPT-3.5	text-davinci-003 (Brown et al., 2020)	175B

Table 3: The Language Models employed for style transfer.

generated versions in GYAFC, the picture is a bit differenw when we only look at the neutral versions of the high-perplexity subset, which in comparison yielded better BERTScore and chrF++ values as well as a higher perplexity (which is more in line with the perplexity of the human-generated versions in GYAFC). Overall, the machine-generated neutral versions seem comparably good with the human-generated versions in GYAFC. Examples are provided in Appendix A in Table 6.

4 Model description

4.1 Baseline model

As comparison we carried out style-transfer experiments using a very large language model (the text-davinci-003 version of GPT-3.5, with 175B parameters) without fine-tuning, using a zero-shot approach. We used the following prompt:

"Here are example sentences: {example1} {example2} {example3}
Here is a sentence: {neutral-style comment}
Here is a rewrite of this sentence according to the example sentences: {"

The model performs a style transfer by completing the prompt.

4.2 Fine-tuned models

We fine-tuned a BART models (bart-base) as well as two T5 models (t5-base and flan-t5-base). The models were fine-tuned using the training set, using the task of generating the style-transferred output by completing the prompts:

Input:
"Here are example sentences:
{example1} {example2} {example3}
Here is a sentence: {neutral-style comment}
Here is a rewrite of this sentence according to the example sentences: {"

Output:
"{original version of the neutral comment} }"

We used the style-neutral, LLM-generated versions in the input and the original Reddit versions of the comments in the output.

4.3 Model evaluation

We evaluate the models' performance on the evaluation set, which does not contain comments from the same Subreddits as the training set. In this way we evaluated how the models perform on unseen data and unseen styles.

Meaning equivalence We compute BERTScore (Zhang et al., 2019) and chrF++ (Popović, 2015, 2017) to assess the meaning equivalence between the neutral input and the style-transferred output.

BERTScore measures embedding similarity between tokens in the source text and in the target text. The the similarity are used to computes *recall* by matching each token x in the source to a token in the target $\hat{x}$, and *precision* by matching each token $\hat{x}$ in the target to a token x in the source, with greedy matching (Zhang et al., 2019). Precision and recall are used to compute the $F-$score.

$$R_{\text{BERT}} = \frac{1}{|x|} \sum_{x_i \in x} \max_{\hat{x}_j \in \hat{x}} x_i^\top \hat{x}_j \quad (1)$$

Model		F1-Score	Precision	Recall	chrF++	Perplexity
BART	bart-base, zero-shot	0.48	0.48	0.49	9.75	650.59
	bart-base, 5 epochs	0.81	0.82	0.80	49.09	379.61
T5	t5-base, zero-shot	0.31	0.30	0.33	0.79	16140.79
	t5-base, 5 epochs	0.86	0.88	0.85	56.02	337.97
	flan-t5-base, zero-shot	0.93	0.95	0.92	88.68	829.89
	flan-t5-base, 5 epochs	0.82	0.83	0.82	50.01	547.81
GPT-3.5	text-davinci-003, zero-shot	0.85	0.83	0.87	59.43	151.72

Table 4: BERTScore, chrF++ and perplexity results for the baseline model and the fine-tuned models (after 5 epochs).

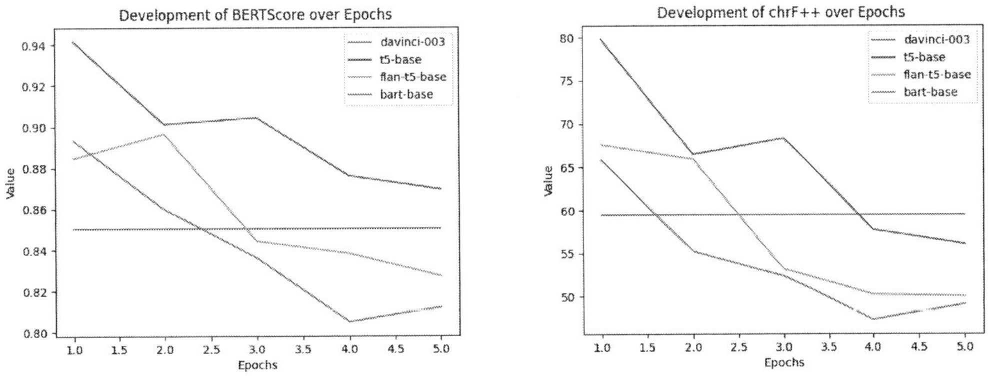

Figure 3: Changes in BERTScore and chrF++ over different epochs.

$$P_{\text{BERT}} = \frac{1}{|\hat{x}|} \sum_{\hat{x}_j \in \hat{x}} \max_{x_i \in x} x_i^\top \hat{x}_j \quad (2)$$

$$F_{\text{BERT}} = 2\frac{P_{\text{BERT}} * R_{\text{BERT}}}{R_{\text{BERT}} + R_{\text{BERT}}} \quad (3)$$

The chrF score (Popović, 2015, 2017) computes *precision* as the percentage of n-grams in the target which have a counterpart in the source, and *recall* as the percentage of n-grams in the source which have a counterpart in the target. For the chrF++ score , the word n-grams are added to the character n-grams and then averaged.

Style transfer In order to evaluate to what extent the style transfer was successful, we compute a general perplexity score using the non-fine-tuned GPT-2. This perplexity indicates how much the style-transferred output differs from the standard language use. We then compute perplexity values for Subreddit-specific fine-tuned language models as described in 3.5, to evaluate to what extent the obtained style for the target Subreddit differed from the style of the other Subreddits.

5 Results

The results of the model evaluation are summarized in Table 4. The fine-tuned models are compared with their own performance before fine-tuning (zero-shot) as well as with the larger baseline model, which is not fine-tuned either. We provide examples of the generated style-transferred comments in Appendix C.

5.1 Meaning equivalence

The results of this evaluation are summarized in Table 4 and Figure 3. The BERTscore and the chrF++ scores on the smaller non-finetuned models show that fine-tuning is indeed necessary for these models. The BERTscore and the chrF++ scores actually worsened with further fine-tuning on the training set, both as compared to the earlier epochs of the same models and to the baseline. This was probably a consequence of the style adaptation as well, as the models progressively differentiated themselves from the standard language use. However, after 5 epochs the fine-tuned models still yielded satisfactory measures of semantic similarity to the neutral input and considerably better scores compared to

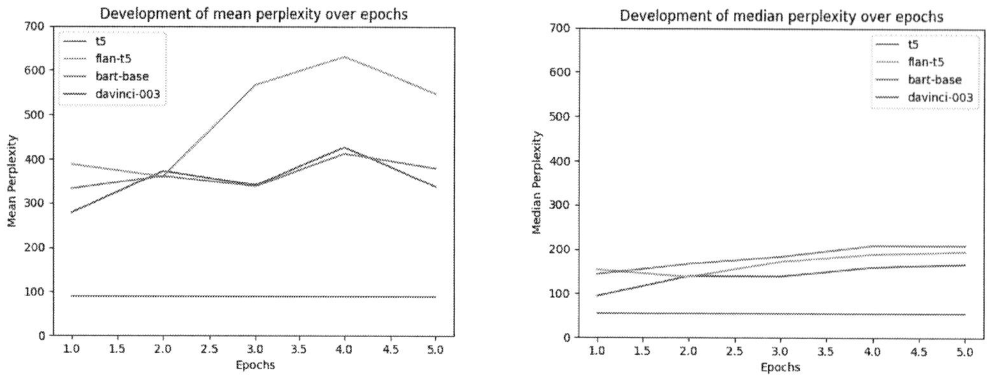

Figure 4: Changes in mean and median GPT-2 perplexity over different epochs.

Model		TrueReddit	TwoXChromosomes	wallstreetbets	worldnews
BART	bart-base	154.82	128.04	115.90	176.27
T5	t5-base	177.43	74.15	118.92	507.51
	flan-t5-base	74.50	107.30	105.29	487.38
GPT-3.5	text-davinci-003	68.14	56.43	92.18	89.69

Table 5: Within-style subbredit-specific perplexity for the four styles in the evaluation set, for the baseline and the fine-tuned models after 5 epochs.

their non-fine-tuned versions. As an exception, it is worth noting that flan-t5-base yielded better scores in the zero-shot version. This happened because the model tended to simply copy the source text.

5.2 General perplexity

The results of this evaluation are summarized in Table 4 and Figure 4. A high perplexity here shows a style differentiation from standard use. All fine-tuned models yield higher perplexity values compared to their zero-shot versions as the fine-tuning progresses – and higher than the baseline.

5.3 Subreddit-specific perplexity

Subreddit-specific perplexity scores were computed for style-transferred outputs, in order to evaluate the match between output style and target style.

Perplexity scores for target-style language models For the four Subreddits in the evaluation set, Table 5 shows the perplexity scores for the matching fine-tuned Subreddit-specific language model, obtained on the style-transferred outputs from the fine-tuned models and the baseline model. The outputs of all fine-tuned models yield particularly high perplexity when the target style is "worldnews" - but this is not the case for the outputs generated by the baseline model for the same target style. Note that the "worldnews" Subreddit did not seem to be a particularly dishomogeneous one during the dataset evaluation.

Comparison between target vs. other styles All style-transferred outputs of the fine-tuned style transfer models yielded the lowest perplexity scores for the Subreddit-specific language models of the corresponding target style compared to other Subreddit-specific language models. The only exception was the model flan-t5-base, whose outputs for the target style "worldnews" yielded the lowest perplexity scores for language model corresponding to the style "offbeat" instead. It is worth mentioning here again that the styles used in the evaluation were not the same styles using during fine-tuning of the style-transfer models. Figure 5 in Appendix C compares different style-specific perplexities for TrueReddit-style comments generated by the different models.

6 Discussion

The dataset evaluation showed that the different bubbles / Subreddits are sufficiently distinguishable from one another and that the quality of our machine-generated neutral-style translations is comparable to that achieved with similar, human-generated datasets.

We left 4 Subreddits aside for the evaluation, only using 16 for fine tuning, in order to evaluate if the fine-tuning improved the style transfer task itself and not a transfer to a particular style.

The style transfer capability of the fine-tuned models was explored using measures of semantic similarity / meaning equivalence between texts such as BERTscore and chrF++ as well as perplexity as a measure of style similarity. Our results show that scores such as BERTscore and chrF++, are improved after fine-tuning compared to the zero-shot scenario, but then decrease as we fine-tune for style transfer. It probably comes with the task of style transfer that, as the model learn to specialize for a specific social media bubble, the semantic similarity decreases. While we argue that BERTscore and chrF++ are more suitable than token-based (n-gram based) measures such as BLEU to assess meaning equivalence in style transfer and paraphrasing tasks, we also observe that the differences between the Subreddits do not only pertain to the style but also to the semantic content, which is probably also causing the semantic similarity scores to decrease with fine tuning. Similarly, topic differences between the Subreddits may also influence the perplexity scores, as a language model will be more "surprised" when encountering text with a very specific style and topic content which differs from those of the average texts it was trained and fine-tuned on.

7 Conclusion

For many downstream tasks it is tempting to use a LLM and to go for a zero-shot approach, in particular for a task such as style transfer, where style itself is a concept which is difficult to pinpoint, let alone finding specific style categories to be applied. Working with examples as prompts has the advantage of sidestepping the issue of defining what a particular style should look like.

However, we show that some fine-tuning of smaller models such as BART and T5 models is also a viable option. These models, when fine-tuned with a small amount of data to learn the style transfer from one social medial bubble to another, despite being much smaller than GPT-3.5, can achieve comparable or better results in performing new, arbitrary style transfers in the Subreddit domain.

For the fine-tuning itself we provide a dataset of different Subreddits under the assumption that to each Subreddit / social media bubble corresponds a characteristic, identifiable style. Just because a comment comes from one specific Subreddit however does not imply that the comment itself will have an identifiable style, some may be less marked. Thus we use perplexity as computed by a LLM (GPT-2) as a proxy to evaluate how stylistically charged a comment is and select 150 high-perplexity comments for each of 20 Subreddits. For the selected comments, we create a neutral-style version for each comment using a LLM (GPT-2). The neutral-style versions are used to create prompts which help the models learn the task of style transfer during fine-tuning. Note that steps requiring the use of a LLM are only involved in the database creation - once the database is created, it is enough to fine-tune smaller models for the task.

Four Subreddits were kept aside for evaluation purposes. Note that the fine-tuning is performed on different styles than the ones used in the evaluation. The semantic overlap between neutral versions and target-style versions was evaluated using BERTscore and chrF++, while the style match was evaluated using perplexity scores of language models. GPT-2 was used as a generic LLM to measure the match with a nonmarked use of language. Then it was fine-tuned to obtain style-specific language models to evaluate the match between the generated outputs and the different styles. The evaluation showed satisfactory results for the smaller, fine-tuned models (BART and T5) when compared to the outputs generated by a LLM (GPT-3.5).

Of course GPT-3.5, a much larger model, can already achieve very good results with a zero-shot approach, without fine-tuning - but we argue that it makes more sense to employ the relatively small resources required to fine-tune a smaller model for the style transfer task rather than following a zero-shot approach.

Limitations

Our goal is to teach the models a general task of style transfer, which is why we use different styles in the training and testing phases. However, we acknowledge that the style of Reddit posts, however different between different Subreddits, may still be rather homogeneous.

This work is limited to English and to social media language - in particular, we looked at comments of a maximum length of 512 tokens. We make a few assumptions during our work, probably the biggest assumption is that the language use learned by a LLM such as GPT-2 reflects the non-marked, standard use of the English language. We also assumed that, if a language model learns the style of a (collection of) texts, then the perplexity of that language model can be used as a proxy for the style match between a text and a target style.

We also assume that perplexity on the one hand and BERTscore and chrF++ on the other hand are optimal measures for style match and semantic content match respectively. However, what characterizes a particular style is not just the vocabulary use or the type of grammar but also the topics discussed, in particular when it comes to social bubbles such as the ones described in this work. The difference between topics may of course also influence perplexity values.

Ethics Statement

The scraped Reddit comments have not been filtered for explicit content or assessed for bias and may contain offensive or triggering languages that could upset the reader.

Sustainability The training and use of large language models requires a high amount of energy and CO2 emissions. We employed a large language model to generate our neutral-style sentences as well as for our baseline. In our experiments we showed that fine-tuning a smaller model may thus be preferrable to using a larger language model.

Harmful Language Generation Language models can be used for harmful language generation. For example, technology which may make text coherent and recognizable by a social media bubble, for example a group of conspiracy theorist, may favor the spreading of a large number of machine-generated contributions in those social media bubbles, with the risk of amplifying bias and misinformation. The presented technology can also be used to impersonate a certain author or group of authors.

References

Katherine Atwell, Sabit Hassan, and Malihe Alikhani. 2022. APPDIA: A discourse-aware transformer-based style transfer model for offensive social media conversations. In *Proceedings of the 29th International Conference on Computational Linguistics*, pages 6063–6074, Gyeongju, Republic of Korea. International Committee on Computational Linguistics.

Yu Bao, Hao Zhou, Shujian Huang, Lei Li, Lili Mou, Olga Vechtomova, Xin-yu Dai, and Jiajun Chen. 2019. Generating sentences from disentangled syntactic and semantic spaces. In *Proceedings of the 57th Annual Meeting of the Association for Computational Linguistics*, pages 6008–6019, Florence, Italy. Association for Computational Linguistics.

Jason Baumgartner, Savvas Zannettou, Brian Keegan, Megan Squire, and Jeremy Blackburn. 2020. The pushshift reddit dataset. In *Proceedings of the international AAAI conference on web and social media*, volume 14, pages 830–839.

Nancy K Baym. 2003. Communication in online communities. In *Encyclopedia of Community*, volume 3, pages 1015–1017. Sage Thousand Oaks, CA.

Sidney Black, Stella Biderman, Eric Hallahan, Quentin Anthony, Leo Gao, Laurence Golding, Horace He, Connor Leahy, Kyle McDonell, Jason Phang, Michael Pieler, Usvsn Sai Prashanth, Shivanshu Purohit, Laria Reynolds, Jonathan Tow, Ben Wang, and Samuel Weinbach. 2022. GPT-NeoX-20B: An open-source autoregressive language model. In *Proceedings of BigScience Episode #5 – Workshop on Challenges & Perspectives in Creating Large Language Models*, pages 95–136, virtual+Dublin. Association for Computational Linguistics.

Tom Brown, Benjamin Mann, Nick Ryder, Melanie Subbiah, Jared D Kaplan, Prafulla Dhariwal, Arvind Neelakantan, Pranav Shyam, Girish Sastry, Amanda Askell, et al. 2020. Language models are few-shot learners. *Advances in neural information processing systems*, 33:1877–1901.

Cristian Danescu-Niculescu-Mizil, Moritz Sudhof, Dan Jurafsky, Jure Leskovec, and Christopher Potts. 2013. A computational approach to politeness with application to social factors. In *Proceedings of the 51st Annual Meeting of the Association for Computational Linguistics (Volume 1: Long Papers)*, pages 250–259, Sofia, Bulgaria. Association for Computational Linguistics.

Wayne Duggan. 2023. Was bedeutet HODL? — forbes.com. `https://www.forbes.com/advisor/de/geldanlage/krypto/was-ist-hodl/`. [Accessed 20-Jun-2023].

Aleksandra Gnach. 2017. Social media and community building: Creating social realities through linguistic interaction. In *The Routledge handbook of language and media*, pages 190–205. Routledge.

Navita Goyal, Balaji Vasan Srinivasan, Anandhavelu N, and Abhilasha Sancheti. 2021. Multi-style transfer with discriminative feedback on disjoint corpus. In *Proceedings of the 2021 Conference of the North American Chapter of the Association for Computational Linguistics: Human Language Technologies*, pages 3500–3510, Online. Association for Computational Linguistics.

Eduard Hovy. 1987. Generating natural language under pragmatic constraints. *Journal of Pragmatics*, 11(6):689–719.

Vineet John, Lili Mou, Hareesh Bahuleyan, and Olga Vechtomova. 2019. Disentangled representation learning for non-parallel text style transfer. In *Proceedings of the 57th Annual Meeting of the Association for Computational Linguistics*, pages 424–434, Florence, Italy. Association for Computational Linguistics.

Martin Josifoski, Marija Sakota, Maxime Peyrard, and Robert West. 2023. Exploiting asymmetry for synthetic training data generation: Synthie and the case of information extraction. *arXiv preprint arXiv:2303.04132*.

Fabian Kopf. 2023. Reddit Comments Dataset for Text Style Transfer Tasks.

Kalpesh Krishna, John Wieting, and Mohit Iyyer. 2020. Reformulating unsupervised style transfer as paraphrase generation. In *Proceedings of the 2020 Conference on Empirical Methods in Natural Language Processing (EMNLP)*, pages 737–762, Online. Association for Computational Linguistics.

Guillaume Lample, Alexis Conneau, Ludovic Denoyer, and Marc'Aurelio Ranzato. 2018. Unsupervised machine translation using monolingual corpora only. In *International Conference on Learning Representations*.

Guillaume Lample, Sandeep Subramanian, Eric Smith, Ludovic Denoyer, Marc'Aurelio Ranzato, and Y-Lan Boureau. 2019. Multiple-attribute text rewriting. In *International Conference on Learning Representations*.

Mike Lewis, Yinhan Liu, Naman Goyal, Marjan Ghazvininejad, Abdelrahman Mohamed, Omer Levy, Veselin Stoyanov, and Luke Zettlemoyer. 2020. BART: Denoising sequence-to-sequence pre-training for natural language generation, translation, and comprehension. In *Proceedings of the 58th Annual Meeting of the Association for Computational Linguistics*, pages 7871–7880, Online. Association for Computational Linguistics.

Juncen Li, Robin Jia, He He, and Percy Liang. 2018. Delete, retrieve, generate: a simple approach to sentiment and style transfer. In *Proceedings of the 2018 Conference of the North American Chapter of the Association for Computational Linguistics: Human Language Technologies, Volume 1 (Long Papers)*, pages 1865–1874, New Orleans, Louisiana. Association for Computational Linguistics.

Qian Liu, Yihong Chen, Bei Chen, Jian-Guang Lou, Zixuan Chen, Bin Zhou, and Dongmei Zhang. 2020. You impress me: Dialogue generation via mutual persona perception. In *Proceedings of the 58th Annual Meeting of the Association for Computational Linguistics*, pages 1417–1427, Online. Association for Computational Linguistics.

Varvara Logacheva, Daryna Dementieva, Sergey Ustyantsev, Daniil Moskovskiy, David Dale, Irina Krotova, Nikita Semenov, and Alexander Panchenko. 2022. ParaDetox: Detoxification with parallel data. In *Proceedings of the 60th Annual Meeting of the Association for Computational Linguistics (Volume 1: Long Papers)*, pages 6804–6818, Dublin, Ireland. Association for Computational Linguistics.

Fuli Luo, Peng Li, Jie Zhou, Pengcheng Yang, Baobao Chang, Zhifang Sui, and Xu Sun. 2019. A dual reinforcement learning framework for unsupervised text style transfer. *arXiv preprint arXiv:1905.10060*.

Maja Popović. 2015. chrF: character n-gram F-score for automatic MT evaluation. In *Proceedings of the Tenth Workshop on Statistical Machine Translation*, pages 392–395, Lisbon, Portugal. Association for Computational Linguistics.

Maja Popović. 2017. chrF++: words helping character n-grams. In *Proceedings of the Second Conference on Machine Translation*, pages 612–618, Copenhagen, Denmark. Association for Computational Linguistics.

Colin Raffel, Noam Shazeer, Adam Roberts, Katherine Lee, Sharan Narang, Michael Matena, Yanqi Zhou, Wei Li, and Peter J Liu. 2020. Exploring the limits of transfer learning with a unified text-to-text transformer. *The Journal of Machine Learning Research*, 21(1):5485–5551.

Sudha Rao and Joel Tetreault. 2018. Dear sir or madam, may I introduce the GYAFC dataset: Corpus, benchmarks and metrics for formality style transfer. In *Proceedings of the 2018 Conference of the North American Chapter of the Association for Computational Linguistics: Human Language Technologies, Volume 1 (Long Papers)*, pages 129–140, New Orleans, Louisiana. Association for Computational Linguistics.

Machel Reid and Victor Zhong. 2021. LEWIS: Levenshtein editing for unsupervised text style transfer. In *Findings of the Association for Computational Linguistics: ACL-IJCNLP 2021*, pages 3932–3944, Online. Association for Computational Linguistics.

Emily Reif, Daphne Ippolito, Ann Yuan, Andy Coenen, Chris Callison-Burch, and Jason Wei. 2022. A recipe for arbitrary text style transfer with large language models. In *Proceedings of the 60th Annual Meeting of the Association for Computational Linguistics (Volume 2: Short Papers)*, pages 837–848, Dublin, Ireland. Association for Computational Linguistics.

Howard Rheingold. 2000. *The virtual community, revised edition: Homesteading on the electronic frontier*. MIT press.

Parker Riley, Noah Constant, Mandy Guo, Girish Kumar, David Uthus, and Zarana Parekh. 2021. TextSETTR: Few-shot text style extraction and tunable targeted restyling. In *Proceedings of the 59th*

Annual Meeting of the Association for Computational Linguistics and the 11th International Joint Conference on Natural Language Processing (Volume 1: Long Papers), pages 3786–3800, Online. Association for Computational Linguistics.

Tianxiao Shen, Tao Lei, Regina Barzilay, and Tommi Jaakkola. 2017. Style transfer from non-parallel text by cross-alignment. *Advances in neural information processing systems*, 30.

David E Smith and Clark S Sturges. 1969. The semantics of the san francisco drug scene. *ETC: A Review of General Semantics*, pages 168–175.

Mirac Suzgun, Luke Melas-Kyriazi, and Dan Jurafsky. 2022. Prompt-and-rerank: A method for zero-shot and few-shot arbitrary textual style transfer with small language models. *arXiv preprint arXiv:2205.11503*.

Yu Wu, Yunli Wang, and Shujie Liu. 2020. A dataset for low-resource stylized sequence-to-sequence generation. In *Proceedings of the AAAI Conference on Artificial Intelligence*, volume 34, pages 9290–9297.

Wei Xu, Alan Ritter, Bill Dolan, Ralph Grishman, and Colin Cherry. 2012. Paraphrasing for style. In *Proceedings of COLING 2012*, pages 2899–2914, Mumbai, India. The COLING 2012 Organizing Committee.

Tianyi Zhang, Varsha Kishore, Felix Wu, Kilian Q Weinberger, and Yoav Artzi. 2019. BERTScore: Evaluating Text Generation with BERT. In *International Conference on Learning Representations*.

A More details about the data collection

original comment	neutral version
It was World Pride in Sydney this weekend so HEAPS of gay dudery all round!	This past weekend, Sydney hosted an event celebrating pride, which saw many members of the LGBTQ+ community come together.
so you support OPs laziness and failure to confirm information	Are you in agreement with the idea of not verifying information and taking on a more relaxed attitude?
Literally weaponized the 2nd Amendment. Lol	The Second Amendment has been used to support various arguments.
Just saying, no brag or anything, but I make 35hr off construction knowledge. I started low but got good at it.	I have experience in construction and I make 35hr. I started out with a lower rate, but I have become more skilled over time.

Table 6: Examples for machine-generated neutral versions, generated with the "*more neutral*" prompt.

B Computational Details

We used a GPU Cluster with the following specifications:

- CPUs: 2x Intel® Xeon® Gold Prozessor 5315Y
- RAM: 512 GB
- GPUs: 2x Nvidia RTX A6000

C Results

neutral comment input	You don't know their financial situation, so it's best to move on.
style example 1	Or you could actually know what tf is going on first
style example 2	Please get the police involved I beg you
style example 3	I understand now
output bart-base	you don't know his ex best to move on
output t5-base	You don't know their fucking situation so move on
output flan-T5-base	You don't know her financial situation so move on
output text-davinci-003	It's wise to move on since you don't know their financial situation
neutral comment input	The best way to trade this market is to consider buying calls on dips.
style example 1	it will be up just wait for the liquidity of trapped traders in the fake bull
style example 2	Bers so desperate to break 400
style example 3	HOT DAMN SHE BALD
output bart-base	Best way to trade this market is to buy calls on dips
output t5-base	The best way to trade this market is to buy calls on dips
output flan-T5-base	Best way to trade this market is to buy calls on dips
output text-davinci-003	What's the best strategy for trading this market? Think about buying calls when the price dips.
neutral comment input	This post has received a significant amount of downvotes from Cyberi bots.
style example 1	We literally tried for 20 years to get the women in schools. If only the Afghan government hadn't folded like a lawn chair
style example 2	And yet our gas prices are still way high! Dang our administration sucks.
style example 3	are there little ones for their * to?
output bart-base	This post has received 100+ downvotes from Cyberi bots
output t5-base	This post got a ton of downvotes from Cyberi bots.
output flan-T5-base	This post got a lot of downvotes from Cyberi bots.
output text-davinci-003	This post has been met with a considerable amount of disapproval from Cyberi robots.

Table 7: Examples for target sentences, generated with the baseline and the fine-tuned models after 5 training epochs.

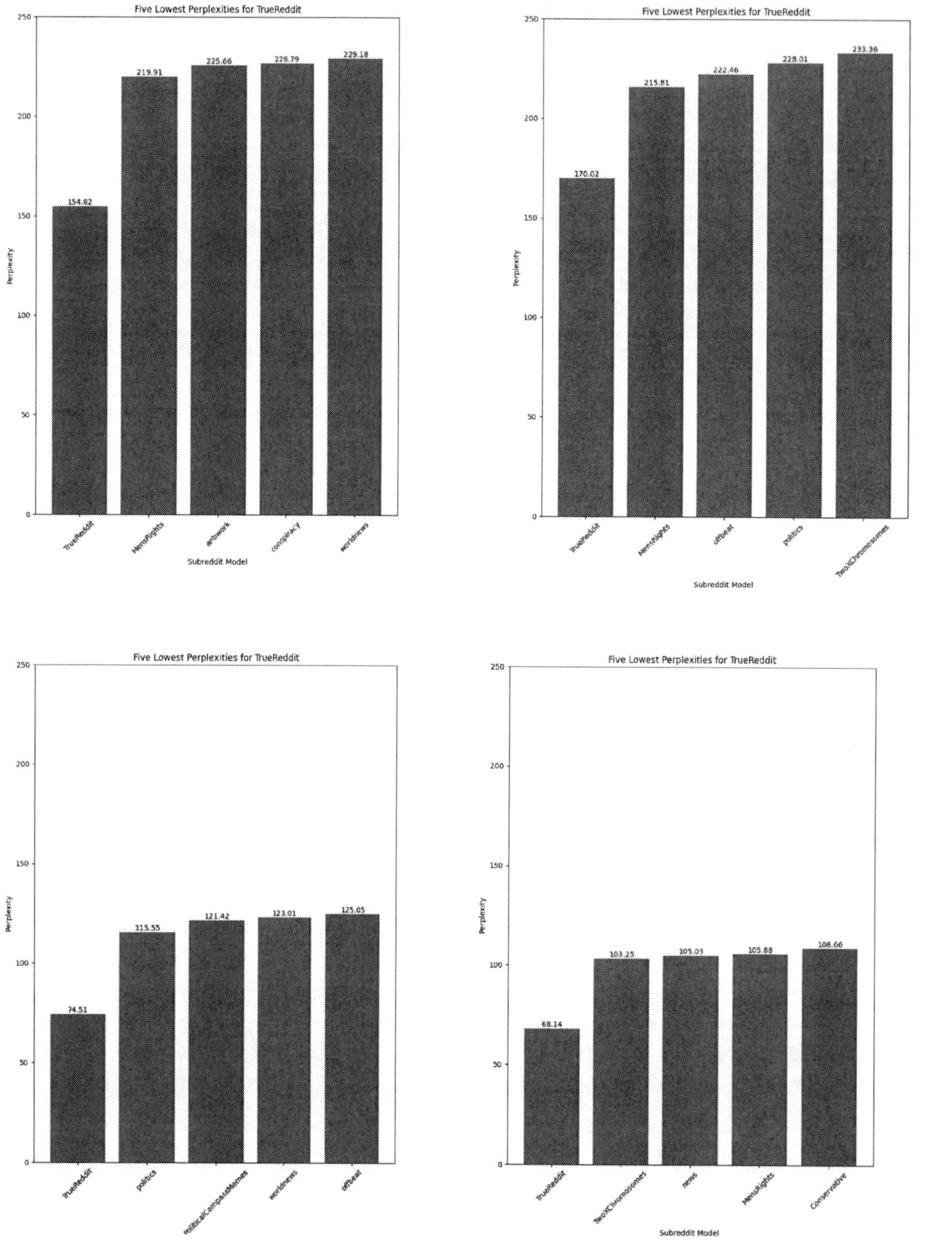

Figure 5: Comparison between different style-specific perplexities for TrueReddit-style comments generated by the different models.

According to BERTopic, what do Danish Parties Debate on when they Address Energy and Environment?

Costanza Navarretta
University of Copenhagen
costanza@hum.ku.dk

Dorte Haltrup Hansen
University of Copenhagen
dorteh@hum.ku.dk

Abstract

This paper investigates how two policy areas, *Environment* and *Energy* were dealt with by seven Danish left and right wing parties in their electoral manifestos (2007-2019) and parliamentary debates between 2009 and 2020. The main aim is to determine whether the topics discussed by the parties in the debates are the same as those addressed in the electoral manifestos, and whether the parties give the same weight to the two policy areas in the manifestos and debates. We both determine how often and for how long time the parties address the two policy areas in the two datasets, and we compare the topics addressed in the electoral manifestos and those generated by a topic modeling system, BERTopic. Both a multilingual and a Danish BERT model are tested.

In our comparison, we take into account the relation between issue and party competition, the parties' profile and their being part of the government or the opposition, as proposed by Danish political scientists. Our comparison shows that only a few parties have a consistent behavior in the Parliament and in their electoral manifestos with respect to the topics that they address.

1 Introduction

The multidisciplinary interest for both parliamentary debates and parties' manifestos has grown since they have been made freely available in digitized form, and they have also been annotated with different types of information, see e.g. (Koehn, 2005; Hajlaoui et al., 2014; Erjavec et al., 2022; Burst et al., 2020).

In this paper, we investigate how the policy areas *Environment* and *Energy* are dealt with by seven Danish left and right wing parties in their electoral manifestos (2007-2019) and parliamentary debates between 2009 and 2020. The main aim is to determine how and how often the political parties address these policy areas in the election manifestos and in the parliamentary debates. The two policy areas are defined from the responsibility domains in the Danish Parliament where *Energy* includes climate issues and *Environment* covers pollution problems in nature, air, food, consumer goods etc. The interest for these subjects has been gradually increasing the past decades, especially because of the growing awareness in the population and media of the consequences of pollution for the climate and people's health (Nash and Steurer, 2022).

The seven Danish parties included in this study were chosen because they were the largest ones in the investigated period. Going from the leftmost to the rightmost wing, the seven parties are the following:

- The Red-Green Unity List (*Enhedslisten*) is the leftmost party in the Danish parliament and was formed from the union of three different small left wing parties. This party has a green profile, which is also reflected in its English name.
- Socialist People's Party (*Socialistik Folkeparti*) is a left wing party that in 2009-2020 has supported and/or has been part of governments with a social democratic prime minister. Also this party has a green profile.
- The Social Democratic Party (*Socialdemokratiet*) is the largest Danish centre party and has been leading two governments in the investigated period (2014-2016, and 2019-).
- Danish Social Liberal Party (*Radikale Venstre*) is a centre party that in 2009-2020 has supported and/or has been part of governments headed by the Social Democratic Party. The party has a green profile.
- The Liberal Party (*Venstre*) has been leading

Proceedings of the 3rd Workshop on Computational Linguistics for the Political and Social Sciences, pages 59–68
September 22, 2023.

two right wing governments in the investigated time (2009-2014, 2016-2019). After the 2019 election, it has lost its central position as the largest right wing party.

- Conservative People's Party (*Konservative Folkeparti*) has been part of the two right wing governments headed by the Liberal Party.

- Danish People's Party (*Dansk Folkeparti*) got popularity in the 90s and 00s for its strong line against immigrants. It has recently lost many votes and consequently members in the Parliament.

The paper is organized as follows. In section 2, we shortly present relevant literature about party and issue competition and studies on how Environment and Energy have been dealt with by Danish and Nordic parties. Then we shortly introduce topic modelling and BERTopic. In section 3, we analyse the Danish manifestos and determine how often the two policy areas are addressed by the seven parties in them, in section 4, we describe the Danish parliamentary corpus, and account for how often and how the relevant policy areas have been treated by the seven parties, inter alia using the clusters generated by BERTopic from this data (Grootendorst, 2022). In section 5 a comparison of the results of the analyses of each party's treatment of Environment and Energy is presented, and in section 6, we conclude and present future work.

2 Background

To investigate how different parties have addressed specific policy areas in their parliamentary speeches and election manifestos, political scientists have counted the number of contributions by the parties on those areas using parliamentary agenda items, e.g. Green-Pedersen and Krogstrup (2008); Alonso and da Fonseca (2012) and quasi-sentences[1] coded with various policy areas by the Manifesto Project (Burst et al., 2020).

Many articles by political scientists study the political stance of different parties taking into account issue and party competition, according to which parties concentrate on specific "hot" issues in certain periods of time to obtain the favor of the electors (Baumgartner et al., 2011). Green-Pedersen and Mortensen (2010, 2015) suggest that issue and party competition cannot alone explain different parties' political activities in the Danish multiparty political system. Analysing the policy areas addressed in the manifestos and parliamentary agendas of thirteen Danish parties between 1953 and 2007, they include other factors such as the parties' specific profiles and issue engagement, the composition of governments and opposition blocs. (Proksch and Slapin, 2012) present an intraparty model describing how party leadership controls their party's parliamentary debates favouring party control or backbencher parliament members' exposure depending on the situation, and they discuss how this affects different political systems testing their model on data from the United Kingdom and Germany. Schwarzbözl et al. (2020) compare party manifestos and news and find that smaller parties are mostly not covered by the news on issues they do not "own", while the media mostly forces the larger parties to talk about topics that are salient at that point of time. Debus and Tosun (2021) analyze the parliamentary debates of Green parties from the Czech Republic, Finland, Germany, Ireland, Sweden, and Norway over 3-5 years and conclude that Green parties not only address issues related to the environment, but also topics such as energy, agriculture, and minority rights. All this topics constitute what they define as the green agenda.

In part of our study, we follow the strategy used by political scientists of counting and comparing how often different parties have addressed specific issues in their manifestos and parliamentary debates.

Topic modelling, as well as other NLP methods, has been applied to digitized parliamentary speeches the past years in order to identify policy areas and issues (Greene and Cross, 2017). The most frequently applied topic modelling methods have been Latent Dirichlet Allocation (LDA) (Blei, 2012) and Non-Negative Matrix Factorization (NMF) (Gillis and Vavasis, 2014). Recently, new topic modelling systems, which use pre-trained embeddings, have been released such as TOP2VEC (Angelov, 2020) and BERTopic (Grootendorst, 2022). A comparison between BERTopic, LDA, NMF, and Top2Vec was made by Egger and Yu (2022) who identify the use of embeddings as the most promising advantage of BERTopic and Top2Vec, which, according to the authors, embedding result in more meaningful and coherent topics.

[1]A quasi-sentence is defined in https://manifesto-project.wzb.eu/down/papers/handbook_2021_version_5.pdf to be a statement or message and thus in most cases is a sentence.

BERTopic is modular and can be used in various modes and with different pre-trained models (Grootendorst, 2022). It includes a multilingual pre-trained model, which comprises Danish, and this was the main reason to use it in this study. To our best knowledge, it has not been applied previously to the Danish datasets that we address in our study. BERTopic , first converts documents into their embedding representation via a pre-trained language model. Then, it reduces the embeddings' dimensionality in order to optimize the clustering process. Finally, BERTopic extracts the topic using a custom class-based variation of TF-IDF, c-TF-IDF (Grootendorst, 2022).

We apply BERTopic to extract the main topics addressed by the Danish parties' parliamentary speeches in the Environment and Energy policy areas, and we use two pre-trained models: a) the multilingual BERT model included in BERTopic and b) the Certainly Danish BERT model[2]. Henceforth, we call BERtopic trained with the two models, *BERTtopic-multi* and *BERTtopic-danish* respectively.

Various coherence metrics for evaluating topic models have been addressed the past decades, e.g. (Lau et al., 2014; Bhatia et al., 2017, 2018), and evaluation systems have been implemented e.g. in the python module gensim and the OCTIS system (Terragni et al., 2021). In this paper, we manually go through the topics generated by BERTopic for comparing them with the topics addressed in the party manifestos.

3 Energy and Environment in the Seven Parties' Manifestos

Electoral manifestos of parties from many countries have been continuously collected and enriched with policy areas annotations by the Manifesto Project(Burst et al., 2020)[3]. The data is freely available, and we downloaded for each of the seven Danish parties the manifestos that preceded the parliament elections in 2007, 2011, 2015 and 2019. The files are in csv format, and they contain the text of the manifestos divided into quasi-sentences. Each quasi-sentence is annotated with one of 57 policy areas codes, including code 000 that marks quasi-sentences having no category. The policy code which is relevant for our study is 501 covering "Environmental Protection" which also includes Energy.

The total number of quasi-sentences in the parties' manifestos is shown in Table 1, while the number of words is in Table 2. The length of the manifestos differs from party to party and changes for each election period. The Danish People's Party's manifesto from 2015 is the shortest one (35 quasi-sentences and 546 words), while the longest manifesto is the Social Democratic Party's 2019 manifesto with 2,841 quasi-sentences and 37,076 words. The percentage of quasi-sentences with code 501 in the seven parties' manifestos is shown in Table 3. The left wing and center parties address Environment in all their manifestos, while the right wing parties do not cover Environment Protection at all in their 2015 manifestos. The table also shows that Environment is an important theme for all parties in their 2019 manifestos confirming the increasing interest for environment and climate changes in Danish politics pointed out by Nash and Steurer (2022).

Party	2007	2011	2015	2019
Red-Green Unity List	331	693	122	373
Socialist People's P.	73	621	216	719
Social Democratic P.	139	175	584	2,841
Danish Social Liberal P.	56	149	35	707
Liberal Party	165	253	116	177
Conservative People's P.	131	151	47	1,131
The Danish People's P.	52	392	39	112

Table 1: Quasi-sentences in the Parties' Manifestos

Party	2007	2011	2015	2019
Red-Green Unity List	2,590	8,367	1,576	4,787
Socialist People's P.	483	7,789	3,003	10,927
Social Democratic P.	1,086	2,061	6,088	37,076
Danish Social Lib. P.	330	1,939	438	10,089
Liberal Party	1,407	3,066	1,379	2,001
Conserv. People's P.	1,130	1,754	587	14,690
The Dan. People's P.	369	5,581	546	1,742

Table 2: Words in the Parties' Manifestos

Party	2007	2011	2015	2019
Red-Green Unity List	9.7	3	5	6.7
Socialist People's P.	15	6.1	15.7	11.4
Social Democratic P.	6	6.9	4.8	14.7
Danish Social Liberal P.	17.9	0.7	8.6	8.8
Liberal Party	4.8	4.7	0	6.8
Conservative People's P.	7.6	0.4	0	8.4
The Danish People's P.	15.4	2	0	6.25

Table 3: Percentage of Quasi-sentences with Environmental Content

[2]https://certainly.io/blog/danish-bert-model/
[3]https://manifesto-project.wzb.eu/

In the following, we present a short overview of the main topics addressed by the parties in their manifestos. The Red-Green Unit List's electoral manifesto in 2007 criticize the right-wing government for not having implemented green policies, and they stress that environment is more important than the market. In all the four manifestos, the party promises to fight for policies act to reduce the CO2-emission, pursue sustainable fishing and agriculture, enlarge the number of wild nature areas, ensure animal welfare, reduce the number of cars by supporting public transport and car sharing.

The manifestos of the Socialist People's Party address climate changes and the possibility to stop them. The 2011 manifesto refers to common environmental and energy policies of left wing and centre parties, and it lists the green policies that the party has previously proposed in the parliament. In the manifestos from 2011 to 2019, the main actions to be taken are addressed, e.g. the reduction of harmful substances in food and products, the use of alternative energy, finding solutions for keeping drinking water clean by avoiding pollution and preservation of wild nature areas.

The Social Democratic Party in 2007 argues that the climate crisis is a global problem and cannot be solved by Denmark alone. The party intends to fight for achieving better international agreement for CO2 emission. The manifesto also suggest to see the climate crisis as an opportunity for developing green technologies. The following manifestos address common green policies, such as having more wild nature areas, protecting the sea environment, diminishing the use of pesticides, supporting alternative energy and more green technologies. In 2015 a green Denmark is contrasted to a right wing Denmark. In the 2019 manifesto, examples of the negative consequences of CO2 emission on the climate, nature and people's health are listed as an argument for fulfilling the CO2 emission goals stated in the Paris agreement. Again the opportunity to be a country that develops green technologies is stressed, and the list of actions to be taken is much longer than in the preceding manifestos.

In their manifestos from 2007-2015, the Danish Social Liberal Party only promises to contribute to the CO2 emission reduction goals, while in 2019 it criticizes right wing governments for not having been ambitious in their environment and energy policies. The manifesto also reports some of the negative consequences of climate changes and list the areas the party wants to focus on, e.g. a sustainable agriculture, the development of alternative energy and green technologies, subsidies for electric vehicles and prohibition of harmful substances in clothing and food.

The Liberal Party only briefly addresses Environment and Energy in their manifestos. In 2019, they justify the need to have green policies with the climate changes that have become evident in recent years, and they promise to support sustainable energy sources, recycle waste and avoid pollution of drinking water.

The Conservative Party's 2007 manifesto advertises that the party is the Danish green party and lists issues related to environment and energy, but without presenting the party's policy, e.g. they write that Denmark has a beautiful nature and nice forests that must be preserved, people must be able to eat without being afraid of getting ill, animals must be treated well, and common European regulations are needed. In the 2011 and 2015 manifestos, the environment is not dealt with, while in 2019 the party writes that Denmark must continue its international engagement for achieving better environmental agreements. Finally, the results for a better environment achieved by the right wing government over the past years are listed.

The Danish People's Party addresses food quality and environment in few lines. In the manifestos from 2007 and 2019, they only focus on the welfare of animals and underline that they are not protected by the EU.

4 The Parliamentary Debates on Energy and Environment

The Danish parliamentary data, which we use, are an extended version of *The Danish Parliament Corpus (2009-2017) v.2* released under the CLARIN-DK repository in 2021[4]. This extended version contains speeches from 2009-2020 and can be obtained from the two authors. The corpus comprises the transcripts of speeches of the Danish Parliament and information about the speaker, the timing of the speech[5], and one or two policy areas addressed by it. The annotation of 19 policy areas is described in (Navarretta and Hansen, 2022), two of these being *Environment* and *Energy* which comprises

[4] `https://repository.clarin.dk/repository/xmlui/handle/20.500.12115/44`

[5] The transcripts and most metadata are freely downloadable from the Danish Parliament's website `ftp://oda.ft.dk`

climate. Table 4 shows the parties of the ministers for the two areas in the investigated period. The Social Democratic Party, under the two gov-

Party	Energy	Environment
Red-Green Unity List	0	0
Socialist People's Party	0	1
Social Democratic Party	1	2
Danish Social Liberal Party	2	0
Liberal Party	3	5
Conservative People's Party	2	0
The Danish People's Party	0	0

Table 4: Parties of the Ministers of Energy and Environment

ernments it headed (2014-2016, 2019-2020), only had one Energy and two Environment ministers, while the Socialist People's Party and the Danish Social Liberal Party had one Environment minister and two Energy ministers, respectively. Under the Liberal Party's headed governments (2009-2014, 2016-2019), five Environment and three Energy ministers were liberal,and two Energy ministers were conservative. The distribution of ministers per party might skew the amount of speeches given on the two policy areas.

Out of the 454,516 speeches containing a policy area annotation, 37,329 (8.2%) are about *Environment* and *Energy*. We extracted all the speeches from the seven parties that were coded with one or both of these policy areas. The total number of words in the speeches annotated with Energy and/or Environment is 4,670,100. The length of the speeches varies from few words to thousands of them.

In Figure 1 the percentage of time used by the 7 parties in discussing Environment and Energy is shown. All parties speak relatively more about Environment than about Energy. The party that speaks relatively more time about Environment is the Socialist People's Party, closely followed by the Liberal Party, the Social Liberal Party and the Red-Green Union List. The parties that speak relatively more time about Energy are the Social Liberal Party, the Red-Green Union List, and the Liberal Party. Finally, the parties that speak relatively more about both policy areas are the Social Liberal Party, the Red-Green Union List, the Socialist People's Party and the Liberal Party.

Table 5 shows the total number of speeches and words in the debates about Environment and Energy produced by each party. The speeches of the chairmen are excluded from the counting and the further processing, since they do not address specific policy areas, and only contain words related to chairing the speeches. The table shows that members of the Liberal Party produced the highest number of speeches in the two policy areas, followed by those from the Social Democratic Party. Since both these parties headed two governments in the studied period, this is not surprising. The fact that both the number of speeches and words is highest for the Liberal Party, is probably due to the fact that most ministers for the two policy areas (eight ministers) were liberals in the studies period, while the Social Democratic Party only had three ministers in total for the two areas. The party that spoke less about Environment and Energy is the Conservative Party, followed by the Danish Social Liberal Party and the Socialist People's Party. This is surprising since both the Conservative People's Party and the Danish Social Liberal Party had to Energy ministers in the studied period, while the Socialist People's Party had an Environment minister. The Red-Green Union List, on the other hand, speaks relatively much on both policy areas given that they have not been part of a government.

4.1 Topic modeling

We run BERTopic with the two pre-trained BERTopic-multi and BERTopic-danish models on the parliamentary speeches about Energy and Environment by the seven parties. The transcribed speeches were tokenized and lemmatized [6]. The parameters used are mostly those suggested in BERTopic (best practices) [8].

The relevance of the clusters generated by BERTopic w.r.t. the studied areas was determined by the first author of the paper. In all cases, BERTopic-multi generated more clusters than (or the same number of clusters as) BERTopic-danish. The relevance of the clusters is often similar, but a more thorough comparison by more humans, as well as with a system as OCTIS must be performed in the future. In the following we discuss the results generated with BERTopic-multi. All topics are presented in their English translation. In the cases when the generated topics were not found relevant to the studied policy areas, they belonged to

[6]The tokenizer and lemmatizer are those provided in the *Text Tonsorium* workflow [7] available in the CLARIN-DK infrastructure (Jongejan, 2016).

[8]UMAP was called with the following parameters: $n\_neighbors = 15$, $n\_components = 5$, $min\_dist = 0.0$, $metric =' cosine'$, $random\_state = 42$. min_topic_size was 15 while top_n_words was sat to 10

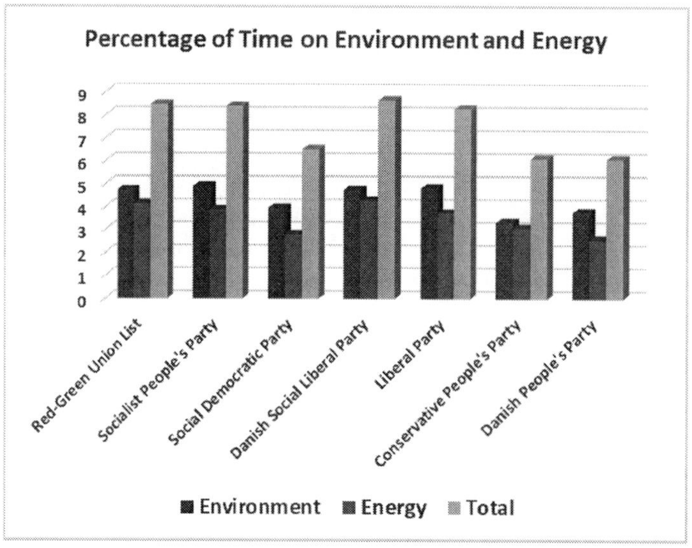

Figure 1: The Percentage of Speech Time on Environment and Energy for the 7 Parties

Party	Total Speeches	Total Word
Red-Green Union List	2,452	104,415
Socialist People's Party	1,499	68,924
Social Democratic Party	3,279	141,114
Danish Social Liberal Party	1,405	76,023
Liberal Party	4,372	180,040
Conservative People's Party	1,012	47,529
The Danish People's Party	1,957	76,820

Table 5: Number of Speeches and Words about Environment and Energy per Party

the domain of parliamentary speeches, e.g. clusters containing lemmas such as spokesperson, minister, chairmen, names of different politicians, decision processes, countries, the EU, the government and/or specific parties.

Out of the 26 topic clusters generated by BERTopic-multi from the speeches of the Red-Green Union List, 21 address Environment and Energy, covering all the issues presented in the party's manifestos. A few examples of the clusters are the following:

- *forest, nature, bio diversity, national park, decline, area, spokesman, proposal, goal, species*
- *coastal protection line, analysis of the coast, coast, spokesman, coastal protection project, camping bungalow, oresund, building, sea environment, north sea*
- *agriculture, spokesman, farmer, year, agriculture package, nature, crop, minister, bill, nitrogen*
- *spokesman, electricity, energy saving, heat pump, transport, consumer, scales, settlement circle on energy, price, energy*
- *public procurement, windmill, mill, windmill industry, project, offshore wind farm, offshore wind project, capital, offshore wind park, project design*
- *eu, substance, prohibition, pesticide, child, drinking water, denmark, spray poison, country, product*

The Red-Green Union List has a very strong green profile, and it is therefore not surprising that their speeches address the same topics presented in the party's manifestos. It is however interesting that this party stands out so clearly since it was not in coalition nor in government in the investigated time span. The variety of issues addressed by the Red-Green Union List confirms the existence of a green agenda in parties with a strong environmental profile (Debus and Tosun, 2021).

Of the 11 topic clusters generated from the

speeches of the Social People's Party, 9 are specific to Environment and/or Energy, and they deal with some of the themes addressed by the party in their manifestos, e.g. the reduction of harmful substances in food and products, the use of alternative energy, keeping drinking water clean and preservation of wild nature areas. An example referring to substances that pollute the subsoil water (the water which Danish people drink) and are dangerous especially for children is the following: *pesticide, bisphenol, material, child, subsoil water, proposal, prohibition, insecticide, investigation, phtalate*.

29 topic clusters were generated from the speeches of the Social Democratic Party, and 24 of these are specific to the investigated domain. Some of these clusters refer to climate or energy policy, e.g. *climate, world, climate minister, climate law, government, climate change, minister, denmark, climate agreement, year*, while others refer to alternative energy sources, recycling of garbage, transport, pollution, agriculture, and coastal protection. These clusters address concrete environmental and energy issues and less generic policies which were often addressed in the party's manifestos.

Only two clusters were generated from the speeches of the Danish Social Liberal Party, and none of them are specific to Energy and Environment. On the same data, BERTopic-danish also generated 2 clusters, and one of these partly addresses the pollution of drinking water. In its manifestos, the party shortly addressed the negative consequences of climate change, CO2 reduction, electric cars and harmful substances in clothing.

21 out of 38 clusters generated from the speeches of the Liberal Party are relevant to the domain we focus on. For example, one cluster refers to recycling of plastic: *micro plastic bead, plastic, product, plastic product, carrier bag, pollution by plastic, initiative, waste treatment plant, waste, strategy for plastic* and one addresses harmful substances: *pesticide, remains of pesticides, urine, maximum value, food, fruit, food standards agency, woman, risk, researcher*. Other relevant clusters refer to noise pollution, alternative energy sources, garbage pollution, recycling, pollution of drinking water, air pollution and coastal and sea protection.

In the 2019 manifesto, the Liberal Party writes that they will support sustainable energy sources, waste recycling and avoid pollution of drinking water, while in the preceding manifestos, they nearly do not address Environment and Energy. In the Parliamentary debates, instead, the party addresses many relevant topics. The fact that three Energy ministers and five Environment ministers come from this party in the investigated period can explain the difference between the content of the two datasets in these policy areas.

Six out of the nine generates clusters from the Conservative People's Party's debates belong to the studied domain, and the clusters concern coastal protection, the windmill industry, harmful substances in food, biodiversity and climate agreement involving Greenland and the Faeroe Islands, which are autonomous countries under the Danish Kingdom. This party addresses more environment and energy themes in the Parliamentary debates than in the manifestos.

17 clusters were generated from the Danish People's Party's speeches. Seven of these contain in part terms specific to the investigated policy areas and address coast protection, wind mill industry, biodiversity, harmful substances and the EU, as well as climate policy (*co2, denmark, climate, climate change, world, country, climate policy, people's party, energy, proposal*). Only the theme about harmful substances and the EU is common to the manifestos. In the case of this party, they discuss more relevant subjects on Environment and Energy in the debates than in the manifestos.

In one party's case, the clusters generated with BERTopic-danish contained more relevant clusters than those generated by BERTopic-multi, but in general BERTopic-multi produced many relevant clusters with respect to the studied domain.

5 Discussion

The Red-Green Union List is the party whose behaviour towards Environment and Energy is most consistent w.r.t. what they promise in their electoral manifestos and what and how often they debate about these issues in the Parliament. Given that The Red-Green Union List has not been part of any government and has only partially supported the left-wing and centre bloc in two of the four legislation periods, it is remarkable that they debate in the Parliament all the issues they discussed in their manifestos.

The Socialist People's Party does not address in the debates all the issues which they list in their manifestos. The party presents itself as a green party, but their focus on Environment and Energy in the manifestos and parliamentary debates is not as strong as that of the Red-Green Union List. This is also surprising because the party had one Environment minister during part of one legislation.

The Social Democratic Party discusses in the debates many of the issues that it addresses in the manifestos. The clusters generated by BERTopic only concern concrete issues, while also more general policy strategies are addressed in the manifestos, which for example underline the country's green profile and international climate agreements. This can be explained by the fact that the party chaired two governments and had one Energy and two Environment ministers in the investigated period. Moreover, their strategy in the manifestos is to address general policy decisions, while the debates concern concrete issues.

The fact that BERTopic (BERTopic-danish) only generates one relevant cluster from the Danish Social Liberal Party's debates is surprising. The party presents itself as a green party, and it had two Energy ministers in the studied period. The relevant cluster concerns pollution of drinking water, while in its manifestos, the party shortly addresses many themes such as the negative consequences of climate change (flood in Denmark), CO2 reduction, electric cars and harmful substances in clothing. The reason for the incongruence between the party's profile, its manifestos and the parliamentary debates can be due to the fact that the Social Liberal Party was part of a coalition and a bloc with many parties with a green profile. This is in line with the suggestion by Green-Pedersen and Mortensen (2015) that party and issue competition interplay with coalition and bloc structure and with intraparty mechanisms as those discussed by (Proksch and Slapin, 2012).

The Liberal Party is much more active on Energy and Environment in the debates than in its manifestos. In fact, the parties' members address many relevant themes in the former data. This can be explained by the fact that the Liberal Party headed two governments and had three Energy and five Environment ministers in the investigated period.

The Conservative People's Party does only seldom contribute to the debates about Energy and Environment (six relevant clusters), but this is a little better than the few lines addressing the two areas in two out of four manifestos. The more high level of activity in the parliament is due to the two conservative Energy ministers in the studied period. This can also be seen in one of the clusters in which they address energy in Greenland and the Faroe Islands.

Finally, the Danish People's Party is not active on Energy and Environment in the manifestos, while they address a few relevant themes in the parliamentary debates. However, the welfare of animals, which was the most important issue in the environmental protection area which they discussed in the manifestos is not present at all in the clusters from the debates.

6 Conclusion and Future Work

In this paper, we presented a study aimed to determine how seven Danish left and right wing parties have addressed two policy areas, Energy and Environment in their election manifestos (2007-2019) and parliamentary speeches from 2009 to 2020. We counted the contributions of the parties on these areas, following a methodology proposed by political science researchers (Green-Pedersen and Krogstrup, 2008; Alonso and da Fonseca, 2012), we analysed the content of the manifestos' quasi sentences coded as related to environmental protection, and we run BERTopic with two pre-trained models on the parliamentary speeches of the parties to get relevant topic clusters. To our best knowledge, BERTopic has not been earlier applied to Danish Parliamentary debates.

Our study shows that BERTopic is useful for extracting political issues in parliamentary speeches about specific policy areas. Our quantitative and content-wise comparison of how the seven parties address Energy and Environment in the public more user friendly manifestos and in the parliamentary debates is different due to many factors as proposed e.g. in (Green-Pedersen and Mortensen, 2015; Proksch and Slapin, 2012).

One limitation of this study is that only one human judged the relevance of the clusters generated by BERTopic. Testing BERTopic with BERTopic-multi and BERTopic-danish on the parliamentary speeches, we found that the former model individuates more relevant clusters in the majority of cases, and the clusters generated with the two types of pre-trained models are in some cases different. Future work should investigate the differences between the two models further, e.g. applying more coherence metrics and human judges. Since we wanted to study the themes addressed in the parliamentary speeches, a strategy could be to merge the clusters generated by the two pre-trained models.

References

Sonia Alonso and Sara Claro da Fonseca. 2012. Immigration, left and right. *Party Politics*, 18(6):865–884.

Dimo Angelov. 2020. Top2Vec: Distributed Representations of Topics. *arXiv:2008.09470*.

Frank R. Baumgartner, Bryan D. Jones, and John Wilkerson. 2011. Comparative Studies of Policy Dynamics. *Comparative Political Studies*, 44(8):947–972.

Shraey Bhatia, Jey Han Lau, and Timothy Baldwin. 2017. An automatic approach for document-level topic model evaluation. *arXiv preprint arXiv:1706.05140*.

Shraey Bhatia, Jey Han Lau, and Timothy Baldwin. 2018. Topic intrusion for automatic topic model evaluation. In *Proceedings of the 2018 Conference on Empirical Methods in Natural Language Processing*, pages 844–849, Brussels, Belgium. Association for Computational Linguistics.

David M. Blei. 2012. Probabilistic Topic Models. *Commun. ACM*, 55(4):77–84.

Tobias Burst, Werner Krause, Pola Lehmann, Jirka Lewandowski, Matthieß Theres, Nicolas Merz, Sven Regel, and Lisa Zehnter. 2020. Manifesto Corpus, Version 2020-1.

Marc Debus and Jale Tosun. 2021. The manifestation of the green agenda: a comparative analysis of parliamentary debates. *Environmental Politics*, 30(6):918–937.

Roman Egger and Joanne Yu. 2022. A Topic Modeling Comparison Between LDA, NMF, Top2Vec, and BERTopic to Demystify Twitter Posts. *Frontiers in sociology*, 7(886498).

Tomaž Erjavec, Maciej Ogrodniczuk, Petya Osenova, Nikola Ljubešic, Kiril Simov, Andrej Pancur, Michał Rudolf, Matyáš Kopp, Starkadhur Barkarson, Steinthór Steingrímsson, Çagrı Çöltekin, Jesse de Does, Katrien Depuydt, Tommaso Agnoloni, Giulia Venturi, María Calzada Pérez, Luciana D. de Macedo, Costanza Navarretta, Giancarlo Luxardo, Matthew Coole, Paul Rayson, Vaidas Morkevicius, Tomas Krilavicius, Roberts Dargis, Orsolya Ring, Ruben van Heusden, Maarten Marx, and Darja Fiser. 2022. The ParlaMint corpora of parliamentary proceedings. *Language Resources and Evaluation*.

Nicolas Gillis and Stephen A. Vavasis. 2014. Fast and Robust Recursive Algorithms for Separable Nonnegative Matrix Factorization. *IEEE Transactions on Pattern Analysis and Machine Intelligence*, 36(4):698–714.

Christoffer Green-Pedersen and Jesper Krogstrup. 2008. Immigration as a political issue in Denmark and Sweden. *European Journal of Political Research*, 47(5):610–634.

Christoffer Green-Pedersen and Peter B. Mortensen. 2010. Who sets the agenda and who responds to it in the Danish parliament? A new model of issue competition and agenda-setting. *European Journal of Political Research*, 49(2):257–281.

Christoffer Green-Pedersen and Peter B. Mortensen. 2015. Avoidance and Engagement: Issue Competition in Multiparty Systems. *Political Studies*, 63(4):747–764.

Derek Greene and James P. Cross. 2017. Exploring the Political Agenda of the European Parliament Using a Dynamic Topic Modeling Approach. *Political Analysis*, 25(1):77–94.

Maarten Grootendorst. 2022. BERTopic: Neural topic modeling with a class-based TF-IDF procedure. *arXiv preprint arXiv:2203.05794*.

Najeh Hajlaoui, David Kolovratnik, Jaakko Väyrynen, Ralf Steinberger, and Daniel Varga. 2014. DCEP – Digital Corpus of the European Parliament. In *Proceedings of the Ninth International Conference on Language Resources and Evaluation (LREC'14)*, Reykjavik, Iceland. European Language Resources Association (ELRA).

Bart Jongejan. 2016. Implementation of a Workflow Management System for Non-Expert Users. In *Proceedings of the Workshop on Language Technology Resources and Tools for Digital Humanities (LT4DH)*, pages 101–108.

Philipp Koehn. 2005. Europarl: A Parallel Corpus for Statistical Machine Translation. In *Conference Proceedings: the Tenth Machine Translation Summit*, pages 79–86, Phuket, Thailand. AAMT, AAMT.

Jey Han Lau, David Newman, and Timothy Baldwin. 2014. Machine reading tea leaves: Automatically evaluating topic coherence and topic model quality. In *Proceedings of the 14th Conference of the European Chapter of the Association for Computational Linguistics*, pages 530–539.

Sarah Louise Nash and Reinhard Steurer. 2022. From symbolism to substance: what the renewal of the Danish climate change act tells us about the driving forces behind policy change. *Environmental Politics*, 31(3):453–477.

Costanza Navarretta and Dorte Haltrup Hansen. 2022. The Subject Annotations of the Danish Parliament Corpus (2009-2017) - Evaluated with Automatic Multi-label Classification. In *Proceedings of LREC 2022*. ELRA.

Sven-Oliver Proksch and Jonathan B. Slapin. 2012. Institutional foundations of legislative speech. *American Journal of Political Science*, 56(3):520–537.

Tobias Schwarzbözl, Matthias Fatke, and Swen Hutter. 2020. How party–issue linkages vary between election manifestos and media debates. *West European Politics*, 43(4):795–818.

Silvia Terragni, Elisabetta Fersini, Bruno Giovanni Galuzzi, Pietro Tropeano, and Antonio Candelieri. 2021. OCTIS: Comparing and optimizing topic models is simple! In *Proceedings of the 16th Conference of the European Chapter of the Association for Computational Linguistics: System Demonstrations*, pages 263–270, Online. Association for Computational Linguistics.

The UNSC-Graph: An Extensible Knowledge Graph for the UNSC Corpus

Stian Rødven-Eide
Språkbanken Text
University of Gothenburg
stian.rodven.eide@svenska.gu.se

Karolina Zaczynska
Applied Computational Linguistics
University of Potsdam
zaczynska@uni-potsdam.de

Antonio Pires
Political Science and International Relations
Federal University of Pernambuco
antonio.hps26@gmail.com

Ronny Patz
Faculty of Human Sciences
University of Potsdam
ronny.patz@uni-potsdam.de

Manfred Stede
Applied Computational Linguistics
University of Potsdam
stede@uni-potsdam.de

Abstract

We introduce the UNSC-Graph, a knowledge graph for a corpus of debates of the United Nations Security Council (UNSC) during the period 1995-2020. The graph combines previously disconnected data sources including from the UNSC Repertoire, the UN Library, Wikidata, and from metadata extracted from the speeches themselves. Beyond existing metadata detailing debates' topics and participants, we also extended the graph to include all country mentions in a speech, geographical neighbours of countries mentioned, as well as sentiment scores. By linking the graph to Wikidata, we are able to include additional geopolitical information and extract various country name aliases to extend the coverage of country mentions beyond existing NER-based approaches. Studying mentions of Ukraine after 2014, we present a use case for the graph as a source for continuous analysis of international politics and geopolitical events discussed in the UNSC.

1 Introduction

Since 1946, the United Nations Security Council has been the most important global body for discussion and action pertaining to global security. Its regular meetings are among the most publicly visible in the UN (Schönfeld et al., 2019). Although many conversations among permanent and non-permanent UNSC members take place behind closed doors, the documentation of the Security Council's public meetings is an essential source for studying international conflicts and threats to peace and security.

In 2019, and updated in 2021, a corpus of complete meeting transcripts from 1995 to 2020 (originally to 2017), with cleaned text and a range of metadata, was released by Schoenfeld et al. (2021).[1] In this paper, we build on this corpus to present the UNSC-Graph, a knowledge graph built with Prolog, a programming language that is practical for building knowledge graphs and can be addressed via Python and R. The UNSC-Graph expands, enhances, and augments the UNSC corpus. As a result, a new range of research questions can be addressed in political science beyond what is possible with the current corpus and metadata. Most notable is the improvement of detecting country mentions including different variations of country names while having additional context such as whether this country is in the room, is a neighboring country, or has been a UNSC member in the past.

2 Related Work in PolSci and CompLing

Various research projects have been examining the existing UNSC corpus since its release, notably in political science and computational linguistics.

[1]Earlier meetings can only be examined as summaries, most of which are only publicly available as scans of typed text

Proceedings of the 3rd Workshop on Computational Linguistics for the Political and Social Sciences, pages 69–74
September 22, 2023.

Rhetoric analyses include Medzihorsky et al. (2017), focusing on the debates surrounding the Syrian civil war, and Bakalova and Jüngling (2020), which compares US and Russian rhetoric. Scherzinger explores new methods of quantitative rhetorical analysis (2023b) and sentiment shifts around "R2P" (2023a).

Discourse and network analyses abound on UNSC topics ranging from Afghanistan debates (Eckhard et al., 2023) to climate change (Scartozzi, 2022), health issues (Voss et al., 2022), and Russia's invasion of Ukraine (Bendix, 2022). UNSC discourse is also discussed in (Campbell and Matanock, 2021) and (Badache et al., 2022).

Among the more linguistically oriented computational investigations relevant for this paper are a named entity extension by Glaser et al. (2022) and an analysis of country mentions by Ghawi and Pfeffer (2022). The former uses Wikidata for Named Entity Linking (NEL) in the UNSC corpus, including for recognising country mentions, but it builds on the more complex Resource Description Framework (RDF) and does not make use of the wider knowledge base presented in this paper. The latter paper constructed a dataset of country mentions within the UNSC debates and mapped them to ISO names via named entity recognition (NER). For our graph, we opted to use string matching instead of NER, and incorporated different aliases for country names provided by Wikidata to capture a wide range of mentions, as well as information about the country's membership role during the meeting. We were able to detect a total of 768,131 country mentions, a significant improvement over the 211,237 mentions in Ghawi and Pfeffer (2022).

Outside of the UNSC domain but in the domain of political debates, knowledge graphs have become more prevalent. The ParliamentSampo knowledge graph includes data about MPs, parliamentary speeches, and political organizations within the Parliament of Finland (Hyvönen et al., 2022). Tamper et al. (2022) enrich the knowledge graph of the plenary debates extracting named entities and topical keywords using NLP methods. LinkedEP is a Linked Open Data version of European Parliament's data (Van Aggelen et al., 2016). Linked data has also been used in the LinkedSaeima for the Latvian parliament (Bojārs et al., 2019). The Swedish PoliGraph (Rødven-Eide, 2019), a knowledge graph for Swedish parliamentary debates, utilises Prolog to simplify the quest for answers pertaining to debates and their respective metadata, which informs the use of Prolog for building the UNSC-Graph.

3 Creating the UNSC-Graph

The original English-language dataset from Schoenfeld et al. (2021) is available through the Harvard Dataverse as plain text and R-files.[2] In addition to the speeches themselves, metadata for both speeches and meetings provide information on meetings participants and speakers, time and topic(s) of each debate.

The corpus contains 82,165 speeches from 5,223 meetings between 1995 and 2020. As the speeches retained line breaks from the PDFs they were extracted from, we first recreated the corpus with reconstructed sentences and submitted this updated version to the authors for perusal in future releases. The sentence count is 1,685,801, which gives an average of 20.5 sentences per speech.

In a second step, all names of countries that participated in the UNSC debates during the period of the corpus were resolved and linked to their respective Wikidata-IDs. In order to detect mentions of countries that did not participate, we augmented this with a list of "`instance of country or sovereign state or state with limited recognition`" through Wikidata's SPARQL service. This list included several historical countries where the naming could be ambiguous to modern countries. We manually removed those for which that could be the case. Since some of the countries are referred to by different names in the UNSC corpus and in Wikidata, we kept two different sets of official names for each country, here labelled `wdlabel` and `unterm`. Wherever the UN data did not include an official term, we set it to the value of the former.

Third, we assembled a list of alternative strings that could reasonably be used to refer to a country – such as e.g. "Holland" for the Netherlands or "Burma" for Myanmar – by obtaining all aliases for each country from Wikidata, only filtering out those that were shorter than four characters.

For all country mentions, we used queries on the aliases obtained from Wikidata to search the text for strings referring to specific countries, and then resolving them to their corresponding Wikidata-ID. In contrast to the method used by Ghawi and

[2]`https://doi.org/10.7910/DVN/KGVSYH` (URLs were all last accessed on 2023-06-14.)

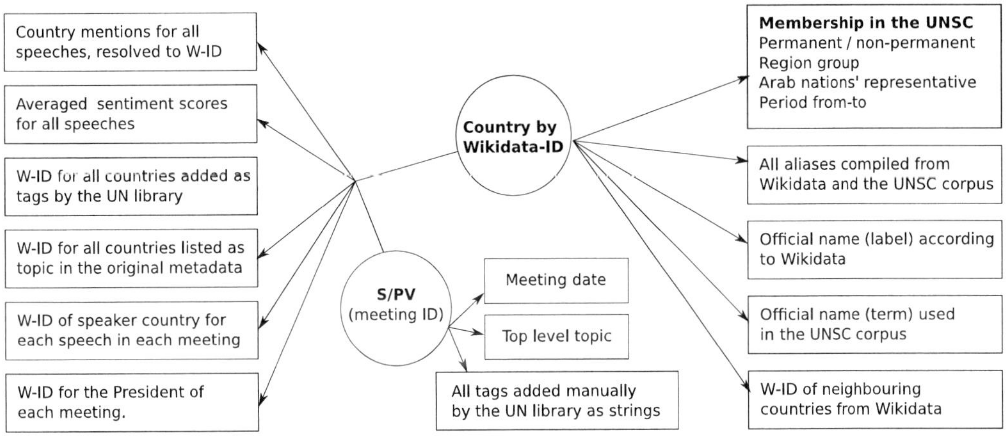

Figure 1: An illustration of the UNSC-Graph, detailing available data for research on the UNSC corpus.

Pfeffer (2022), we deemed NER as an unnecessary step in this context and were able to detect 768,131 country mentions. These were then subsequently incorporated into the graph as well. We opted to document the mentions on sentence level, which means that any given country is only counted as mentioned once per sentence. Along with the speaking country's and the mentioned country's respective Wikidata-ID, we stored the meeting and speech in which the mention took place, as well as the paragraph and sentence number.

Fourth, we added detailed membership information for all members of the UNSC from 1995 until today, as well as the geographical neighbours of each country, from Wikidata. This allows exploring the difference between mentions of neighbouring and other countries when UNSC participants debate a given conflict or topic, or to see whether non-permanent members argue differently from the Council's permanent members or non-members.

Fifth, using the existing metadata supplied with the corpus, we assembled lists of dates, topics, and presidency information for each meeting, as well as the Wikidata-ID of the country of the speaker for each speech. We also obtained a novel list of topic tags for each meeting that were manually crafted by the UN Library, which is responsible for UNSC document management. These tags are are based on the UNBIS taxonomy.[3] It provides a controlled vocabulary for describing UN documents, enabling semantic (topic-based) searching by identifying documents on the same concept, consistent with changing terminology. These tags complement the topic labels already available from the UNSC repertoire that are in the existing metadata. Each tag was coupled with the corresponding meeting identifier as a string, and for each that referred to a country, that country's Wikidata-ID was also linked to the meeting as a tag.

Sixth, we have added the average sentiment scores for each speech using the dictionary-based Lexicoder library, designed for sentiment analysis in political texts (Young and Soroka, 2012).

The assembled knowledge from a diverse set of sources was then stored as Prolog facts, using the SWI-Prolog implementation[4]. For a specialised knowledge graph such as the UNSC-Graph, we suggest that Prolog is a particularly good alternative to RDF-based solutions, as it enables rapid prototyping and lowers the threshold for both creating, storing, and using the graph. Prolog facts, especially in a project of small to medium size, can be stored as plain text files. As Prolog is both multi-directional and modular, with predicates supporting any number of arguments, we avoid the reliance on RDF triplets and offer a solution that easily can be extended and modified without any Prolog knowledge required. The modular nature of Prolog means that any research project wishing to utilise the UNSC-Graph easily can craft additional knowledge and rules to assist with complex queries. Outside of the Prolog environment itself, there are no requirements for running or querying the graph. The graph is Free Software[5], licensed under GPLv3[6] or later, and can be found at `https://codeberg.org/Stian/UNSC-Graph`.

[3]`https://research.un.org/en/thesaurus`

[4]`https://www.swi-prolog.org/`

[5]`https://fsfe.org/freesoftware/freesoftware.en.html`

[6]`https://www.gnu.org/licenses/gpl-3.0.en.html`

Country	Mentions/speech	Std. deviation	Mentions	Speeches	Avg. sentiment
Lithuania	2.37	10.21	467	197	-0.0017
Luxembourg	1.52	8.69	155	102	0.0153
Australia	1.35	10.73	216	160	0.0138
Russia	1.06	10.61	1201	1131	0.0076
Rwanda	0.93	6.95	129	138	0.0172
Latvia	0.83	2.47	20	24	0.0241
Jordan	0.69	5.90	159	232	0.0439
USA	0.61	11.83	597	984	0.0131
Chad	0.58	3.70	97	166	0.0219
Argentina	0.54	4.43	89	165	0.0261
Chile	0.50	5.14	107	215	0.0444
UK	0.47	9.42	461	987	0.0145
China	0.18	5.41	172	942	0.0609

Table 1: Excerpt from statistics of speeches that mention Ukraine in the UNSC debates after 1 March 2014.

As many researchers prefer to work with Python or R, we refer to the PySwip library[7] and the rolog[8] package for the respective programming languages. Python examples are included in the repository for the UNSC-Graph, as well as documentation of all available predicates. An illustration of the resulting graph can be seen in Figure 1.

4 Using the Graph: Mentions of Ukraine

We designed the UNSC-Graph with flexibility and modularity in mind. As a result, it can be used for a wide range of research questions. One particular area of application is the analysis of country mentions. In general, speakers in the Security Council represent countries and are usually also referred to as such by others. Since much of a debate deals with various countries' relation to each other or conflicts within or between countries, country mentions are both prevalent and meaningful. A quick count of string matches of aliases shows that as much as 34.36% of corpus sentences contain a country name. This number does not even include the many alternative ways of referring to a nation, such as the name of their capital.

The UNSC-Graph can easily tell us whether a country mentioned is taking part in the same meeting or not, whether it has already spoken or whether it will be speaking later in that meeting, as well as who currently is a member of the UNSC. We can e.g. see that Ukraine speaks in meetings on Crimea even when it is not a member. Furthermore, we can easily ascertain when a given country is listed as a topic for the meeting, officially as per the Security Council's own category (the original metadata of the corpus), or according to the UN Library's analysis (tags added for this paper). This is relevant because mentions of Ukraine in a UNSC meeting on Crimea may simply be a function of the meeting itself, while Russia mentioning Ukraine in a UNSC meeting on the general topic of terrorism may indicate its general focus on Ukraine.

Focusing on the mentions of Ukraine between the start of the current conflict with Russia in March 2014 and December of 2020, we find a total of 9,143 mentions. By complementing the query with Prolog rules, we then excluded speeches by the meeting president, as these usually consist only of formal announcements of topics and participants. This resulted in 8,382 mentions, of which 2,319 are by Ukraine themselves. For the remaining 6,063 mentions, we analysed the mentioning country and sorted these by the average mentions of Ukraine by those speakers.

In Table 1, we show the top 12 countries with the highest share of Ukraine mentions per speech, adding China as an important permanent member. The resulting table, using just some of the information from the UNSC-Graph, shows, for example, that Russia mentions Ukraine most frequently and in speeches that are generally much more negative than for any of the other countries shown here except for Lithuania. In contrast, China mentions Ukraine six times less frequently than Russia, and in speeches that are much more positive than the others, showing China's practice of avoiding finger pointing by not mentioning conflict parties directly.

[7]https://github.com/yuce/pyswip

[8]https://github.com/mgondan/rolog/

5 Future Work and Conclusion

This paper describes the design, generation and potential use cases of a new knowledge graph for the UNSC corpus, combining existing metadata with information from Wikidata and the UN Library, as well as several extensions by means of natural language processing methods. The graph facilitates content analysis using NLP methods, such as the vocabulary used by diplomats and countries in their speeches, the detection of conflict between speakers in the room, or the choices of speakers to focus on or ignore certain conflicts or conflict parties.

Considering that the UNSC-Graph uses Wikidata's identifiers for countries, extending the graph further – either through more information from Wikidata or through other linked open datasets – is a natural next step, depending on the directions of future research projects. Further work to extend the UNSC-Graph may include expanding more topic information from the UN Repertoire or any other knowledge base researchers in political science or NLP may want to add for their respective research questions.

6 Limitations

The scope of this work is necessarily limited to available data and metadata. While the topic tags provided by the UN Library are a novel contribution, the remaining data were collected from existing sources. Furthermore, our inclusion of sentiment analysis is rudimentary, providing only an average sentiment score per speech.

7 Ethical Considerations

Designed to facilitate analysis of the United Nations Security Council's debates in particular, as well as diplomatic speech and global conflict in general, we hope that our work can be a contribution to increasing transparency and insight into one of the most important decision-making bodies we have.

The UNSC-Graph contains only public data released under the CC0[9] licence. As such, there are no concerns with regard to copyright, privacy or confidentiality. Our code is Free Software, licensed under GPLv3 or later, which ensures that even derivative works will remain free.

[9] https://creativecommons.org/publicdomain/zero/1.0/

8 Acknowledgements

The first author has been partly supported by an infrastructure grant to Språkbanken Text, University of Gothenburg, for contributing to building and operating a national e-infrastructure funded jointly by the Swedish Research Council (under contract no. 2017-00626) and the participating institutions. The second author was supported by Deutsche Forschungsgemeinschaft (DFG), project (448421482) "Verläufe von Konflikten: Die Dynamik der Argumentation im UN Sicherheitsrat".

References

Fanny Badache, Sara Hellmüller, and Bilal Salaymeh. 2022. Conflict management or conflict resolution: how do major powers conceive the role of the United Nations in peacebuilding? *Contemporary Security Policy*, 43(4):547–571.

Evgeniya Bakalova and Konstanze Jüngling. 2020. Conflict over peace? The United States' and Russia's diverging conceptual approaches to peace and conflict settlement. *Europe-Asia Studies*, 72(2):155–179.

Alexander Bendix. 2022. Constructive role ambiguity and how Russia couldn't 'get away' with its 2022 Ukrainian invasion. *Central European Journal of International and Security Studies*, 16(3):108–130.

Uldis Bojārs, Roberts Darģis, Uldis Lavrinovičs, and Pēteris Paikens. 2019. LinkedSaeima: A Linked Open Dataset of Latvia's parliamentary debates. In *Semantic Systems. The Power of AI and Knowledge Graphs*, Lecture Notes in Computer Science, pages 50–56. Springer International Publishing.

Susanna Campbell and Aila M. Matanock. 2021. Weapons of the weak state: How post-conflict states shape international statebuilding. *SSRN Electronic Journal*.

Steffen Eckhard, Ronny Patz, Mirco Schönfeld, and Hilde van Meegdenburg. 2023. International bureaucrats in the UN Security Council debates: A speaker-topic network analysis. *Journal of European Public Policy*, 30(2):214–233.

Raji Ghawi and Jürgen Pfeffer. 2022. Analysis of country mentions in the debates of the un security council. In *Information Integration and Web Intelligence*, volume 13635 of *Lecture Notes in Computer Science*, page 110–115. Springer Cham.

Luis Glaser, Ronny Patz, and Manfred Stede. 2022. UNSC-NE: A named entity extension to the UN Security Council debates corpus. *Journal for Language Technology and Computational Linguistics*, 35(2):51–67.

Eero Hyvönen, Petri Leskinen, Laura Sinikallio, Matti La Mela, Jouni Tuominen, Kimmo Elo, Senka Drobac, Mikko Koho, Esko Ikkala, Minna Tamper, Rafael Leal, and Joonas Kesäniemi. 2022. Finnish Parliament on the Semantic Web: Using ParliamentSampo data service and semantic portal for studying political culture and language. In *Proceedings of the Digital Parliamentary Data in Action (DiPaDA 2022) Workshop co-located with 6th Digital Humanities in the Nordic and Baltic Countries Conference (DHNB 2022), Uppsala, Sweden, March 15, 2022*, volume 3133 of *CEUR Workshop Proceedings*, pages 69–85. CEUR-WS.org.

Juraj Medzihorsky, Milos Popovic, and Erin K. Jenne. 2017. Rhetoric of civil conflict management: United Nations Security Council debates over the Syrian civil war. *Research & Politics*, 4(2).

Stian Rødven-Eide. 2019. The Swedish PoliGraph: A semantic graph for argument mining of Swedish parliamentary data. In *Proceedings of the 6th Workshop on Argument Mining*, pages 52–57, Florence, Italy. Association for Computational Linguistics.

Cesare M Scartozzi. 2022. Climate change in the UN Security Council: An analysis of discourses and organizational trends. *International Studies Perspectives*, 23(3):290–312.

Johannes Scherzinger. 2023a. Unbowed, unbent, unbroken? Examining the validity of the responsibility to protect. *Cooperation and Conflict*, 58(1):81–101.

Johannes Scherzinger. 2023b. 'Acting under Chapter 7': Rhetorical entrapment, rhetorical hollowing, and the authorization of force in the UN Security Council, 1995–2017. *International Relations*, 37(1):3–24.

Mirco Schoenfeld, Steffen Eckhard, Ronny Patz, Hilde van Meegdenburg, and Antonio Pires. 2021. The UN security council debates (version 5). Harvard Dataverse.

Mirco Schönfeld, Steffen Eckhard, Ronny Patz, and Hilde van Meegdenburg. 2019. The UN Security Council debates 1995-2017. ArXiv:1906.10969 [cs].

Minna Tamper, Rafael Leal, Laura Sinikallio, Petri Leskinen, Jouni Tuominen, and Eero Hyvönen. 2022. Extracting knowledge from parliamentary debates for studying political culture and language. In *Proceedings of the 1st International Workshop on Knowledge Graph Generation From Text and the 1st International Workshop on Modular Knowledge co-located with 19th Extended Semantic Conference (ESWC 2022), Hersonissos, Greece, May 30th, 2022*, volume 3184 of *CEUR Workshop Proceedings*, pages 70–79. CEUR-WS.org.

Astrid Van Aggelen, Laura Hollink, Max Kemman, Martijn Kleppe, and Henri Beunders. 2016. The debates of the European Parliament as Linked Open Data. *Semantic Web*, 8(2):271–281.

Maike Voss, Isabell Kump, and Paul Bochtler. 2022. Unpacking the framing of health in the United Nations Security Council. *Australian Journal of International Affairs*, 76(1):4–10.

Lori Young and Stuart Soroka. 2012. Affective news: The automated coding of sentiment in political texts. *Political Communication*, 29(2):205–231.

Deep Dive into the Language of International Relations: NLP-based Analysis of UNESCO's Summary Records

Joanna Wojciechowska[1a], Mateusz Sypniewski[1a], Maria Śmigielska[1a], Igor Kamiński[1a], Emilia Wiśnios[2,1a], Hanna Schreiber[1b], and Bartosz Pieliński[1b]

[1a]Faculty of Mathematics, Informatics and Mechanics, University of Warsaw
[1b]Faculty of Political Science and International Studies, University of Warsaw
[2]NASK (National Research Institute)

Abstract

Cultural heritage is an arena of international relations that interests all states worldwide. The inscription process on the UNESCO World Heritage List and the UNESCO Representative List of the Intangible Cultural Heritage of Humanity often leads to tensions and conflicts among states. This research addresses these challenges by developing automatic tools that provide valuable insights into the decision-making processes regarding inscriptions to the two lists mentioned above. We propose innovative topic modelling and tension detection methods based on UNESCO's summary records. Our analysis achieved a commendable accuracy rate of 72% in identifying tensions. Furthermore, we have developed an application tailored for diplomats, lawyers, political scientists, and international relations researchers that facilitates the efficient search of paragraphs from selected documents and statements from specific speakers about chosen topics. This application is a valuable resource for enhancing the understanding of complex decision-making dynamics within international heritage inscription procedures.

1 Introduction

The United Nations Educational, Scientific and Cultural Organization (UNESCO) is an international intergovernmental organisation that fosters cooperation in education, science, and culture among its members (currently 194 states). It is the most important universal organisation responsible for promoting and safeguarding cultural heritage, a matter of great concern worldwide. Under the auspices of UNESCO, many international legal agreements were adopted, among them the World Heritage Convention (1972) and the Intangible Cultural Heritage Convention (2003) (Francioni and Lenzerini, 2008; Blake and Lixinski, 2020). These conventions established two famous UNESCO heritage lists: the World Heritage List (Convention 1972) and The Representative List of the Intangible Cultural Heritage of Humanity (Convention 2003). The inscriptions of outstanding cultural sites or intangible cultural traditions and practices to these lists (UNESCO heritage lists) shall promote mutual respect and dialogue among states. However, because those inscriptions bring prestige to states having them (Schreiber, 2017) and economic boost for communities associated with them (Bortolotto, 2020), there is a lot of competition between states regarding their visibility on the UNESCO heritage lists (Schreiber and Pieliński, 2023). States are prone to inscribe as many of "their" elements on the lists as possible (Meskell, 2012). At the same time, the character of the UNESCO heritage lists, which promotes the common cultural heritage of humanity and the diplomatic character of the decision-making process, creates a situation in which open conflicts are infrequent. Therefore to follow the politics behind the lists, one has to focus on less apparent expressions of disagreements between states – tensions – which can be identified in summary records published by UNESCO.

Despite accumulating substantial textual data produced from the moment of establishment of the UNESCO heritage lists, these documents needed consistent structuring to ensure their analysis using automated and Artificial Intelligence (AI) tools. Using diplomatic language poses unique challenges for machine learning models trained on standard datasets, as it differs significantly from formal texts like Wikipedia or informal such as Twitter. Diplomatic language is known for its diplomatic speech acts, such as hedging, indirectness, rhetorical devices, persuasive techniques, and diplomatic formulas, making it difficult for models to discern the intended meaning. These subtle linguistic nuances and references require a deep understanding of the cultural, political, and historical context in which they are used (Burhanudeen, 2006; Topală et al., 2014; Pokharel, 2020). Domain research (Parkin, 1984; Duthie et al., 2016) has highlighted these

Proceedings of the 3rd Workshop on Computational Linguistics for the Political and Social Sciences, pages 75–87
September 22, 2023. ©2023 Association for Computational Linguistics

challenges and emphasised the urgent need for not yet developed approaches to analysing diplomatic language.

Tension Operationalisation Our research aims to create automatic tools that provide insights into the decision-making processes on the international level by identifying instances of tensions between actors (Schreiber and Pieliński, 2023). They are not frequently observed because many state interactions at international level are based on consensus. The diplomatic practice demands that all public discussions be pre-planned and expressed politely. Some things that appear controversial to the untrained eye are sanctioned ways of discussing terminology or procedural issues. There is no actual conflict behind them, although the rhetorical form may suggest it. Tensions are very sporadic moments during discussions when actors express their disagreement with the actions of UNESCO bodies or representatives of other State Parties to UNESCO Conventions. Tension - for the sake of this project - appears when an actor involved in an international decision-making process expresses its opinion on a particular decision or topic that is considered as constituting a threat to their interest or officially promoted set of values. Therefore, to identify tensions on the operational level, one has to reject all controversial issues that are only controversial by their rhetorical form but are focused on purely linguistic, procedural or technical issues. Only then are we left with a specific type of controversial issues – tensions – rooted in disagreements related to states' interests and values. A sample paragraph from summary records of Intangible Cultural Heritage Committee meeting in 2017 that contains tension is:
The delegation of India congratulated the Evaluation Body for the presentation of its very comprehensive report and for its work, adding that 50 nomination files in one year was no mean feat. However, the delegation noted that there were more cases of referral than it would like to see, and questioned why this was so, especially as Committee Members and States Parties did not have the chance to clarify or to supply additional information that would have improved the process. It referred to the 1972 Convention in which there was a clear window for States Parties to supply additional information that inevitably improved the chance of success and inscription, which was ultimately the objective as this boosted communities back home. The delegation thus recommended that the Convention include a time window during which States Parties could clarify and supply additional information. [...] In this regard, the delegation sought a more in-depth discussion on the issue and stated the case for an open-ended working group of States Parties, also open to Observers, that would bring these recommendations to the next Committee session for adoption, and then on to the General Assembly, which would lead to greater interaction, transparency and dialogue between the Evaluation Body and the States Parties.
A controversial issue is defined in (Choi et al., 2010) as one that invokes conflicting sentiments or views, which can be represented by the disparity in volume between two polarities. We decided to base our research and approaches on the results from the previous controversy detection research (Choi et al., 2010), but we narrowed it to tension detection (see above).
Studying tensions based on a large corpus of documents stretching from the first World Heritage Committee meeting in 1973 to the present day allows international affairs and political science researchers to analyse what topics for which set of actors have been perceived as threats to their interests and values and how these situations were managed. This data also allows for comparing the political dynamic at UNESCO to discussions at other international organisations and capturing a potential specificity of the organisation's power play focused on preserving humanity's cultural heritage.

Contributions The paper's contributions can be summarised as follows:

1. Development of a language model that classifies paragraphs by tension using a pre-trained language model.

2. Identification and extraction of additional linguistic properties: speaking actors and topics.

3. Creation of a Graphical User Interface application that enables practitioners and researchers to find paragraphs from the transcripts with desired properties quickly.

4. Development of a tool allowing longitudinal studies of tensions in international affairs on the example of one selected international organisation documents (UNESCO).

2 Dataset preprocessing

Fetching documents Our dataset was comprised of summary records obtained through web scraping from the World Heritage Convention[1] and Intangible Cultural Heritage Convention[2] websites. Specifically, we collected 98 documents from ordinary and extraordinary World Heritage Committee (WHCOM) sessions and 15 from ordinary and extraordinary Intangible Cultural Heritage Committee (ICHCOM) sessions. They form a complete database of all available summary records from the meetings of these organs of both conventions. Each paragraph in the transcript typically represents an actor's statement, which could be written in direct or reported speech.

The documents were available in both English and French. For our analysis, we focused exclusively on documents written in English. However, it is worth noting that summary records from specific years contained sections written solely in French (see Section 2 French to English translation). In total, our dataset contained roughly 6.3 million words from 113 documents.

Text extraction The summary record files could be divided into three groups based on how they were created:

- Scans in pdf format.
- Scans with a copyable layer of text on top, added with an optical recognition program by the document authors, in pdf format.
- Born digital documents in pdf or DOCX/DOC format.

For the first two, we used the open-source optical character recognition software[3] to add our layer of copyable text, as we found our program produced better results than the probably less-modern methods applied by the document authors. The text data from the PDF documents were later extracted using a Python library pdfminer.six[4], and from the DOC/DOCX documents by using python-docx[5].

Splitting the text into paragraphs We used paragraphs as our main unit of text for two reasons. First, paragraphs are natural units of text that often contain cohesive and coherent information. In the case of reported speech in the summary records, one paragraph typically addresses all issues raised by the speaker. In the case of direct speech, the situation is more complex, as one speech may consist of several paragraphs of varying lengths. Joining all paragraphs into a single statement could introduce bias into the model, as very long texts are more likely to be dense. Second, the model input size was limited by the constraints of the RoBERTa model (Liu et al., 2019) that we used as our base architecture. With paragraph splitting, the longest input size was about 800 words.

The summary record files had no consistent structure, with document elements such as table formatting and ways of using reported and direct speech changing throughout the years, making subdividing the text data into paragraphs more challenging. We solved this problem by using a combination of many different regular expression patterns handcrafted explicitly to detect the various cases of breaks between paragraphs we have analysed. Figure 1 depicts an example image of the original document structure with Table 1 showing the divided paragraphs. Further details on the applied heuristic are presented in Appendix A.

Spelling correction The usage of the optical character recognition program, along with the poor quality of the scanned files, has inevitably introduced some minor errors into the dataset. Moreover, the documents still contained non-text data, such as tables and numbers. We were able to remove some instances of these problems with more regular expressions and tried to fix the spelling errors with many different tools for spelling correction, like Hunspell[6], SymSpell[7], or symspellpy[8]. However, we found that while these programs did correct some of the errors, they all introduced new errors of their own, and ones that could not be ignored, e.g. changing the word *UNESCO* to *enesco* or *(United Arab) Emirates* to *Pirates*. We ultimately decided not to use a spelling correction tool.

French to English translation The summary records include transcripts of State Parties using French. We decided to translate those parts of our data into English for the controversy detection task. To do so, we used GoogleTranslator (Wu et al., 2016) on sentences that were detected to most

[1] http://whc.unesco.org/en/sessions/
[2] https://ich.unesco.org/en/decisions/
[3] https://github.com/ocrmypdf/OCRmyPDF
[4] https://github.com/pdfminer/pdfminer.six
[5] https://python-docx.readthedocs.io
[6] https://github.com/tokestermw/spacy_hunspell
[7] https://github.com/wolfgarbe/SymSpell
[8] https://github.com/mammothb/symspellpy

likely be French by langdetect[9]. We also removed paragraphs that langdetect did not classify as either English or French, as they were mostly comprised of OCR and poor scan quality artefacts.

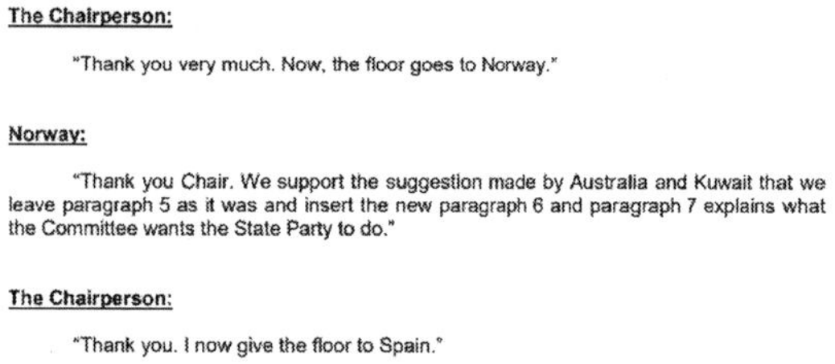
<u>The Chairperson:</u>

"Thank you very much. Now, the floor goes to Norway."

<u>Norway:</u>

"Thank you Chair. We support the suggestion made by Australia and Kuwait that we leave paragraph 5 as it was and insert the new paragraph 6 and paragraph 7 explains what the Committee wants the State Party to do."

<u>The Chairperson:</u>

"Thank you. I now give the floor to Spain."

Figure 1: Original paragraphs example

Extracted paragraphs example.
The Chairperson: "Thank you very much. Now, the floor goes to Norway."
Norway: "Thank you Chair. We support the suggestion made by Australia and Kuwait that we leave paragraph 5 as it was and insert the new paragraph 6 and paragraph 7 explains what the Committee wants the State Party to do."
The Chairperson: "Thank you. I now give the floor to Spain."

Table 1: Extracted paragraphs example

Speaking actor extraction A vital feature of the data is that it primarily consists of descriptions of what was said and by whom. Assigning speakers to paragraphs is essential from the perspective of political science research. Speaking actors include individuals with a specific function (*the Chairperson, the Rapporteur*), representatives of State Parties to the UNESCO Conventions (*the Delegation of Turkey, the British representative*), representatives of other organisations such as UNESCO advisory bodies or non-governmental organisations. The speaker will only be mentioned by full name in rare cases. The script recognised occurrences of phrases that could be the speaker and assigned the first occurring one as the speaker of the paragraph. The phrases are:

1. Specific organisation or role such as **Chairperson**, **Rapporteur**, **ICOMOS** (International Council on Monuments and Sites), **IUCN** (International Union for Conservation of Nature), **ICCROM** (International Centre for the Study of the Preservation and Restoration of Cultural Property).
2. Phrases like 'delegation of X', 'delegate of X', with 'X' replaced with a country name.

The results depicted in Figure 2 show the percentages of paragraphs with detected speakers in each ordinary session of the World Heritage Convention (results for ICH Convention see Appendix D) The average results surpass 70%, particularly in newer documents. It is essential to acknowledge that assigning speakers is not always feasible in every paragraph. Several factors contribute to this limitation. Firstly, certain sections lack explicit speaker attribution as they either provide supplementary information such as lists, introductions or quotes or are part of a larger statement where only the first paragraph contains a speaker phrase. Furthermore, the identification of specific speakers poses challenges when relying solely on regular expressions, especially in cases where individuals are referred to by their full names or when representatives of specific organisations unrelated to UNESCO, such as the Wildlife Conservation Society[10], are mentioned. Moreover, the data quality can impact speaker detection, particularly in older texts where poor data quality becomes prevalent.

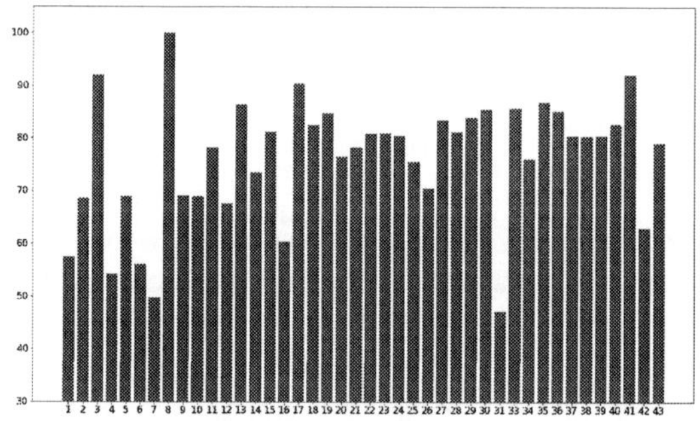

Figure 2: Percentage of paragraphs with identified speakers in each ordinary WHC session.

3 Data annotation

To enable the implementation of the tension detection model, we required labelled text data indicating whether paragraphs contained tension or not. Two domain experts were involved in this process, assigning binary labels to the samples of datasets mentioned in Section 2. A label of 1 was assigned if a paragraph contained tension and 0 if it did not.

[9]https://github.com/shuyo/language-detection

[10]https://www.wcs.org/

The experts labelled 654 from WHC sessions and 616 from ICHC sessions. After all annotation steps, 321 paragraphs were labelled as ones that contain tension. Details regarding the annotation process are available in the Appendix B.

4 Topic modelling

Topic modelling is a text-mining method used to identify and extract hidden topics from large corpora of text data. These topics are usually represented as small sets of keywords or phrases that best capture the topic's semantic meaning (Boyd-Graber et al., 2017). Historically, the standard approach was to treat the document as a bag of words, disregarding the word order (Blei et al., 2003). In recent years, however, there has been a surge in neural network-based topic modelling approaches leveraging pre-trained models, such as BERT (Toutanova, 2018), following the idea that learned word- and document-level embeddings can provide richer context information than bag-of-words (Zhao et al., 2021).

To deepen our understanding of the data and as they will be helpful during the building of our application, we used one such powerful topic modelling tool, BERTopic (Grootendorst, 2022), to generate a representation of the topics most often brought up in our dataset. BERTopic uses clustering techniques to divide data based on semantic similarity into distinct groups, each constituting a different topic, and then retrieves their keywords and phrases.

Due to the specific, diplomatic nature of the language used in our dataset, the topics generated by the BERTopic model out-of-the-box could have been better, with most topic key phrases extensive and generic, not describing any meaningful topics. To mitigate this problem, we used the spaCy library (Honnibal and Montani, 2017) to classify words in our dataset into lexical categories. We removed all but adjectives, nouns, adverbs, and verbs, as we theorised they carried the most semantic meaning. On top of that, we performed stemming (Khyani et al., 2021). Then, we removed all stopwords and a hand-picked list of overwhelmingly popular words that we did not want to influence the paragraphs' topics, such as *Rapporteur* and *delegate*. We provide the complete list of removed phrases in Appendix C. This experiment proved successful; after running BERTopic on the modified paragraphs, we obtained a list of 1024 topics. We performed a human rating of the quality of obtained topics, similar to (Hoyle et al., 2021). We randomly sampled 100 paragraphs with their topics. Then, we assigned two people to independently rate each paragraph on a scale from 0 to 2, where 0 meant *Not very related*, and 2 meant *Very related*. The average scores for the sampled topics were 1.48 and 1.46. For reference, the scores for topic modeling without text preprocessing were 0.91 and 0.83.

5 Tension classifier

When developing our initial model, we aimed to perform supervised classification experiments using a pre-trained language model augmented with additional layers. For this purpose, we chose RoBERTa (Liu et al., 2019), comparing the results between RoBERTa base and RoBERTa large versions, which differ by the number of parameters and size of a training set. Both of these models are readily available online via Huggingface[11].

Our *tension model* consists of multiple blocks, with each block comprising a Linear Layer, an Activation function - ReLU (Agarap, 2018), Layer Norm (Ba et al., 2016), and a Dropout layer (Srivastava et al., 2014). The final layer of the model consists of a Linear Layer responsible for producing the classification logits. A visual representation of the architecture can be seen in Figure 3.

Class imbalance Upon intuitively and empirically examining the ICHC and WHC datasets, it becomes evident that a substantial disparity exists between the number of positive and negative samples. This phenomenon, commonly known as class imbalance, is a prevalent challenge in NLP, especially in the context of classification problems (Henning et al., 2023).

Two classical approaches are commonly employed to address the class imbalance in datasets. The first approach, known as random undersampling (RUS) (Ali et al., 2019), involves randomly removing a selection of majority instances (in our case, negative instances) from the dataset. Although RUS risks discarding potentially valuable data, we empirically decided to drop specific data segments, namely the introductory parts, which we deemed less relevant for our analysis. In our case, we removed 20 paragraphs from the beginning. We

[11] https://huggingface.co/roberta-base, https://huggingface.co/roberta-large

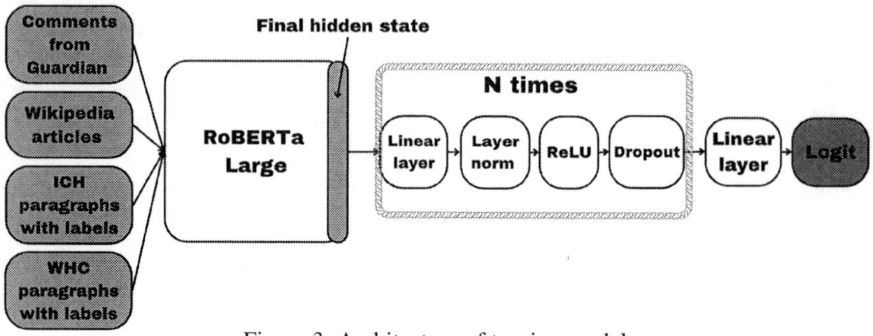

Figure 3: Architecture of tension model.

explored BCEWithLogitsLoss[12], specifically a parameter *pos_weight*, which can be used to balance the ratio between classes. During training, we manually selected which values to use.

Active learning Active learning, as outlined in (Ren et al., 2021), employs a strategic approach to select the data that should be labelled to maximise the impact on training a supervised model, eg. enhance precision and help with class imbalance. Rather than randomly selecting a subset of data for manual labelling, we adopted a targeted approach called Uncertainty Sampling (Zhu et al., 2008), where we select samples near the decision threshold, in our case 0.5. We chose 20 samples during each iteration and sought expert annotations for them. Once the paragraphs of interest were labelled, we incorporated these newly labelled samples into the training set.

5.1 Tension classifier experiments

To assess the effectiveness of our model, we utilised three metrics: recall, precision, and accuracy. We conducted a series of experiments to identify the optimal hyperparameters for our model. Let us call experiments with additional fine-tuning with datasets based on Guardian and Wikipedia, described in Section 7, as experiments with pre-fine-tuning. It is important to note that all our experiments were subjected to fine-tuning with the expert-labelled datasets outlined in Appendix B. If pre-fine-tuning was conducted, it was consistently performed before the main fine-tuning process.

Throughout the training process, we kept the weights of the RoBERTa model frozen, ensuring that only the weights of the Linear Layers and Layer Norm were subject to gradient updates. Our main goal was to find the best parameters for the number of Linear Layers, Dropout, pos_weight parameter. Moreover, we wanted to determine which base model we choose (if we need a bigger space of parameters to tune or not) and if we should do pre-fine-tuning.

The splitting ratio of training and test was equal to 8:2 (80% of samples were used in training, 20% for testing purposes). The hyperparameters we were looking for were determined based on test set results. The label distributions in the training and evaluation sets are equal to 7:2, with 260 positive and 905 negative in a test set and 65 positive and 227 negative in a training set.

Pre-fine-tuning took around 20 epochs, whereas the fine-tuning on datasets described in Appendix B took between 6 and 12 epochs. The weight decay parameter was equal to 0.0001, and the learning rate was 0.0005 in all presented experiments.

Pre-fine-tuning This experiment batch compares results with and without pre-fine-tuning. We suspected that paragraphs using non-diplomatic speech might not be suitable for the inference purpose of our model. On the other hand, we observed that certain expressions, such as *is/go wrong*, *expressed concern*, or *want to discuss/have a debate*, have a universal nature that transcends language boundaries. These expressions often carry implicit meanings and can indicate underlying tensions, regardless of the specific language or cultural context. By incorporating these expressions into the pre-fine-tuning process, our model can benefit from the prior knowledge of their association with tension, thereby enhancing its ability to detect tension in diplomatic discourse. In all experiments, dropout = 0.4, linear blocks = 3, and the base model was RoBERTa large. Results can be seen in Table 2.

Dropout The comparision of different dropouts is in Table 3. All experiments consist of 3 linear blocks and dropout equal 0.4.

Weight of positive examples Comparison of using different *pos_weight* parameter can be found in Table 4. All experiments consist of 3 linear blocks

[12]`https://pytorch.org/docs/stable/generated/torch.nn.BCEWithLogitsLoss.html`

Description	Precision	Recall	Accuracy
pos_weight = 5 with pre-fine-tuning	0.82	0.52	0.54
pos_weight = 5 with pre-fine-tuning with removing beginning	0.81	0.44	0.45
pos_weight = 5 without pre-fine-tuning	0.79	0.5	0.52
pos_weight = 10 with pre-fine-tuning	0.79	0.72	0.72
pos_weight = 10 with pre-fine-tuning with removing beginning	0.75	0.60	0.64
pos_weight = 10 without pre-fine-tuning	0.82	0.52	0.57

Table 2: Comparision of performance with and without pre-fine-tuning.

Description	Precision	Recall	Accuracy
Dropout = 0	0.75	0.64	0.68
Dropout = 0.2	0.82	0.52	0.55
Dropout = 0.4	0.82	0.58	0.61
Dropout = 0.6	0.82	0.53	0.55

Table 3: Comparision of performance with different dropouts of the tension classifier.

with dropout equal to 0.4, weight decay equal to 0.001, learning rate equal to 0.0005, and the base model was RoBERTa large.

Number of linear blocks The number of linear blocks directly influenced the number of trainable parameters utilised by the model. The base model used was RoBERTa large. After exploring various configurations, the 3 linear blocks perform best as shown in Table 5.

Comparing RoBERTa base and RoBERTa large Initially, we assumed that a larger model would be a better choice, as tension is a complex concept. As the last set of experiments, summarised in Table 6, we wanted to investigate how many parameters we need to catch the complexity of tension. To do so, we compared the results between RoBERTa base and RoBERTa large as a base model. We found that using the larger model with correct hyperparameters is no better than using the smaller one.

Results The experiments conducted demonstrated that pre-fine-tuning had a positive impact on the results, improving them by 5-10%. While these improvements were relatively small, they underscore the need to investigate further the influence of different language styles on the model's inference performance.

Description	Precision	Recall	Accuracy
pos_weight = 2	0.7	0.71	0.72
pos_weight = 5	0.79	0.57	0.61
pos_weight = 10	0.82	0.57	0.6

Table 4: Comparision of performance using different *pos_weight* values.

Description	Precision	Recall	Accuracy
N = 3, Dropout = 0.6	0.82	0.53	0.55
N = 2, Dropout = 0.6	0.80	0.61	0.64
N = 1, Dropout = 0.6	0.79	0.65	0.68
N = 3, Dropout = 0.4	0.82	0.58	0.61
N = 2, Dropout = 0.4	0.80	0.61	0.64
N = 1, Dropout = 0.4	0.79	0.65	0.68

Table 5: Comparision of performance for different numbers of layers (N) in the tension classifier.

We analyse the effect of various hyperparameters on the model's performance. Setting the dropout to 0 resulted in the highest accuracy, although it did not necessarily yield the best precision. A dropout value of 0.4 was chosen as a compromise to balance accuracy and precision. Additionally, we found that setting the *pos_weight* to 2 improved the overall accuracy. Surprisingly, the findings revealed that employing only one linear block achieved the best recall while maintaining comparable precision and overall accuracy. It proves that a simpler model architecture can effectively capture the relevant features and achieve optimal recall.

6 Application

We have developed an application specifically designed for researchers of global heritage regimes and UNESCO diplomats to facilitate their search for information within selected speeches. Previously, these individuals had to devote hours to studying extensive summary records to locate relevant fragments for their research or diplomatic practice. However, our application is intended to drastically reduce the time required for this task, enabling users to quickly find the specific statements they need. The application offers the following filtering options for the displayed paragraphs:

- **session**: specifies the sessions from which the paragraphs are displayed.
- **actor**: specifies the speakers of the paragraphs.

Description	Precision	Recall	Accuracy
RoBERTa base, *pos_weight* = 5, *do* = 0.4 with pre-fine-tuning	0.74	0.70	0.72
RoBERTa base, *pos_weight* = 10, *do* = 0.4 with pre-fine-tuning	0.8	0.36	0.33
RoBERTa base, *pos_weight* = 5, *do* = 0.4 without pre-fine-tuning	0.79	0.34	0.30
RoBERTa base, *pos_weight* = 5, *do* = 0.6 without pre-fine-tuning	0.70	0.76	0.71
RoBERTa base, *pos_weight* = 2, *do* = 0.4 with pre-fine-tuning	0.7	0.71	0.72
RoBERTa base, *pos_weight* = 10, *do* = 0.4 with pre-fine-tuning	0.79	0.72	0.72

Table 6: Comparision of performance between RoBERTa base and RoBERTa large as a base model.

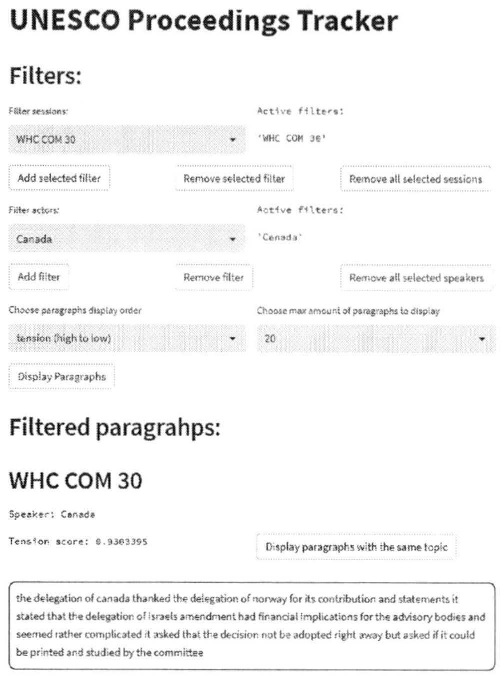

Figure 4: Sample screen from the application.

Furthermore, users can specify the number of paragraphs to be displayed and the preferred order of presentation, either by tension or by date. In conjunction with each presented paragraph, the application provides additional details, including the speaker's identity, a tension score, and a convenient button that enables users to reveal all paragraphs related to the selected paragraph. All these features are presented in Figure 4.

7 Related work

Recent research on controversy (and, in our case, tension) detection is not broad. We found only one model available publicly, which detects controversy, specifically in the Guardian16 corpus[13] and is described in further detail at (Kim and Allan, 2019), where it is additionally stated that a generic document without implicit or explicit topic annotations cannot only rely on inherent topic annotation. The subset of data involving comments has similar issues to other Twitter-based controversy datasets (Chang et al., 2023), as the language used is exceptionally informal and often consists of short sentences. It differs from our dataset, as diplomatic language is significantly more formal. Another popular dataset idea in the controversy classification community contains labelled articles fetched from Wikipedia (Bykau et al., 2021). The method for building this dataset was first described in (Dori-Hacohen et al., 2016) and later expanded upon in a doctoral dissertation (Shiri Dori-Hacohen, 2017). From that point, researchers build their Wikipedia-derived datasets (Jasper Linmans, 2018) where positive examples were based on Wikipedia's *List of controversial issues*[14] for their own need, but rarely making the produced textual data public. IBM researchers used original description (Dori-Hacohen et al., 2016) to produce a downloadable dataset named *dataset_ii.csv*[15].
In addition, they extracted 3561 concepts, crowd-annotated later, from Wikipedia pages under edit protection, assuming that many of these would be controversial. This dataset was named *dataset_iii.csv*[16]. The average pairwise Cohen Kappa agreement on this task was 0.532. Table 7 illustrates each dataset's negative (0s) and positive samples (1s) and thus shows an imbalance between classes that are needed to address. It's worth noting that this set of textual data was never used together in controversy detection research.

[13] https://drive.google.com/file/d/1g6yh77tBgWlgXcKCLULLBVcUt7Xvs1JE/view

[14] https://en.wikipedia.org/wiki/Wikipedia:List_of_controversial_issues

[15] https://research.ibm.com/haifa/dept/vst/debating_data.shtml

[16] https://research.ibm.com/haifa/dept/vst/debating_data.shtml

Name of the dataset	Non-tension	Tension	Total
Guardian	439	281	720
Wiki ii	608	605	1213
Wiki iii	2720	841	3561
Guardian + Wiki	3767	1727	5494
Guardian + Wiki + Comments	100435	172093	272528

Table 7: Number of positive and negative samples for each dataset.

8 Conclusions

During our research, we have successfully developed a pioneering tool for the computational analysis of UNESCO World Heritage Convention (WHC) and Intangible Culture Heritage Convention (ICHC) proceedings. This tool encompasses many features and functionalities, catering to the diverse needs of diplomats and political scientists analysing these important textual resources.
To achieve the primary goal of detecting tensions within the text, we harnessed the power of pre-trained language models and enhanced them by incorporating additional layers. By doing so, we have successfully created a classifier that operates in the complex and multifaceted domain of political science, specifically within the realm of UNESCO proceedings.
The development of our tool marks a significant advancement in the field, providing researchers and practitioners with a robust solution for computational analysis and exploration of tensions within these important discourse contexts.
Our findings contribute to understanding tension in a specific domain and provide valuable insights for further research in related areas.

9 Limitations and future work

While the proposed methodology for analysing diplomatic documents presented in this paper offers significant contributions to the field, it is important to acknowledge certain limitations and potential areas for improvement. These limitations include:

- **Scalability**: Annotating controversies is time-consuming and resource-intensive. Creating a large annotated dataset requires significant effort and expertise. As a result, the current dataset size may not be sufficient to capture the full complexity and variability of tensions. Future research should aim to overcome scalability challenges and develop strategies for efficiently creating larger annotated datasets, for example, by adding more active learning loops.

- **Generalisation to Other Political Organizations**: The proposed methodology's effectiveness in detecting tensions in other political organisations is uncertain. Different political organisations often have distinct ideologies, rhetoric, and controversies that may not align with the training data. The model may not effectively capture tensions' unique characteristics and dynamics in diverse political contexts. Our model is based only on the UNESCO dataset, but we suspect it can represent the language political scientists use well. We plan to create a model fine-tuned on datasets containing diplomats' speeches that can be used in the diplomatic language in NLP tasks.

- **Variability in Speaker References**: Identifying speakers solely through regular expressions may be challenging when multiple ways of referring individuals or groups exist. Speakers can be referred to using various forms, such as names, pronouns, titles, or descriptions. Regular expressions alone may not capture all possible variations and may lead to inaccurate or incomplete speaker detection. Developing a robust tool for detecting speaking actors in any reported speech data would enhance detection and facilitate generalisation to other problems.

- **Extending range of tension:** In this work, we've focused only on binary classification of tension. However, in real-world scenarios, tension is often a nuanced and multi-dimensional concept that cannot be adequately captured by a simple binary classification. Future work could explore the possibility of extending the range of tension by considering a more fine-grained approach.

Acknowledgements

All experiments were performed using the Entropy cluster funded by NVIDIA, Intel, the Polish National Science Center grant UMO-2017/26/E/ST6/00622 and ERC Starting Grant TOTAL. This article describes a Team Programming Project completed at the University of Warsaw in the academic year 22/23. Hanna Schreiber and

Bartosz Pieliński wish to acknowledge that their contribution to this paper was carried out within the framework of the research grant Sonata 15, "Between the heritage of the world and the heritage of humanity: researching international heritage regimes through the prism of Elinor Ostrom's IAD framework," 2019/35/D/HS5/04247 financed by the National Science Centre (Poland).

References

Abien Fred Agarap. 2018. Deep learning using rectified linear units (relu). *arXiv preprint arXiv:1803.08375*.

Haseeb Ali, Mohd Salleh, Kashif Hussain, Ayaz Ullah, Arshad Ahmad, and Rashid Naseem. 2019. A review on data preprocessing methods for class imbalance problem. pages 390–397.

Jimmy Lei Ba, Jamie Ryan Kiros, and Geoffrey E. Hinton. 2016. Layer Normalization.

Janet Blake and Lucas Lixinski. 2020. The 2003 UNESCO Intangible Heritage Convention: A Commentary.

David M. Blei, Andrew Ng, and Michael Jordan. 2003. Latent Dirichlet allocation. *JMLR*, 3:993–1022.

Chiara Bortolotto. 2020. Commercialization without over-commercialization: normative conundrums across heritage rationalities. *International Journal of Heritage Studies*, 27(9):857–868.

Jordan Boyd-Graber, Yuening Hu, and David Mimno. 2017. Applications of Topic Models. *Foundations and Trends® in Information Retrieval*, 11(2-3):143–296.

Hafriza Burhanudeen. 2006. Diplomatic language: An insight from speeches used in international diplomacy. *Akademika*, 67(1):37–51.

Siarhei Bykau, Flip Korn, Divesh Srivastava, and Yannis Velegrakis. 2021. Fine-Grained Controversy Detection in Wikipedia.

Rong-Ching Chang, Ashwin Rao, Qiankun Zhong, Magdalena Wojcieszak, and Kristina Lerman. 2023. #RoeOverturned: Twitter Dataset on the Abortion Rights Controversy.

Yoonjung Choi, Yuchul Jung, and Sung-Hyon Myaeng. 2010. Identifying Controversial Issues and Their Sub-topics in News Articles. In *Intelligence and Security Informatics*, pages 140–153, Berlin, Heidelberg. Springer Berlin Heidelberg.

Shiri Dori-Hacohen, David Jensen, and James Allan. 2016. Controversy Detection in Wikipedia Using Collective Classification. In *Proceedings of the 39th International ACM SIGIR Conference on Research and Development in Information Retrieval*, SIGIR '16, page 797–800, New York, NY, USA. Association for Computing Machinery.

Rory Duthie, Katarzyna Budzynska, and Chris Reed. 2016. *Mining Ethos in Political Debate*, volume 287 of *Frontiers in Artificial Intelligence and Applications*, pages 299–310. IOS Press, Netherlands. This research was supported in part by EPSRC in the UK under grant EP/M506497/1 and in part by the Polish National Science Centre under grant 2015/18/M/HS1/00620.

Francesco Francioni and Federico Lenzerini. 2008. The 1972 World Heritage Convention: a Commentary.

Maarten R. Grootendorst. 2022. BERTopic: Neural topic modeling with a class-based TF-IDF procedure. *ArXiv*, abs/2203.05794.

Sophie Henning, William Beluch, Alexander Fraser, and Annemarie Friedrich. 2023. A Survey of Methods for Addressing Class Imbalance in Deep-Learning Based Natural Language Processing.

Matthew Honnibal and Ines Montani. 2017. spaCy 2: Natural language understanding with Bloom embeddings, convolutional neural networks and incremental parsing. To appear.

Alexander Hoyle, Pranav Goel, Andrew Hian-Cheong, Denis Peskov, Jordan Boyd-Graber, and Philip Resnik. 2021. Is Automated Topic Model Evaluation Broken? The Incoherence of Coherence. In *Advances in Neural Information Processing Systems*, volume 34, pages 2018–2033. Curran Associates, Inc.

Evangelos Kanoulas Jasper Linmans, Bob van de Velde. 2018. Improved and Robust Controversy Detection in General Web Pages Using Semantic Approaches under Large Scale Conditions.

Divya Khyani, BS Siddhartha, NM Niveditha, and BM Divya. 2021. An interpretation of lemmatization and stemming in natural language processing. *Journal of University of Shanghai for Science and Technology*, 22(10):350–357.

Youngwoo Kim and James Allan. 2019. Unsupervised Explainable Controversy Detection from Online News. *ECIR 2019*.

Yinhan Liu, Myle Ott, Naman Goyal, Jingfei Du, Mandar Joshi, Danqi Chen, Omer Levy, Mike Lewis, Luke Zettlemoyer, and Veselin Stoyanov. 2019. RoBERTa: A Robustly Optimized BERT Pretraining Approach. *CoRR*, abs/1907.11692.

Mary McHugh. 2012. Interrater reliability: The kappa statistic. *Biochemia medica : časopis Hrvatskoga društva medicinskih biokemičara / HDMB*, 22:276–82.

Lynn Meskell. 2012. The rush to inscribe: Reflections on the 35th Session of the World Heritage Committee, UNESCO Paris, 2011. *Journal of Field Archaeology*, 37(2):145–151.

David Parkin. 1984. Political Language. *Annual Review of Anthropology*, 13:345–365.

Surendra Pokharel. 2020. Diplomatic language: An analysis of salutations from speeches used in international diplomacy. *Journal of International affairs*, 3(1):180–193.

Pengzhen Ren, Yun Xiao, Xiaojun Chang, Po-Yao Huang, Zhihui Li, Brij B. Gupta, Xiaojiang Chen, and Xin Wang. 2021. A Survey of Deep Active Learning.

Hanna Schreiber. 2017. Intangible cultural heritage and soft power - Exploring the relationship. *International Journal of Intangible Heritage*, pages 43–57.

Hanna Schreiber and Bartosz Pieliński. 2023. Inviting all humanity to an elite club? Understanding tensions in UNESCO's global heritage regimes through the lens of a typology of goods. *International Journal of Cultural Policy*, 29(1):113–129.

James Allan Shiri Dori-Hacohen. 2017. Controversy Analysis and Detection.

Nitish Srivastava, Geoffrey Hinton, Alex Krizhevsky, Ilya Sutskever, and Ruslan Salakhutdinov. 2014. Dropout: A Simple Way to Prevent Neural Networks from Overfitting. *Journal of Machine Learning Research*, 15(56):1929–1958.

Raluca-Maria Topală et al. 2014. Morphological characteristics of the diplomatic language. *Cultural Intertexts*, 1(01+ 02):308–319.

Jacob Devlin Ming-Wei Chang Kenton Lee Kristina Toutanova. 2018. BERT: Pre-training of Deep Bidirectional Transformers for Language Understanding .

Yonghui Wu, Mike Schuster, Zhifeng Chen, Quoc V. Le, Mohammad Norouzi, Wolfgang Macherey, Maxim Krikun, Yuan Cao, Qin Gao, Klaus Macherey, Jeff Klingner, Apurva Shah, Melvin Johnson, Xiaobing Liu, Łukasz Kaiser, Stephan Gouws, Yoshikiyo Kato, Taku Kudo, Hideto Kazawa, Keith Stevens, George Kurian, Nishant Patil, Wei Wang, Cliff Young, Jason Smith, Jason Riesa, Alex Rudnick, Oriol Vinyals, Greg Corrado, Macduff Hughes, and Jeffrey Dean. 2016. Google's Neural Machine Translation System: Bridging the Gap between Human and Machine Translation.

He Zhao, Dinh Phung, Viet Huynh, Yuan Jin, Lan Du, and Wray L. Buntine. 2021. Topic modelling meets deep neural networks: A survey. *CoRR*, abs/2103.00498.

Jingbo Zhu, Huizhen Wang, Tianshun Yao, and Benjamin K. Tsou. 2008. Active Learning with Sampling by Uncertainty and Density for Word Sense Disambiguation and Text Classification. In *Proceedings of the 22nd International Conference on Computational Linguistics - Volume 1*, COLING '08, page 1137–1144, USA. Association for Computational Linguistics.

A Details about splitting text into paragraphs

The primary regular expression was designed to identify sentence beginnings following vertical breaks. By carefully considering exceptions, such as page endings, we achieved a high success rate in locating the majority of paragraphs. Additionally, we dedicated efforts to creating multiple specialised regular expressions capable of detecting unique patterns observed in specific summary records, such as bullet points or slides.

B Details about expert-labelling

Our experts labelled two sessions: 35 WHC ordinary session[17], which encompassed 654 paragraphs, and 12 ICHC ordinary session[18], which consisted of 616 paragraphs. Initially, there was a notable discrepancy in their annotations, primarily due to the lack of strict guidelines for labelling the positive class. However, once stricter guidelines were established, the distribution between paragraphs containing tension and those that did not change, as indicated in Table 8.

The row *Consistent annotation from beginning* statistic provides valuable insights into the level of agreement between our expert annotators regarding the presence or absence of tension in the annotated paragraphs.

Our analysis revealed that, in the ICHC dataset, 39 paragraphs received a unanimous label indicating the presence of tension. Similarly, in the WHC dataset, 17 paragraphs were consistently identified by both annotators as containing tension.

After the data was labelled and before the conflicts were resolved, we computed the score of their annotations, called the Cohen kappa score (McHugh, 2012), which measures the compatibility of two annotators in categorical classification. The Cohen kappa score for paragraphs from 12 ICHC COM was equal to: 0.2205, and for paragraphs from 35, WHC COM: 0.1148. The low score was the effect of an insufficient description of tension in annotation guidelines. Together with domain experts we've fixed the guidelines. Its final version is available in subsection B.1.

Initially, 404 paragraphs from WHC and ICHC datasets exhibited complexities in achieving unanimous annotation agreement. However, through

[17] `https://whc.unesco.org/en/sessions/35COM`

[18] `https://ich.unesco.org/en/12com`

rigorous examination and expert discourse, a consensus was reached, and additional 166 paragraphs from the 35 WHC COM dataset and 99 paragraphs from the 12 ICHC COM dataset were labelled as positive.
These findings highlight the inherent challenges associated with the annotation process and underscore the significance of expert discussions and consensus-building to ensure the accurate classification of tension within the analysed paragraphs.

Description of a subset	0s	1s	Total
Full 35 WHC	471	183	654
Full 12 ICHC	478	138	616
Full 35 WHC and 12 ICHC	949	321	1270
Consistent annotation of full 35 WHC and 12 ICHC after the first annotation stage	810	56	866
35 WHC without introduction	451	183	634
12 ICHC without introduction	458	138	596
35 WHC and 12 ICHC without introduction	909	321	1230

Table 8: Details about the annotation of datasets.

B.1 Annotation guidelines

Annotation was done by two researchers and co-authors of this paper. The first annotator was a political scientist with extensive expertise in text analysis (Bartosz Pieliński). The second one was international affairs researcher and long-time UNESCO cultural heritage expert (Hanna Schreiber). Each annotator was presented with the annotation guidelines as stated below.

Introduction In this task, you aim to detect tensions in UNESCO Summary Records, transcriptions from UNESCO sessions. Tensions refer to controversial issues rooted in disagreements related to states' interests and values. The annotation task involves classifying paragraphs as either indicating tension (1) or not indicating it (0). You should follow the guidelines below to ensure consistency and accuracy in annotation process.

Annotation schema

- **Tension** Mark a paragraph as indicating tension if (1) there is a controversy between participants of a discussion, and (2) the controversy relates to the interests or values of at least one of the actors taking part in the discussion.
- **No Tension** Mark a paragraph as not indicating tension if (1) there is no controversy between participants of a discussion or if (2) there is a controversy, but it is not related to the interests or values of at least one of the actors taking part in the discussion.

Document Segments Each document is splitted into paragraphs. They may vary in length, ranging from a single word to several sentences. You should read and analyse each segment to determine its classification based on the provided annotation schema.

Annotator Instructions

- Familiarise yourself with the topic of the research and the context of diplomacy documents.
- Focus on identifying any indications of tension, disagreement, or conflicting positions within the segment.
- Make the annotation judgment based solely on the content of the segment itself; do not consider information from other parts of the document or external sources.
- Use your best judgment and avoid making assumptions or inferences beyond what is explicitly stated in the text.
- If you encounter ambiguous segments or are uncertain about the classification, mark them for review, and consult with the research team.

Annotation Process

- Use the annotation tool provided by the research team to mark each segment as tense or non-tense.
- Pay close attention to sentence boundaries and ensure the annotation accurately represents the segment's overall meaning.
- If a document segment contains a mix of tense and non-tense elements, consider the dominant tone and classify it accordingly.
- Do not modify the original document or alter the text in any way during the annotation process.

Inter-Annotator Agreement (IAA) To ensure the reliability of the annotations, at least two annotators will independently review each document segment. The research team will provide a guideline for handling cases of ambiguous or challenging segments to promote consistent annotations.

Confidentiality and Data Handling Treat all research documents and data as confidential and only use them for the purpose of this research project. Do not share or discuss any document content or results with unauthorised individuals or outside the research team.

Annotation Completion and Review Inform the research team once you have completed the annotation task. Participate in review meetings with the research team to address any questions, concerns, or discrepancies in the annotations.

By following these guidelines, you can contribute to the creation of a reliable dataset for detecting tensions in diplomacy documents, facilitating the research's success and impact.

C Removed phrases

The full list of hand-picked phrases we removed from consideration during topic modelling is provided below. Moreover, we omitted all descriptions of nationalities and country names.

- chairperson
- committee
- cultural
- delegate
- delegation
- heritage
- iccrom
- icomos
- iucn
- lesion
- outstanding
- party
- property
- rapporteur
- representation
- session
- representative
- site
- state
- world

D ICH speaker extraction

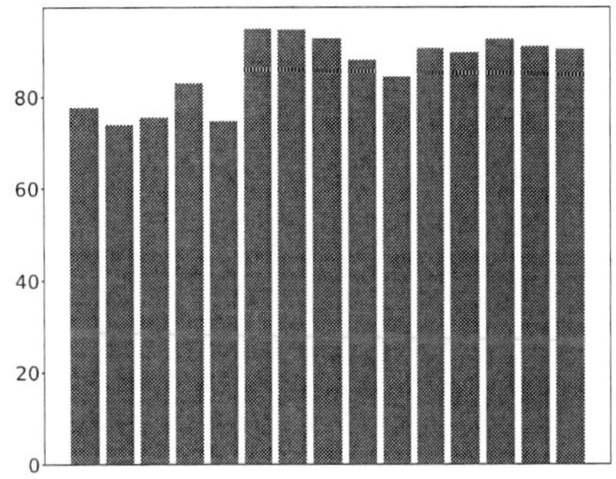

Figure 5: Percentage of paragraphs with identified speakers in each ordinary ICH session.

Evaluating the Quality of the GermaParl Corpus of Plenary Protocols (v2.0.0)

Christoph Leonhardt and Andreas Blätte
University of Duisburg-Essen
{christoph.leonhardt, andreas.blaette}@uni-due.de

Abstract

Parliamentary debates play a key role for the democratic process and for law-making. Scholarly interest in this material benefits greatly from the emergence of new datasets and corpora of parliamentary protocols. Here we combine the presentation of a second, extended version of GermaParl with an evaluation of the data quality of this corpus of plenary protocols in the German Bundestag. For this purpose, about 1 per cent of all protocols have been annotated manually to create a gold standard against which the structurally annotated corpus is compared. Results indicate that GermaParl can be considered a trustworthy resource for a broad set of research questions.

1 Introduction

The increasing availability of large collections of text enables researchers to address new substantive research questions and paves the way for a multitude of new methodological approaches (Hurtado Bodell et al., 2022, p. 1). Whether qualitative discourse analysis or computationally elaborate text-as-data approaches, corpora are the foundation for many new research avenues. In particular, research on legislative debates (Fernandes et al., 2021) benefits from the emergence of corpora of parliamentary proceedings (Sebők et al., 2021).

It has become common sense that the pure existence of new (parliamentary) data is not enough. Availability and reusability matters, and the FAIR principles (Wilkinson et al., 2016) are becoming a cornerstone of data-driven research. But as research moves beyond experimental explorations of new methods, concerns about data quality receive increasing attention: Sound data quality is a precondition for trustworthy research and valid findings. While this is not at all unique for new, large datasets, the volume of the data, their often complex structure and intricate processing pipelines make quality control particularly important for big data.

Relevant key concerns for data quality depend on the type of data. Analyzing Twitter tweets requires awareness for and scrutiny of the technical sampling issues faced. For large corpora of newspaper articles, the presence of (near) duplicates can heavily distort results and needs to be controlled. For parliamentary data, turning raw material into semi-structured data formats (such as XML) in an automated process without a realistic possibility to hand-check output manually throughout entails many potential sources of errors. This is increasingly debated and there is an emerging concern with the quality of resources used for conducting large-scale data-driven research.

The emerging literature on data quality in big data settings emphasizes the need for rigorous quality control. The "Total Error Framework" (RatSWD, 2023, pp. 9–10) and the "Framework for Total Corpus Quality" (Hurtado Bodell et al., 2022) are important contributions to the evolving practice of evaluating data quality. They build on the "Total Survey Error Framework" established in survey methodology (Hurtado Bodell et al., 2022; RatSWD, 2023). These frameworks have an integrative view for the quality of the data. The "Framework for Total Corpus Quality" includes a concern for the transparency of its preparation and its usability to assess the way they facilitate fruitful research. As Hurtado Bodell et al. (2022, p. 12) put it:

> "We suggest that it is now time to turn to a systematic analysis of the role of data quality in scientific inference from textual data. It is time to open the door into the messy data kitchen".

We here apply these considerations to a corpus we prepared and released earlier this year.[1]

[1] An evaluation of a resource conducted by its authors is not independent and can be perceived to have limited value due to the obviously lacking critical distance. However, we think

Proceedings of the 3rd Workshop on Computational Linguistics for the Political and Social Sciences, pages 88–100
September 22, 2023.

GermaParl v2.0.0, released in May 2023, is a comprehensive update of GermaParl, as an established corpus of parliamentary protocols described in Blätte and Blessing (2018). As data quality has always been a key concern of the curation project, previous presentations of GermaParl had a focus on the data preparation workflow, which is designed to facilitate continuous improvements of the data (Blätte et al., 2022). Going beyond our earlier work with its procedural focus, this contribution addresses the question which level of substantive data quality has been achieved.

Our analysis is also inspired by the work of Paul Ramisch who recently addressed the issue of data quality from the perspective of historical source criticism (2023). In his work, he evaluated the quality of another corpus of debates of the *Bundestag* using a gold standard approach. While his approach – by explicitly taking into account the representation of the contents of speeches – is more comprehensive than the one we will employ, it inspired us to evaluate the quality of our corpus by comparing the processed data with a sample of the raw data. We thus feel intellectually indebted to the work presented by Ramisch (2023).

We proceed as follows: After a brief overview of the GermaParl corpus and its preparation process, the framework used to estimate data quality is introduced. Based on an explanation how a benchmark dataset has been prepared, the actual assessment of the data quality of the corpus is presented. The contribution concludes with a discussion of the results and an outlook.

2 The GermaParl corpus of parliamentary debates

2.1 Data Formats and Preparation

The GermaParl corpus includes all proceedings of the German *Bundestag* from 1949 to 2021 and is published in two different formats:

- **TEI/XML:** A structurally annotated TEI/XML format. Text is segmented into individual utterances. This version is available on GitHub.[2]
- **CWB:** An indexed version of the corpus, imported into the Corpus Workbench (CWB) (Evert and Hardie, 2011). It is structurally and linguistically annotated and available via Zenodo.[3]

An outline of preparation procedures is important to convey where potential errors in the data might be introduced. In a nutshell, the data preparation process starts with downloading the raw data from the website and online archives of the *Bundestag*. It is processed in a pipeline that includes cleaning, preprocessing, the structural annotation of the text as well as the enrichment of the data with additional information. For the CWB version of the corpus, the text is linguistically annotated. Finally, the data is imported into the CWB.

Three aspects of the data preparation are particularly important:

Preprocessing: The raw data is retrieved from the websites of the German *Bundestag* using different file formats (TXT, PDF and XML). All file formats already include digitized text one way or the other. Concerning PDF, we did not have to perform any form of Optical Character Recognition, as the *Bundestag* has already done that. When the raw protocols were available in more than one file format, data quality was the key consideration to opt for a file format. Each file format required some adjustments to the processing pipeline.

Speaker Annotation: GermaParl is structurally annotated, making it possible to variably create corpus subsets. Most importantly, it is possible to zoom in on individual speeches. The beginning of speeches is detected by matching specifically marked up lines in the protocols using a set of regular expressions. This may result in false positives and negatives. To omit false positives, a list of manually identified mismatches is used rather than refining the regular expressions until they cover all specific cases, making the expression incomprehensibly and error-prone.

Enrichment: To add information to identified speakers which is not part of the initial protocols – such as a speaker's party affiliation or the speaker's full name in some legislative periods – external data sources are used. Predominantly, additional information can be added using deterministic matching

that we offer insights into the specific challenges of curating a corpus of GermaParl's characteristics. By making the evaluation exercise fully transparent, we generate opportunities for third-party checks and a safeguard against manipulation. That being said, we would welcome future independent work comparing different corpora and using different approaches like the one suggested by Ramisch (2023).

[2]https://github.com/PolMine/GermaParlTEI.

[3]https://zenodo.org/record/7949074.

of shared attributes between the protocol and external data. But plenary protocols include errors and inconsistencies, so fuzzy matching is used to consolidate the name of a speaker. Most external information is retrieved from Wikipedia or the *Stammdaten* file of the German *Bundestag*.[4] If a speaker could not be identified on Wikipedia, alternative resources such as the Munzinger encyclopedia[5] are used selectively. To increase the usability of GermaParl, metadata at the speaker level has been harmonized. Most importantly, variations of parties and parliamentary groups are consolidated.

As elaborated on in Blätte et al. (2022), the workflow includes manual steps, yet it is fully automated and reproducible by design (see Blätte and Leonhardt (2023) for a full description). This is the prerequisite for an efficient and sustainable evolution of the resource, including successive improvements of data quality.

2.2 Data Report

GermaParl v2.0.0 comprises 273 million tokens, covering 72 years of parliamentary debates in 4341 individual protocols.[6] It provides a number of different annotation levels which are comprehensively documented in the online documentation of the resource (Blätte and Leonhardt, 2023).

The structural annotation of GermaParl covers metadata at the protocol and the speaker level. One important purpose of these attributes is to create subcorpora for synchronic and diachronic analyses according to relevant criteria. Table 1 provides an overview of the key structural attributes of GermaParl.[7]

The corpus is linguistically annotated. Aside from tokenization and sentence segmentation, Part-of-Speech tags (Universal Dependencies Tag Set provided by Stanford CoreNLP (Manning et al., 2014) and the Stuttgart-Tübingen Tag Set provided by TreeTagger (Schmid, 1994)) and lemmata (provided by TreeTagger (Schmid, 1994)) are added at the token level. While named entities, added by Stanford CoreNLP (Manning et al., 2014), are part of the linguistic annotation, they are implemented as structural attributes, reflecting that this annotation layer can span more than one token. The same applies to the annotation of sentences.

2.3 Getting Started with GermaParl

The XML version of GermaParl serves as a persistent interchange data format. It is relevant for technically oriented users that are used to process XML and that have own pipelines and infrastructures for handling large corpora. Yet given the size and the structure of the data, many users from the social sciences and the humanities will find the XML variant of GermaParl overwhelming. The CWB version provides this group of users with a linguistically annotated resource in a data format suitable for efficient data analysis.

The CWB version of the corpus can be analyzed with different compatible tools such as the Corpus Workbench itself (Evert and Hardie, 2011) or the Graphical User Interface CQPweb.[8] To access the CWB using the statistical programming language R, we offer the `polmineR` R package which is created and maintained by one of the authors of this contribution (Blätte, 2023). `polmineR` provides fast and reliable access to the functionality of the Corpus Workbench, including the powerful CQP query language. Analyzing large corpora and making use of the rich structural and linguistic annotation layers thus becomes accessible for scholars comfortable with the R programming language. `polmineR` is interoperable and tested to run out of the box and fast on (local) Windows, macOS and Linux machines, even for large corpora such as GermaParl. To download and install the corpus from Zenodo, the R package `cwbtools` (Blätte, 2022) provides convenient auxiliary functionality.

On a system with a working installation of R, the following lines of code suffice to install and run GermaParl.[9]

```
# install cwbtools and polmineR
install.packages("cwbtools") # >= v0.3.8
install.packages("polmineR") # v0.8.8
```

[4]The Stammdaten file can be retrieved from the open data website of the German *Bundestag* (https://www.bundestag.de/services/opendata). It contains comprehensive information on all members of parliament.

[5]`https://www.munzinger.de/`

[6]GermaParl is an evolving resource; future updates will extend its temporal coverage, and fix errors in the data either found by ourselves or reported by users.

[7]This overview describes the CWB version of the corpus. While the structural attributes are essentially identical in the TEI/XML version of the corpus, linguistic annotation was performed only for the CWB version.

[8]`https://cwb.sourceforge.io/cqpweb.php`.

[9]This will install the v2.0.0 release version of the corpus. For future updates, the Zenodo landing page (`https://doi.org/10.5281/zenodo.3735140`) will resolve to the latest version.

Structural Attribute	Description
protocol_lp	Legislative period
protocol_no	Session number
protocol_date	Date of the protocol
protocol_year	Year derived from date
speaker_name	Full name of the speaker
speaker_parlgroup	Parliamentary group of a speaker, corrected errors when necessary
speaker_party	Party affiliation of a speaker, retrieved from Wikipedia or other external resources
speaker_role	Parliamentary role of a speaker, derived from speaker call
p / p_type	paragraph / type of paragraph (speech or stage)
ne / ne_type	named entity / type of named entity

Table 1: Structural Attributes in the GermaParl Corpus

```
# install GermaParl2
cwbtools::corpus_install(
  doi = "10.5281/zenodo.7949074"
)

# test GermaParl2 installation
polmineR::corpus("GERMAPARL2") |>
  size()
```

3 Measurement of Data Quality - Method and Design

3.1 Data Quality as truthful textual representation

GermaParl v2 covers 72 years of parliamentary history, significantly extending the time covered by the v1 release of GermaParl which was limited to 1996 to 2016. The question of data quality needs to be addressed anyway, but given the additional error sources that enter the game for data that is not born-digital (scanning quality, OCR errors), historical data make data quality issues more pressing. If systematic errors remain unknown, the potential of data covering several decades of parliamentary history to uncover long-term trends is significantly impeded.

In this section, we discuss our understanding of corpus quality and how it can be measured. The approach borrows heavily from the "Framework for Total Corpus Quality" presented by Hurtado Bodell et al. (2022). The framework is proposed as "a conceptual framework for assessing the quality of textual data that enables researchers to systematically diagnose a corpus' scientific value along three quality dimensions: total corpus error, corpus comparability, and corpus reproducibility" (Hurtado Bodell et al., 2022, p. 1). As such, it is part of a family of established approaches, most importantly the "Total Survey Error Framework" and related efforts to extend this framework to the realm of big data and unstructured data (Hurtado Bodell et al., 2022; RatSWD, 2023).

In this first take to assess the quality of GermaParl, we focus on the dimension of "total corpus error" (Hurtado Bodell et al., 2022, p. 1). It has three aspects: "source errors, textual representation errors (TREs), and research inference errors (RIEs)" (Hurtado Bodell et al., 2022, p. 4). Within this triad, we will mainly focus on the aspect of "textual representation errors". Since we work with already digitized data, systematically checking the "source errors" (Hurtado Bodell et al., 2022, p. 4) is out of the scope of this contribution.[10] As a multi-purpose corpus which has been created to broadly serve research, "research inference errors" can not be estimated meaningfully either.

Thus, we employ a simplified version of this framework, asking how well the corpus represents the original data in the form published by the *Bundestag* and how truthfully additional information has been added to this data (Hurtado Bodell et al., 2022, pp. 4–5). To do this, we compare the processed TEI/XML version of GermaParl v2.0.0 with the initial raw protocols in form of the PDF files

[10]This does not address whether the transcripts represent everything that happens in parliament truthfully. This question is beyond the scope of this contribution. It has been analyzed and discussed for the German *Bundestag* in-depth in dedicated studies (Burkhardt, 2003, chapter 9). Also errors in the data provided by the German *Bundestag* (Ramisch, 2023, chapter 2) are not evaluated systematically.

which can be retrieved from the "Dokumentations- und Informationssystem für Parlamentsmaterialien" (DIP) of the German *Bundestag*.[11]

When focusing on the "Textual Representation Errors", we are concerned with the question of "How different [...] the processed machine-readable and observed corpus [are]" (Hurtado Bodell et al., 2022, p. 4). Hurtado Bodell et al. (2022) discuss this along four categories that lend structure to our evaluation. For each category, the error itself is described first, followed by potential causes of these errors in GermaParl.

source-to-(digital)-text errors Following Hurtado Bodell et al. (2022, pp. 4–5), transforming the source data into a machine-readable format is a first category of errors. Potential errors comprise flaws introduced by the digitization itself – scan artefacts, for example – or the inclusion of unwanted parts of the source material. We largely omit this aspect from our analysis because of our reliance on digitized text provided by the German *Bundestag*. So digitization errors like random additional or missing characters which might be caused by scan artefacts (Hurtado Bodell et al., 2022, p. 5) are mostly out of our control and are not systematically identified as long as they do not result in a missing speaker call.

text-to-documents errors Hurtado Bodell et al. (2022, p. 5) describe the identification of "cohesive units of text" as the source of "text-to-documents" errors. For the curation of qualitative corpora, the correct segmentation of text to meaningful documents such as speeches is crucial. The relevance of these errors is particularly evident for the assignment of speakers to segments of text in parliamentary corpora. If the beginning of a separate speech is missed, additional chunks of text are incorrectly assigned to the wrong speaker. The same is true for the creation of "faux documents" (Hurtado Bodell et al., 2022, p. 5) if separate speeches are detected where they should not.

These errors concern a step of the corpus preparation pipeline of GermaParl that is truly crucial: The identification of speeches. The sequence of text preprocessing, applying regular expressions, and the handling special cases as well as false positives is essential for the correct assignment of text to speakers, and potentially error-prone.

[11] https://dip.bundestag.de/.

documents-to-corpus errors According to Hurtado Bodell et al. (2022, p. 5) the "accuracy of metadata in a corpus" gives rise to "documents-to-corpus errors".

The capabilities to enrich identified speeches with additional metadata are important for the data quality of GermaParl, as these additional annotations provide plentiful possibilities for analysis. As described in section 2, the enrichment is realized by matching attributes found in the protocols and external data; "documents-to-corpus errors" thus would materialize in mismatches, such as wrongly assigned party affiliations.

processing errors Processing errors arise when transforming the machine-readable corpus from one format to another (Hurtado Bodell et al., 2022, p. 6). For GermaParl, this might be the case when importing the processed XML files into the Corpus Workbench. It must be noted that the TEI/XML version and the CWB version of the corpus differ by design, with the latter including an additional consolidation step to increase usability while the TEI/XML contains some more variations within party and parliamentary group names.

3.2 Research Inference Errors

GermaParl is designed as a multi-purpose resource and is, as such, not concerned with a single research question in mind. As a consequence, other errors identified by Hurtado Bodell et al. (2022, p. 6) are not entirely applicable for our curation project. While "coverage errors" – how far the data represents its stated population – and "text curation errors" – issues caused by the modification and preprocessing of text – might be relevant for corpora like GermaParl as well, this is not systematically addressed in the upcoming evaluation.

3.3 Corpus Comparability and Corpus Reproducibility

Aside from estimating the Total Corpus Error as discussed above, Hurtado Bodell et al. (2022) suggest two more dimensions of corpus quality: Corpus comparability and corpus reproducibility.

Corpus comparability is concerned with how findings based on one resource compare to findings based on another or how findings based on different sections of the same resource are comparable (Hurtado Bodell et al., 2022, p. 6). This is particularly relevant in terms of errors in the data. For diachronic analyses, missing a lot more observations in one period that in another should be avoided (Hurtado Bodell et al., 2022, p. 7). Concerning corpus comparability, as shown in the previous sections, the data sources – while all provided by the German *Bundestag* itself – are not completely homogeneous. While not in our control, it seems obvious that the "within-corpus comparability" (Hurtado Bodell et al., 2022, p. 7) might be limited by different processes to retrieve the data as text. The data quality of the raw data at different points in time is also discussed in more detail by Ramisch (2023, chapter 2). These potential challenges require thorough empirical evaluation in the upcoming sections.[12]

Regarding corpus reproducibility described by Hurtado Bodell et al. (2022, p. 7) as the goal that "two different researchers should be able to create the same corpus from the same observed material", we already presented our approach to reproducibility (Blätte et al., 2022). We are strongly opinionated in this respect: Reproducibility of the data preparation process contributes to the quality of the data not only in the sense that reproducibility is desirable in its own right. Much more than that, it is a way to ensure that a resource can evolve, incrementally increasing data quality. If the preparation workflow is not reproducible, the maintaining a resource is excessively costly.

4 Applying the Total Corpus Error framework

In the previous section, we described what potential errors might be expected. Our focus on the textual representation error informs the need to develop an understanding on what a truthful representation of the debates in the German *Bundestag* would look like. In other words, we need to create a "ground truth" that contains information about which speeches actually occur in the debates, when these debates actually occurred and what additional information should be added. A compiled representation of the true debates allows us to compare these expected speeches with the speeches in the processed corpus. In contrast to the approach by Ramisch (2023, chapter 3) who is also interested in the extent of speeches, we focus on the metadata of each speech by annotating and enriching each line indicating the beginning of an individual speech. Implicitly, these errors correspond to the false assignment of tokens to speakers where the beginning of a new speech is missed. Instead of assigning tokens to the expected but missed speaker, in most cases they will be assigned to the previous speaker instead (see Ramisch (2023, chapter 3.5.2) as well).

The precise steps are discussed in more detail in the following sections.

4.1 Sampling and Ground Truth

When creating this "ground truth", it would be unfeasible to collect the necessary information for each protocol in a larger corpus. Indeed, it is enough to evaluate a representative sample of documents. Hurtado Bodell et al. (2022, p. 8) assessed a stratified random sample of newspaper pages. We also annotate a representative sample of parliamentary protocols. To account for the changing appearance of the protocols, changes in parliamentary procedures or the changing composition of parties in the *Bundestag*, each legislative period should be included in the sample with at least two sessions. Our overall target was to annotate one per cent of the entire corpus.[13]

To organize the collection of information, a codebook outlining the annotation task was created. It contained information about how document-level metadata and speeches should be identified and documented (allowing the identification of potential text-to-documents errors) and how the metadata of speeches should be enriched with additional information (the full name and the party affiliation) to facilitate the identification of documents-to-corpus errors. The coders were provided with specific instructions about which resources to use to add metadata if possible.

The annotation task was assigned to four coders: one author of this contribution and three student assistants with a background in political science. Each protocol was initially coded by a single coder. With the categories being formal rather than evaluative and the codebook quite specific, the risk of "coder bias" – an important limitation in quantitative content analysis (Riffe et al., 2005, p. 123) – was considered as neglectable. To guarantee that the corpus is compared against an accurate ground truth, obvious remaining flaws such as missing

[12]The comparability to other corpora is no aspect of the data quality of GermaParl. However, it can be noticed that the XML version is currently TEI-inspired. Future versions of GermaParl are envisaged to adhere to the encoding standards of the ParlaMint project (Erjavec et al., 2022)

[13]Similarly, Ramisch (2023, chapter 3) manually annotated two protocols per legislative period, using the XML files provided by the German *Bundestag*.

speakers, typos in the gold standard or falsely assigned additional information were consolidated. Some of these flaws were noticed when the initial gold standard annotation was initially compared against the processed data and corrected accordingly. In sum, to ensure completeness and accuracy, after the initial annotation each protocol was looked at by at least one, sometimes also a second, additional coder – i.e. with access to the previous annotation – to iteratively create a complete and accurate gold dataset.

To ensure the comparability of the added data in the ground truth and the processed data in the corpus, minor harmonization steps were performed on the ground truth such as the adoption of a party abbreviation from GermaParl as well as the adoption of variations in speaker names – the removal or addition of middle initials, for example. The goal is to identify corresponding entities, not necessarily verbatim matches.

It has to be noted that this approach potentially comes with some limitations and biases which are discussed in the respective section on limitations at the end of this contribution.

Ultimately, the coded sample comprised 51 protocols (1.17 per cent of all protocols). Table 3 (see appendix) shows the number of annotated speakers per legislative period. For each protocol, the occurring speakers and additional metadata were documented in order of occurrence along with document-level metadata.

4.2 Estimation of Corpus Quality

The final measure of corpus quality is the proportion of correct assignments over different subsets of the corpus. First, we analyze the metadata at protocol level to estimate documents-to-corpus errors.[14]

For the speaker level, this measure includes both the assignment of tokens to the correct speaker (addressing potential text-to-documents errors) as well as assigning the correct metadata to the correct speaker (addressing potential documents-to-corpus errors). We compare each speaker in the gold standard representing the initial data with the corresponding observation in the processed data. This comparison can result in five different states:

- **full match:** Same speaker matched in processed data, metadata identical.
- **partial match:** Same speaker matched in processed data, metadata (partially) different.
- **missing:** Speaker not matched in the processed data.
- **mismatch:** Different, unexpected speaker matched.
- **only in GermaParl:** Speaker occurs in the processed data but not in the gold standard, indicating false positives or overlooked speakers when creating the ground truth

In particular, we are interested in the accuracy of the representation of the data split according to different comparative dimensions. These dimensions are the general accuracy of the data, as well as the accuracy per legislative period, parliamentary role and parliamentary group.

4.2.1 Protocol Level Annotation

To assess documents-to-corpus errors at the level of the entire protocol, the question is whether each protocol is enriched with the correct metadata. Thus, the metadata of the protocols – the legislative period, the session number and the session date – was documented for all protocols which were included in the gold standard evaluation. As table 2 indicates, this error is not very prominent in our sample. One wrong date resulted from a session taking place on two separate days – only the first date is reported in the processed data.

Attribute	Matching	Documents	Correct Matches in %
Legislative Period	51	51	100.00
Session	51	51	100.00
Date	50	51	98.04

Table 2: Accuracy of Document Level Metadata in GermaParl

4.2.2 Speaker Level Annotation

Out of 10725 annotated speakers, 10398 are fully matched in the processed data. This represents 96.95 per cent of all speakers. 194 speakers (1.81

[14] For the overwhelming majority of protocols, a single protocol corresponds to a single parliamentary session. While we know that this does not apply for all protocols, we did not encounter multiple sessions in one protocol in our sample, thus making the text-to-documents-error less important at this level.

per cent) were identified, but annotated with metadata which differs from the expected values. 69 speakers (0.64 per cent) are not matched at all. 64 speakers were mismatches. This represents 0.6 per cent. 68 speakers occur only in the processed data and not in the gold standard.

While these overall values are relevant, the accuracy of the data might vary along a set of dimensions. Table 4 in the appendix shows the results of this comparison along these different dimensions. Considering variation over time, we see that the proportion of complete matches is relatively stable over different legislative periods. Noteworthy outliers are the second, the seventh and the 14th legislative period, with a comparatively high number of partial and missing matches. Regarding the parliamentary role of speakers, the accuracy to identify speakers of the federal council (i.e. members of the German *Bundesrat*) is comparatively low. For parliamentary groups, we do not see major deviations. Focusing specifically on mismatches, we identify an increased number of mismatches in the 14th legislative period and for presidential speakers.

Regarding the documents-to-corpus errors, there is relevant variation in the proportion of partial matches. For some cases, the explanation is quite simple: For some governmental and presidential speakers, parliamentary groups are reported in the processed data where they should not. This also explains the high number of partial matches in the "NA" category in the parliamentary group section. Other speakers have false assignments of parliamentary groups or parties. While this might be due to switching parties, this deserves further investigation. While mismatches do not occur very often, they can represent crucial errors in the data. For some instances, these errors are false positives in the sense that the expected speaker and the speaker detected are actually the same person with a different name, for example because of marriage. In our case, this accounts for quite a large number of mismatches: 48 mismatches are caused by a mismatch between the expected speaker "Petra Bläss" and the observed speaker "Petra Bläss-Rafajlovski", for example. For this reason, a more granular analysis of the nature of these mismatches might be relevant. For other cases, more investigation is needed. Speakers found only in GermaParl often correspond with these mismatches. In this case, instead of the expected value in the gold annotation, other speakers were added in the processed data, leaving them unmatched. Currently, errors in the gold standard cannot be ruled out, so that these instances might point to speakers which are in the protocols but were overlooked in the gold standard annotation. But in general, the number of these cases is relatively low.

4.3 Processing Error

The *processing error* is estimated by comparing the observations in both versions, with the proportion of corresponding observations as the central measure. All errors reported for the TEI/XML version will also be part of the CWB corpus.

We assume that the CWB corpus is equivalent to the TEI/XML version of the corpus. There are just cases of a minor harmonization to increase the usability of the CWB resource. The empirical analysis supports this: While most speakers (98.86 per cent) are identical in both versions of the corpus, there are differences in 122 of the speakers identified in the evaluated protocols. For the most part, this concerns the assignment of parliamentary groups (0.62 per cent of all speakers) and parties (0.51 per cent). A preliminary glance at the deviations suggests that both are indeed caused by minor variations in the names of the same entities with the most noteworthy deviation being the inclusion of the CDU as a parliamentary group in the first legislative period in the XML/TEI version of the corpus whereas it has been harmonized to CDU/CSU in the CWB corpus.

5 Discussion

Our overall result of this evaluation exercise is: The overwhelming majority of speakers is identified – representing little text-to-documents errors – and assigned to the correct metadata – suggesting few documents-to-corpus errors. That being said, the data is not yet perfect: Specific groups of speakers are identified more robustly than others.

While for some research questions, the assignment of tokens to reasonable documents will be sufficient, for others the correct assignment of metadata throughout is imperative. Thinking about a continuum between in-depth qualitative analysis of a limited set of debates and speeches and quantitative text-as-data approaches to the data: The latter strand of research will find some noise that does not systematically distort results to be anticipated and acceptable, whereas in-depth qualitative research may require a zero-tolerance take on errors – a standard only a genuine edition could meet. Our findings on data quality convey that GermaParl may be considered a resource meeting sound quality standards for a broad set of analytical approaches to parliamentary speech, though not for all.

While the percentages shown table 4 indicate that the general workflow works well, improvements are possible and will be made. Evaluating missing speakers qualitatively suggests that the quality of the raw data is a limiting factor in this regard. Typos, missing or additional punctuation marks and whitespace as well as missing line breaks limit the effectiveness of our approach. In some instances, the preparation pipeline is able to account for this. However, the occurrence of noise is difficult to anticipate. Other errors concerning partially matched speakers seem to indicate plain inaccuracies in the preparation of the data used to enrich the corpus. Our findings also confirm the prior intuition that rare speakers are more difficult to match than common ones: Speakers from the federal council occur comparatively rarely and in quite a variety of different forms, making the formulation of regular expressions matching all relevant cases challenging.

Finally, while the sample used to generate the ground truth covers a large proportion of the data, we did not encounter all errors which are known to us at the time of writing. For instance, a known data error in GermaParl v2.0.0 is the unintended inclusion of appendices in the final dataset. Depending on the legislative period and the specific document, this either assigns additional content to the last speech – most of the time a presidential speaker – or adds speeches which were only added to the minutes, suggesting these were ordinary speeches. While the first issue seems related to a text-to-documents error, the second issue can be understood as a case of a coverage error because the intended coverage – speeches held in the German *Bundestag* – is exceeded in a portion of the protocols. Errors such as these are publicly documented in the GitHub repository of the resource.[15] Future versions of the will improve data quality by addressing these known errors.

6 Outlook

We envision GermaParl as both a trustworthy and useful resource for a broad set of research questions, and as an evolving resource which allows for continuous updates and improvements. We did not compare the quality of GermaParl to similar resources, i.e. other corpora of parliamentary debates. A comparative contextualization of the reported measures would ideally be provided for by independent researchers. Yet our own evaluation of our resource leaves us with newly-won, quantitatively grounded confidence that – remaining errors notwithstanding – the quality of GermaParl achieved is a solid foundation for current research and further developments.

The qualitative inspection of errors encountered underlines the need to improve the resource continuously in a collaborative and sustainable fashion: It is impossible to anticipate all errors in a corpus as large as GermaParl: It covers 72 years of parliamentary proceedings, 19 legislative periods and includes more than 273 million tokens in 4341 protocols. Thus, user feedback and suggestions are an important aspect for the future development of the corpus, including its data quality.

Limitations

This contribution systematically compares an accurate account of the debates in the German *Bundestag* and its representation in the GermaParl corpus. The "gold standard" has been generated in an iterative process that may have introduced a bias: The identification and correction of speakers which are missing in the ground truth (but are available in the processed data) is potentially easier than the identification of errors which occur in both the ground truth and the processed data. To avoid a potentially lopsided correction of errors which would flatter the results presented, the gold standard dataset was checked iteratively in the process outlined. Our reasoning was to design a process to obtain a gold standard annotation for a technical annotation task with little interpretative leeway that might have caused intercoder disagreement. Still, random noise and annotation errors cannot be ruled out. A consequence of our process is that we do not offer a measure of the intercoder reliability between the four coders in the initial annotation, nor a measure of the difficulty of the annotation task.[16]

A further aspect we do not discuss in depth is that we encountered errors in the PDF files such as missing pages resulting in missing speakers. Relying on the PDF files to create the gold standard

[15] https://github.com/PolMine/GermaParl2.

[16] We gratefully acknowlege our reviewers' discussion of this limitation.

annotation then results in additional errors which are not necessarily caused by errors in GermaParl.

Finally, the current implementation of the algorithm used to compare the gold standard and the processed data is very sensitive for a large number of missing speakers occurring consecutively, flagging all speakers after a specific gap as mismatches even though valid speaker matches would be available later. While the chosen parameters worked well, it is conceivable that this could overestimate the number of mismatches if a number of consecutive speakers is missing in GermaParl.

Ethical Considerations

The parliamentary data we prepared is entirely in the public domain and the data preparation process is fully transparent. We are not aware of a scenario how our work might negatively affect relevant principles of research ethics. As we see it, our contribution is also technically improved access to parliamentary debates that strengthens democratic accountability.

Acknowledgments

The preparation of GermaParl and this evaluation was made possible by funding from KonsortSWD within the National Research Data Infrastructure (NFDI) (Project Number 442494171) as well as from the Text+ consortium within the NFDI (Project Number 460033370). We gratefully acknowledge this support. In addition, we would like to thank our three student assistants Silvia Mommertz, Jan Erik Lutz and Jan Borcherding who supported this work by conducting a part of the manual annotation for this quantitative evaluation with great scrutiny. Finally, the insightful comments of our reviewers are gratefully acknowledged.

References

Andreas Blätte. 2022. cwbtools: Tools to create, modify and manage CWB Corpora. R package version 0.3.8.

Andreas Blätte. 2023. polmineR: Verbs and Nouns for Corpus Analysis. R package version 0.8.8.

Andreas Blätte and Andre Blessing. 2018. The GermaParl Corpus of Parliamentary Protocols. In *Proceedings of the Eleventh International Conference on Language Resources and Evaluation (LREC 2018)*, Miyazaki, Japan. European Language Resources Association (ELRA).

Andreas Blätte and Christoph Leonhardt. 2023. The GermaParl Corpus of Plenary Protocols (v2.0.0) - Documentation. Version 2023-05-23. Technical report.

Andreas Blätte, Julia Rakers, and Christoph Leonhardt. 2022. How GermaParl Evolves: Improving Data Quality by Reproducible Corpus Preparation and User Involvement. In *Proceedings of the Workshop ParlaCLARIN III within the 13th Language Resources and Evaluation Conference*, pages 7–15, Marseille, France. European Language Resources Association.

Armin Burkhardt. 2003. *Das Parlament und seine Sprache. Studien zu Theorie und Geschichte parlamentarischer Kommunikation.* Max Niemeyer Verlag, Berlin, New York.

Tomaž Erjavec, Maciej Ogrodniczuk, Petya Osenova, Nikola Ljubešić, Kiril Simov, Andrej Pančur, Michał Rudolf, Matyáš Kopp, Starkaður Barkarson, Steinþór Steingrímsson, Çağrı Çöltekin, Jesse de Does, Katrien Depuydt, Tommaso Agnoloni, Giulia Venturi, María Calzada Pérez, Luciana D. de Macedo, Costanza Navarretta, Giancarlo Luxardo, Matthew Coole, Paul Rayson, Vaidas Morkevičius, Tomas Krilavičius, Roberts Darģis, Orsolya Ring, Ruben van Heusden, Maarten Marx, and Darja Fišer. 2022. The ParlaMint corpora of parliamentary proceedings. *Language Resources and Evaluation.*

Stefan Evert and Andrew Hardie. 2011. Twenty-first century Corpus Workbench: Updating a query architecture for the new millennium. In *Proceedings of the Corpus Linguistics 2011 conference*, University of Birmingham, GBR.

Jorge M. Fernandes, Marc Debus, and Hanna Bäck. 2021. Unpacking the politics of legislative debates. *European Journal of Political Research*, 60:1032–1045.

Miriam Hurtado Bodell, Måns Magnusson, and Sophie Mützel. 2022. From Documents to Data: A Framework for Total Corpus Quality. *Socius*, 8:1–15.

Christopher Manning, Mihai Surdeanu, John Bauer, Jenny Finkel, Steven Bethard, and David McClosky. 2014. The Stanford CoreNLP natural language processing toolkit. In *Proceedings of 52nd Annual Meeting of the Association for Computational Linguistics: System Demonstrations*, pages 55–60, Baltimore, Maryland. Association for Computational Linguistics.

Paul Ramisch. 2023. Goldstandard-Korpus-Evaluation als Methode digitaler Quellenkritik in den Geschichtswissenschaften am Beispiel des Open-Discourse-Korpus der Bundestagsprotokolle.

RatSWD (Rat für Sozial- und Wirtschaftsdaten). 2023. Erhebung und Nutzung unstrukturierter Daten in den Sozial-, Verhaltens- und Wirtschaftswissenschaften:

Herausforderungen und Empfehlungen. (RatSWD Output Series, 7. Berufungsperiode Nr. 2), Berlin.

Daniel Riffe, Stephen Lacy, and Frederick G. Fico. 2005. *Analyzing Media Messages. Using Quantitative Content Analysis in Research*, 2 edition. Lawrence Erlbaum Associates, Inc. Publishers, Mahwah, New Jersey.

Helmut Schmid. 1994. Probabilistic Part-of-Speech Tagging Using Decision Trees. Manchester, UK.

Miklós Sebők, Sven-Oliver Proksch, and Christian Rauh. 2021. OPTED. Review of available parliamentary corpora. Technical report.

Mark D. Wilkinson, Michel Dumontier, IJsbrand Jan Aalbersberg, Gabrielle Appleton, Myles Axton, Arie Baak, Niklas Blomberg, Jan-Willem Boiten, Luiz Bonino da Silva Santos, Philip E. Bourne, Jildau Bouwman, Anthony J. Brookes, Tim Clark, Mercè Crosas, Ingrid Dillo, Olivier Dumon, Scott Edmunds, Chris T. Evelo, Richard Finkers, Alejandra Gonzalez-Beltran, Alasdair J.G. Gray, Paul Groth, Carole Goble, Jeffrey S. Grethe, Jaap Heringa, Peter A.C 't Hoen, Rob Hooft, Tobias Kuhn, Ruben Kok, Joost Kok, Scott J. Lusher, Maryann E. Martone, Albert Mons, Abel L. Packer, Bengt Persson, Philippe Rocca-Serra, Marco Roos, Rene van Schaik, Susanna-Assunta Sansone, Erik Schultes, Thierry Sengstag, Ted Slater, George Strawn, Morris A. Swertz, Mark Thompson, Johan van der Lei, Erik van Mulligen, Jan Velterop, Andra Waagmeester, Peter Wittenburg, Katherine Wolstencroft, Jun Zhao, and Barend Mons. 2016. The FAIR Guiding Principles for scientific data management and stewardship. *Scientific Data*, 3(160018).

A Appendix

Legislative Period	N Speakers	N Protocols
1	473	4
2	280	3
3	371	2
4	1000	3
5	590	3
6	673	3
7	984	4
8	563	3
9	300	2
10	792	4
11	303	2
12	864	3
13	1050	3
14	370	2
15	548	2
16	271	2
17	350	2
18	263	2
19	680	2

Table 3: Ground Truth - Sample

	annotated speakers	Match Category: full	partial	missing	mismatch	matched speakers*	only in GermaParl
Legislative Period							
1	473	461	7	5	0	97.46	0
2	280	258	18	4	0	92.14	0
3	371	360	1	10	0	97.04	0
4	1000	968	28	4	0	96.80	0
5	590	588	0	2	0	99.66	0
6	673	651	4	15	3	96.73	3
7	984	906	74	3	1	92.07	1
8	563	548	12	2	1	97.34	1
9	300	299	0	1	0	99.67	0
10	792	782	4	5	1	98.74	1
11	303	296	3	4	0	97.69	4
12	864	858	4	2	0	99.31	0
13	1050	1038	0	4	8	98.86	8
14	370	320	0	4	46	86.49	46
15	548	546	0	0	2	99.64	2
16	271	269	0	2	0	99.26	0
17	350	337	13	0	0	96.29	0
18	263	259	0	2	2	98.48	2
19	680	654	26	0	0	96.18	0
Role							
federal_council	17	11	1	5	0	64.71	0
government	1980	1855	104	17	4	93.69	5
mp	4254	4206	12	21	15	98.87	16
parl_commissioner	4	4	0	0	0	100.00	0
presidency	4470	4322	77	26	45	96.69	47
Parliamentary Group							
AfD	48	48	0	0	0	100.00	0
CDU	40	40	0	0	0	100.00	0
CDU/CSU	1482	1461	7	7	7	98.58	7
CSU	6	6	0	0	0	100.00	0
DIE LINKE	74	74	0	0	0	100.00	0
DP	21	20	1	0	0	95.24	0
DP/FVP	1	1	0	0	0	100.00	0
FDP	613	611	1	1	0	99.67	0
FU	22	20	0	2	0	90.91	0
GB/BHE	4	4	0	0	0	100.00	0
GRUENE	371	367	0	1	3	98.92	3
KPD	29	29	0	0	0	100.00	0
NA	6470	6192	181	48	49	95.70	52
PDS	63	60	0	0	3	95.24	3
PDS/Linke Liste	19	19	0	0	0	100.00	0
SPD	1429	1416	1	10	2	99.09	3
fraktionslos	33	30	3	0	0	90.91	0

* fully matched speakers in per cent

The leftmost column indicates the dimensions as they are expected in the gold annotation.

Role "parl_commissioner" refers to the role of parliamentary commissioner in GermaParl.

Parliamentary Group "NA" describes governmental speakers, presidential speakers and other non-MPs.

Table 4: Comparison of Ground Truth and Processed Data

Author Index

Association for Computational Linguistics
209 N. Eighth Street
Stroudsburg, Pennsylvania 18360

ISBN 979-8-3313-1646-4
9 798331 316464

CURRAN ASSOCIATES INC.
proceedings.com